The First Presidential Communications Agency

SUNY series on the Presidency: Contemporary Issues

John Kenneth White, editor

The First Presidential Communications Agency

FDR's Office of Government Reports

Mordecai Lee

State University of New York Press

Published by
State University of New York Press, Albany

Printed in the United States of America

Cover photo: United States Information Center, 1942, looking southwest. Pennsylvania Avenue is on the right side of the picture. The truck at the bottom of the picture is turning southwards onto 14th Street NW. Over the Center's main entrance (where the streetcar is stopped) is the building's title: "US Information." The Commerce Department building is at the top left. Credit: National Archives, Record Group 44, Box 996.

For information, address State University of New York Press, 90 State Street, Suite 700, Albany, NY 12207

Production by Diane Ganeles
Marketing by Michael Campochiaro

Library of Congress Cataloging-in-Publication Data

Lee, Mordecai, 1948–
The first presidential communications agency : FDR's Office of Government Reports / Mordecai Lee.
p. cm. — (SUNY series on the presidency)
Includes bibliographical references and index.
ISBN 0-7914-6359-1 (alk. paper) — ISBN 0-7914-6360-5 (pbk: alk. paper)
1. United States. Office of Government Reports—History. 2. Administrative agencies—United States—History. 3. Roosevelt, Franklin D. (Franklin Delano), 1882–1945. I. Title. II. SUNY series in the presidency.

JK411.L44 2005
352.23'2748'097309044—dc22 2004045402

10 9 8 7 6 5 4 3 2 1

A parent is truly fortunate to be able to watch
the flowering of one's offspring;
in my case my only child, Ethan Garrison Lee,
who was born in 1987.
Every day has been a wonder.

Contents

Illustrations

Figures

Tables

Preface

This book is due to a lucky accident. For a different research project, I was trying to locate an article I had vaguely remembered seeing excerpts of in Albert Lepawsky's *Administration: The Art and Science of Organization and Management*. As I was leafing through the book seeking the passage I wanted, I noticed the abridged version of a different article, about something called the Office of Government Reports (OGR).[1] That article had originally been published in the second issue of *Public Administration Review* in 1941 and was written by the agency's director, Lowell Mellett.[2] Even though I had written my dissertation on federal public relations, and have since published extensively on government public relations, I had never heard of OGR. I started reading those excerpts of Mellett's article and was captivated. I wanted to know more. This book is the result of that idle curiosity.

In the context of the public's views toward American government in the early twenty-first century, OGR almost sounds like a bad joke. An entire government bureaucracy dedicated to reports?! I hope that this volume contributes to an understanding of a forgotten chapter of the modern presidency and in the practice of public relations (in the best sense of the phrase) in government.

My deepest appreciation to the Fromkin Family and the Golda Meir Library of the University of Wisconsin–Milwaukee for the 33rd annual Fromkin Grant in 2002. It financed visits to the Truman Library in Independence, MO, the National Archives in College Park, MD, and the Center for Legislative Archives (maintained for Congress by the National Archives) in Washington, DC. Also, the role of my campus' library in this project was more than financial. Its Archives, Interlibrary Loan, Government Documents Department, microfilm and microfiche collections, and the Human Resources Department were all very helpful as well. To all who helped me, my thanks. The grant culminated in a public lecture at the library's conference center in October 2002 about the US Information Center, the same subject as chapter 8. The lecture and its published version were very different from the chapter in this book since they were oriented toward a lay audience.

This research was also underwritten by a travel grant in 2002 from the Franklin and Eleanor Roosevelt Institute to conduct research at the Roosevelt Library in Hyde Park, NY. My thanks for that financial assistance. The Wisconsin Historical Society in Madison, WI, possessed many OGR and National Emergency Council (NEC) publications in its library as well as a virtually complete collection of Congressional hearings from that era. Similarly, the central branch of the Milwaukee Public Library had complete sets of the *Congressional Record, US Government Manual, Congressional Directory,* and the *Budget of the United States.* I also benefited from archival documents at the Carl Albert Center at the University of Oklahoma and Center for American History at the University of Texas–Austin. Similarly, staff at the Hoover, Eisenhower, Kennedy, Johnson and Ford presidential libraries, the Library of Congress, the US Senate Library, and the Ad Council were exceedingly generous with their time in tracking down obscure documents in their archives, as well as answers to seemingly arcane questions I had put to them long distance. Although too numerous to mention by name, I am indebted to the professionals who helped me at all these institutions. Librarians and archivists are the unsung custodians of civilization.

My gratitude to summer research assistant David Kosalka for copying articles about OGR and its predecessor agency, the NEC, listed in the *New York Times Index*. He also located unindexed references to OGR and NEC in the *Congressional Record* during floor debates on relevant appropriations bills. My appreciation to Alan Ehrenhalt and Rod Ross, two friends who live in Washington, DC, for helping describe Pershing Park, the site near the White House of the US Information Center from 1942–48. My research led me to Yale Professor Emeritus James W. Fesler, who in 1936 had been on the staff of the Brownlow Committee and had studied NEC's field offices. He shared his memories of those long-ago events and so much more. It was a delightful experience I was incredibly fortunate to have had. My program assistant, Andrea Zweifel, patiently proofed what must have seemed like endless revisions of each chapter. She saved me from many embarrassing mistakes.

I greatly benefited from the help of the editorial staff and reviewers of the State University of New York Press. Chapter 4 and some sections of chapter 5 are partly reprinted from an article I had published in *Public Relations Review* (see endnote for copyright permission information).[3] Finally, this book represents a closing of a circle that began in graduate school. My doctoral studies at Syracuse University were underwritten by a Herbert Lehman Fellowship in Public Affairs, awarded by the New York State Board of Regents.

Now, the State University of New York Press is publishing a book that was a direct result of the subsequent academic career the fellowship had made possible. So now, thirty years later, I can publicly express my gratitude to the citizens of New York State for their long-ago financial assistance.

Of course, any mistakes in the book are mine alone, despite the best efforts of so many people who tried to set me straight.

Abbreviations

APR	Administration of Public Relations
BOB	Bureau of the Budget
CPI	Committee on Public Information
EOP	Executive Office of the President
GAO	General Accounting Office (changed in 2004 to Government Accountability Office)
GIS	Government Information Service
IMP	Industrial Mobilization Plan
NEC	National Emergency Council
NRA	National Recovery Administration
NRPB	National Resources Planning Board
OEM	Office for Emergency Management
OFF	Office of Facts and Figures
OGR	Office of Government Reports
OWI	Office of War Information
OWMR	Office of War Mobilization and Reconversion
PBA	Public Buildings Administration
PRA	Public Relations Administration
USIS	United States Information Service
WPC	War Policies Commission
WRB	War Resources Board

Chapter 1

Introduction and Overview

A Federal Agency Dedicated to Government Reports?

In the first half of the twentieth century, the meaning of the phrase "government report" was very different from its common usage now—early in the twenty-first century. In contemporary usage, government reporting has a very negative meaning. It invokes the image of big brother and bureaucrats intruding unnecessarily in the lives of over-regulated Americans, forcing them to fill out long and unnecessary reports about the most private aspects of their businesses or families. This current meaning is nearly a universal one, given the statement in the 1990s by an activist Democratic president that "the era of big Government is over."[1] The idea of a government agency dedicated solely to reports would strike the contemporary observer as absurd, silly, and beyond belief.

Yet, to early public administration theorists and New Deal reformers, a government report was an important element of democracy. It represented two related activities. Administrative agencies fulfilled their democratic accountability to the people by reporting to the citizens about their activities and policies and, in the other direction, reported to the government's leadership about public opinion. During President Franklin Roosevelt's administration, government reporting was viewed as a very laudable and positive activity, directly related to enhancing democracy in the administrative state.

Believing in the importance of an activist government that engaged in public reporting, when FDR created the Executive Office of the President (EOP) in 1939, one of its five original agencies was a new agency called the Office of Government Reports (OGR). Two years later, Congress passed a law giving legislative sanction to OGR by authorizing its eligibility for annual appropriations. In that founding legislation, Congress defined the purposes of the agency, including:

1. Provide a central clearing house through which individual citizens, organizations of citizens, and state or local governmental bodies may transmit inquires and complaints and receive advice and information.

2. Collect and distribute information concerning the purposes and activities of executive departments and agencies for the use of the Congress, administrative officials, and the public.

3. Keep the president informed of the opinions, desires, and complaints of citizens and groups of citizens and of state and local governments with respect to the work of federal agencies.[2]

This congressional declaration of the agency's mission was a forceful and authoritative statement of the general importance of public relations in public administration and specifically of public reporting. However, Congress quickly had second thoughts.

OGR was to be short-lived. A year after its congressional authorization, it was merged into the temporary Office of War Information (OWI) for the duration of World War II. After the war, President Harry Truman dismantled OWI and re-established OGR to its status quo antebellum. In reaction, Congress appropriated only a fraction of the annual funding Truman had requested for fiscal year 1948 and was unwilling to provide any funding for the fiscal year after that. Truman had no choice but to shut down OGR a year and a half after he had restored it. In all, OGR had existed for four and a half years.

What was this OGR? If it was one of the original agencies of the new EOP, it must have been of some importance. After all, in government and politics, nothing happens without a reason. But what led Roosevelt and Truman to try to keep it alive? Up to now, historians and researchers have not been interested in answering that question. Perhaps that OGR barely survived Roosevelt, and the fact that it never became institutionalized within the federal government may have discouraged historical inquiries.

The story of OGR is missing from the record of the Roosevelt and Truman presidencies and from the history of presidential communication activities. Understandably, as an agency that existed only briefly, OGR would be of less interest than some of the lasting and extant legacies of those two presidencies. But failures can also be worth studying. Some of FDR's failures have been studied, even romanticized, including the Federal Arts, Writers and Theatre Projects,[3] Greenbelt cities,[4] and the two film documentaries *The Plow That Broke the Plains* and *The River*.[5]

Given the vital role of EOP in the emergence of the powerful contemporary presidency, a body of literature is gradually developing about it. Yet, again, these books mention OGR only glancingly even though it was one of EOP's original five agencies.[6] One of the other five original EOP agencies that didn't survive very long, the National Resources Planning Board—OGR's counterpart in every way, often mentioned by Congress in the same political breath (see chapter 5)—has been studied.[7] Two recent one-volume histories of the New Deal make no mention of OGR or its predecessor, the National Emergency Council (NEC).[8] Other books on specific aspects of the Roosevelt presidency occasionally mention OGR and NEC, but only briefly.[9] It is discussed briefly in a few articles in academic journals, mostly published contemporaneous to its existence or shortly after its demise.[10] Four unpublished dissertations include brief discussions of OGR, but largely focus on other topics or agencies.[11]

Significance of Studying the Office of Government Reports

When President Roosevelt first created OGR, he had to fight off intense and persistent efforts by the conservative coalition in Congress to kill it. Similarly, when President Truman re-established OGR after World War II, the implacable opposition to OGR by the Republican-majority eightieth Congress overwhelmed him.

This obscure and forgotten agency is significant for three reasons. From the viewpoint of political science and American history, this story is about one round in the ongoing struggle between the presidency and Congress over preeminence.[12] The twentieth century was largely a 100 Years War between the legislative and executive branches of the national government for primacy.[13] Until then, it was indeed accurate to describe the America's form of national government as congressional government.[14] Beginning with Roosevelt, political science largely applauded the emergence of the presidency as the active and primary branch of the federal government. But, the perception that this is "normal" is largely an artificial construct. Gary Wills argued, recently, that Congress was always intended by the writers of the Constitution as the central branch of the three.[15] The slow and steady emergence of the imperial presidency is not necessarily a natural development. Certainly, from time to time during the twentieth century, Congress sought to demonstrate its dominance or at least fight a rear-guard action to protect its central role. The 1920 defeat of the League of Nation's Covenant in the Senate and the passage of the War Powers Act in 1973 over a presidential veto epitomize Congress's ongoing battle to be the alpha branch of government. The story of OGR provides a concrete case study of this struggle between the two branches. FDR largely prevailed through 1941, but Congress had the last word in 1942 and then again in 1948. So, even though we think, almost romantically, of these two presidents as the originators of the powerful modern presidency, this arc of power did not grow in one consistent trend. Both sides fought every round vigorously. Through the events described in this book, one sees the tactics and strategies pursued by both branches of government to prevail over the other. And, contrary to the historical flow of power, here was an example of Congress triumphing over the modern expansionist presidency.

The struggle between the White House and Capitol Hill for preeminence is more than an abstract competition for power. It is about the consequences of predominance. That is why the opposition of the conservative coalition in Congress to FDR's New Deal was especially heated regarding OGR. Congress has consistently been hostile to public-relations expenditures in executive-branch agencies, before Roosevelt and after Truman, and to this day. Often this stance is associated with other so-called unnecessary categories of expenditures, such as consultants, travel, training, fancy offices, and the like. Like these other administrative-overhead activities, Congress views them as wasteful. Yet, the unfailing opposition by Congress to public-information activities in the executive branch has a more substantive motivation than mere across-the-board parsimony. Public relations and other communication programs give public administrators an opportunity not only to *report* directly to the citizenry, but also to generate *public support* for the agency. Since elected officials are dependent on being popular to survive, they are reluctant to take on popular government programs. And an agency's popularity translates into concrete power: higher budgets, more autonomy from legislative intervention and expanded activities. When an agency has strong public support, a legislature looses leverage to control it. In that respect, the struggle to control public reporting is the struggle over who will set the agency's destiny. Choke off the channel of communication to the public and the legislature has more de facto power over the agency. So, irrespective of partisan and political motivations, legislators have an *institutional* interest in minimizing public relations in public administration. No wonder there was so little authentic (as opposed to partisan) support in Congress for OGR. The agency was not merely the public-reporting program of one federal agency, rather it embodied reporting to the public by the entire executive branch—it was the *president's* public-relations agency. A robust OGR was a direct threat to Congress's institutional interests. As an agency that represented direct communication with the citizenry by the executive branch, the stakes were so much higher than just fighting over one agency's public relations. In short, OGR embodied just about everything that Congress loathed.

Executive/legislative squabbles continue to occur up to the present. For example, in 2002 the US General Accounting Office (GAO) (an arm of Congress) filed a lawsuit against the administration in an effort to obtain records of the vice president's energy task force.[16] This unusual step by GAO occurred even though the same party controlled both the presidency and the two houses of Congress. Other examples that echo OGR relate to the conflict in 2004 over predominance in the policy for occupying and rebuilding Iraq and in 2003 when the House passed a bill to undo new Federal Communication Commission rules regarding concentration of media-outlet ownership.[17] Therefore, the conflict between the two branches reflected institutional concerns that occur irrespective of shared partisan affiliation. Part of the OGR story is similar. Even though during the Roosevelt years the majority party in Congress was Democratic, the president still had trouble getting what he wanted approved by Congress. In the same way, regarding OGR, some people on Capitol Hill had wondered why the agency was in the Executive Branch, under the control of the president as his communication agency. Why shouldn't it be under the direction of Congress, as a generic federal-reporting office, they argued.

A close study of the history of OGR identifies the strands in the continuing institutional conflicts between Congress and the president. Those tugs and pulls for political power over half a century ago illuminate ongoing and current struggles. In that sense, OGR serves as a prime case study in a fight over raw political power that is at the heart of the permanent constitutional structure of the federal government.

The second perspective for analyzing the story of OGR is communications and public relations, whether applied specifically to the public sector or generally to society-at-large. By the beginning of the twenty-first century, the governmental process had largely evolved to be dominated by communications.[18] To communicate is to govern; to govern is to communicate. President Reagan's moniker as "the Great Communicator" conveyed in a shorthand that required no further elaboration the explanation of his successes and popularity. Political campaigns now largely consist of TV advertising, a president's agenda and political fate is largely pursued by communication plans and strategies, and many government-to-citizen (G2C) transactions are migrating to e-government. In this context, the effort to establish a permanent presidential communications agency in 1939 comprises a trip wire or early-warning signal of the dawn of the communications age in American government and politics.

Roosevelt had pursued innovative and unprecedented communications strategies to both govern and win elections. According to Winfield, FDR's communication activities, including OGR, had laid the "foundation for the modern presidency."[19] His concept of a permanent communications agency was unparalleled. Today, it is hard to go back to the mindset of the 1930s when such an agency was an astonishing and controversial innovation. Since 1969 every president has had a White House Office of Communications.[20] That such an agency should exist as part of a presidency now seems self-evident. It was Roosevelt who attempted to set such a precedent. Yet, he was thirty years and five presidents ahead of his time. OGR was the false dawn of the communications age in American politics and government. It foretold the coming of the information-drenched twenty-first century. Despite its failure to survive, OGR provided the historical template to the later strong focus of contemporary presidents on media relations. As a presidential agency dedicated to communications, OGR was a forerunner of the institutionalization of such efforts within the modern White House as well as of government-by-publicity.

OGR is also significant in the broader context of the history of public relations and publicity in society in general. Effective human communications have been important since the beginnings of organized society. Yet, the history of the modern era presents a distinct pattern of the rapid development of new communication technologies and practices and a subsequent dramatic increase in the central importance of communications as the primary mode of interconnectness of the human community. Whether the commonly accepted moniker for modern era is eventually to be that of the digital age, the computer era, the Internet age, or the Cybernetic era,[21] the predominance of information exchange as the primary currency of society is unquestionable. The computer had reduced all knowledge to just one binary category, with the resultant explosion in communications and information.

Public relations and publicity have emerged in contemporary history as a central and strategic approach to effectiveness and success in this new era.[22] When Marshall McLuhan famously observed that "the medium is the message,"[23] he was thought to be referring to hardware and technology. Yet his insight is equally valid for software and communications methodologies. Public relations has been one of those elements that McLuhan could have meant, whether knowingly or not. The central insight of public relations has been that *the percep-*

tion of the message is the ultimate measure of all communications. The original roots of public relations in press agentry and publicity were intended to trump the substance of the message through gimmicks, misleading tricks, and ballyhoo.[24] Later, public relations gradually developed respectability under the leadership of pioneers such as Ivy Lee and Edward L. Bernays due to their focus on the substance of corporate actions as well as the consequences of those actions that would lead to a good opinion by the public.[25] Yet the acceleration of communications technologies and techniques throughout the twentieth century led partly to a relapse back to the shortcuts of the earlier times. By the beginning of the twenty-first century, it was commonplace to consider *perception as the message,* at times seemingly wholly divorced from the substance. Public image or brand identification became the cynical currency of modern times. The oft-times wholly artificial personae of public figures—whether in show business, politics, or business—became the only thing that counted. Spin, image, branding, and hype emerged as the public-relations practices that appeared to trump all the others.[26] Despite the best efforts of the public relations profession for nearly a century, the term "PR" was permanently lodged as an epithet in modern usage,[27] to be sneeringly spit out universally by anyone in any context, bound to help win an argument. In that sense, the code phrase PR became a symbol of the era itself, that of persuasion by propaganda, wholly unconnected to facts and substance.

In this broader context, OGR epitomizes an early entity that identified communication as its central function and activity. *What* was communicated was subsumed to the core mission of *communicating.* OGR represented a prototype of the operationalization of the insight that public relations was an end, not just a means. In this view, public relations could, and should, be separated from the substantive work of an organization. Information was an end, in and of itself. OGR represents an important step in the history of public relations.

Public Reporting in Early Public Administration Theory

OGR was the most prominent manifestation of the theory of public reporting that had been nurtured by public administration theorists and practitioners during the 1920s and 30s. The intellectual roots of OGR start with the emergence of the profession of public administration in the United States in the early twentieth century. For good-government reformers (sometimes called "goo goos"—reform minded politicians and professors of government), American politics needed to replace the spoils system, patronage, "no-show" jobs, and the corruption of urban machines. They wanted to substitute it with a new profession of trained managers. These managers would be apolitical, hired and promoted based on merit, specialists in their field, given tenure in their jobs so as to provide continuity regardless of election results. Above all, their focus would be on the delivery of government services in the most efficient method possible. Politicians would determine the ends; heads of bureaus ("bureaucrats") would select the most efficient means. Elected officials would set policy and public administrators would merely implement it as vigorously and successfully as possible. When election results led to a change in policy, perhaps by 180 degrees, the professional manager wouldn't hesitate to administer a new program that was the opposite of the previous administration.

Yet, the promoters of this revolution in the delivery of public services in American government needed to reconcile their vision with democracy. After all, if the purpose of democracy was to give the voters the power to hold elected officials accountable for their decisions, then how could the public hold government administrators—who were protected by civil-service rules from arbitrary firing—equally accountable? So, was born, the theory of government reporting in American public administration.

Government agencies engage in external communications for many different reasons. In some cases, they seek to increase the utilization of their services by engaging in a marketing effort of informing potential clients about the availability of such services. Sometimes agencies seek to maximize public compliance with laws and regulations by broadly disseminating information about those requirements. At other times, the dissemination of information is an end in itself, since the information is the "product" of the agency, such as educational booklets from the US Department of Agriculture on food and nutrition. Other examples of the purposes of external relations include public service campaigns intended to modify mass behavior (e.g., "Only you can prevent forest fires") and seeking assistance of citizens as the "eyes and ears" of an agency (e.g., the 911 system). All these external relations purposes are integrally tied to implementing the agency's mission.

By using communications strategies, an agency is able to increase its efficiency at accomplishing its goals. In other words, these activities have a utilitarian purpose in that they are intended to facilitate the administrative delivery of governmental goods and services.[28]

Beyond these utilitarian communications purposes, the public administrator also has a normative democratic obligation to conduct an additional external-communication program that has no benefit to the efficiency of the administrative process. Called public reporting, this entails enhancing democracy by helping maintain an informed citizenry. Because the government manager is operating in the public sector, he/she has an obligation to report to the public-at-large on agency activities. This is part of the accountability process in a democracy. Since the agency is exercising its powers derived from the sovereignty of the public and is spending public funds, the agency must give an accounting of its performance to its ultimate "bosses." Public reporting focuses on the agency's current and past activities and is for informational and democratic purposes, whereas efforts to enhance citizen participation in agency goals focuses on future activities and are for planning, decision-making, and implementation purposes. Yet the two are very much connected, because effective citizen participation in democracy cannot occur unless it is preceded by efforts to inform the public—hence reporting.

The theory and function of public reporting should not be viewed in isolation. Rather, reporting is a step in the democratic process. There are some effective tools to build the public's credibility and trust in government through public involvement.[29] They include advisory committees, public hearings, citizen participation in decision-making, surveys and questionnaires, public-listening sessions and cards seeking feedback on services. But, public involvement can't occur in a vacuum. The public can't give the government useful feedback if it doesn't have the information needed to develop an informed opinion.[30]

Information is not only needed for voting. Between elections, public opinion is the ongoing gauge that expresses the judgment by the citizenry of how government is performing its mission. Just as with elections, for public opinion to work in a democracy, the citizens need information about what government is doing. Based on the results of this reporting, citizens would then have the information they need to be involved in agency decisions, policies, and operations. They would be able to develop informed judgments and public opinion could coalesce in one direction or the other.[31] In that respect, public reporting is the prerequisite to successful citizen participation in public administration.

Therefore, due to its underpinnings in normative democratic theory, public reporting is unique to the public sector, and is not a mandated activity in the business and nonprofit sectors.[32] Although some private and nonprofit agencies engage in external communication activities that are comparable to public reporting, these efforts are voluntary and goodwill oriented, rather than an absolute requirement.

The theory and profession of public administration had emerged as part of the progressive movement at the beginning of the twentieth century. It sought to reform government, largely to improve its efficiency and professionalism, but also strengthen the democratic accountability of government agencies. Some of the earliest writings by public administration theorists focused on the need to promote democracy simultaneous with the creation of permanent and professionalized administrative institutions that implement government policies. According to (professor, later president) Woodrow Wilson in his seminal article on creating professional public administration in the United States:

> administration in the United States must be at all points sensitive to public opinion . . . The ideal for us is a civil service cultured and self-sufficient enough to act with sense and vigor, and yet so intimately connected with popular thought, by means of elections and constant public counsel, as to find arbitrariness or class spirit quite out of the question.[33]

One way to harmonize public administration with democracy was for government officials to report about their activities to the public. That would make public administrators accountable to the citizenry and thus strengthen democracy in the administrative state. This led to the emergence of public reporting as a feature of the new profession of public administration. In 1928, Herman Beyle stated that "official reports of governmental authorities submitted or made available to the public as an accounting of official conduct might be made a more effective agency for the promotion of good government and an essential foundation of popular rule."[34]

Much of the early literature of government reporting focused on municipal administrators.[35] In 1919, Morris Cooke had described municipal reports as having "the greatest room for improvement" of all aspects of government publicity. He lauded New York City's 1915 annual report as "a neat volume printed in good type filled with many easily grasped facts and altogether enjoyable reading. It is in reality a citizen's handbook."[36] In 1927, Clarence Ridley began a systematic effort to survey municipal reports, recommending more informative and easy-to-read approaches and conducting an annual contest on best reports.[37] A decade later, he passed the project on to Herbert Simon, then his research assistant at the International City Managers' Association.[38] By 1938, public reporting by municipalities was a well-established activity. Simon and Ridley suggested its benefit in helping create an informed citizenry that, in turn, could fulfill its role in a democracy:

> The traditional description of the municipal report as the means by which the public official gives an accounting to the citizenry of his stewardship is therefore a very incom-

> plete picture. The report is equally important in helping the citizen discharge *his* responsibly to his government. Many progressive reports undertake the additional task of educating the citizen on questions of public policy, which he may later have to determine at the polls.[39]

The focus on government reporting was extended to all levels of government, not just municipal administration. One of the earliest textbooks in general public administration, not limited to municipal government, dedicated an entire chapter to the subject of government reports.[40] Reporting became a standard topic in public administration education, appearing in pioneering handbooks and academic reviews of public and municipal administration.[41]

Plan of the Book

This book tells a story that encompasses the three threads in American government in the twentieth century described above. OGR's tale is that of three parallel corners turned—or attempted to be turned—in the evolution of the modern federal government: the struggle for preeminence between presidents and Congress, the transformation of the presidency by the rise of the information age, and reporting by government agencies to the public. These three themes are, respectively, of interest to political science, communications, and public administration.

The story of OGR is largely told chronologically (except for chapter 4). This is intended to help convey the sense of how things seemed at the time of the events described. *During* the struggle over its existence, no one knew if Presidents Roosevelt and Truman would succeed in institutionalizing the agency or if the opposition by the conservative coalition in Congress would prevail. Eric Foner, in his history of Reconstruction, emphasized that the historian "must avoid telescoping the actual course of events into a predetermined linear progress."[42] Therefore, the sequence of the chapters traces the life of OGR chronologically.

The next chapter reviews the work of NEC, OGR's organizational antecedent. Chapters 3, 4, and 5 present the tangled story of Roosevelt's effort to establish a permanent presidential communications agency. Chapters 6 and 7 describe the agency at its zenith—in late 1941 and early 1942. Chapters 8 and 9 cover FDR's fight with Congress and the press over a wartime-headquarters building for OGR, called the US Information Center. Although Roosevelt won the battle to build and open the Information Center, that fight weakened OGR politically so much that Roosevelt reluctantly decided to reverse himself and merge OGR into the wartime Office of War Information. After the war, President Truman re-established OGR, although with slightly different responsibilities, which are described in chapter 10. However, the Republican Eightieth Congress refused to provide continuing funding for the agency and Truman had no choice but to shut it down.

The final chapter examines whether OGR's abolition was authentic or merely de jure. A close examination discloses that nearly all of its functions continued under the aegis of different agencies. Many of OGR's programs exist to this day (2005) in the White House Office of Communications, demonstrating that OGR was indeed the first presidential communications agency. Finally, the chapter analyzes in detail the roots of congressional hostility toward OGR, tying that opposition to the three themes of congressional–presidential relations, the rise of the information age and advocacy for government to engage in public reporting. The fight over OGR's fate was a fight about power, because reporting efforts can increase public support for executive-branch agencies, thus limiting Congress's power to cut programs that are popular with public opinion.

In the years immediately after the OGR blowout, public reporting faded from importance in both theory and practice. This suggests the final significance of telling the story of this unusual federal agency. The demise of OGR contributed to the demise of public reporting. This was a regrettable development if one accepts the theory that public reporting is one way to harmonize the modern administrative state with democracy.

Chapter 2

Origins

The National Emergency Council, 1933–39

Before Roosevelt's presidency, the most significant example of a federal communications agency was the Committee on Public Information (CPI), established by executive order by President Woodrow Wilson in 1917. Its purpose was to be the central source for information about US involvement in World War I. Wilson named former reporter George Creel to head it.[1] During the war, CPI utilized "new public relations and advertising techniques to picture the war as a conflict between good and evil and to publicize America's plans for a peaceful, democratic world order."[2] It was an unprecedented marriage of propaganda and ideology, conducted by an official agency of the national government. But CPI was very controversial with Congress, which was suspicious of the federal government running a propaganda agency, especially one under the control of the president. Furthermore, CPI's successes in whipping up American public opinion in support of a moral crusade "generated unrealistic hopes for a better world. . . . Creel had oversold his product. Propaganda became a scapegoat in the postwar period of delusion."[3]

Franklin Roosevelt had been part of the Wilson administration, serving as assistant secretary of the Navy.[4] He hadn't liked what CPI did, saying that he was "opposed to organizing a single propaganda agency."[5] So, in the run-up to World War II, when he was encouraged to create a successor to CPI, he "displayed little enthusiasm" for doing that.[6] Still, CPI was the only template of an activist-presidential effort at public-information dissemination. When FDR's press secretary Stephen Early created a much more expansive White House press operation than that of previous presidents, he was viewed as having "merely refined and expanded the system that had begun with George Creel."[7]

The first overt action by Roosevelt regarding public reporting and information dissemination after entering the White House (besides Early's work as press secretary) occurred during the first year of his presidency with an expansion of the staff of the National Emergency Council (NEC). As part of his efforts to deal with the Great Depression, FDR created not only an alphabet-soup of confusing ad-hoc agencies to deliver government services and programs, but he also created several "superagencies" that were intended to have power and authority to accomplish centralized coordination of the work of this multitude of agencies. Some of those coordinating bodies included the Special Industrial Recovery Board, the Executive Council, and the Industrial Emergency Committee. He created NEC in November 1933 for "the purpose of coordinating and making more efficient and productive the work of the numerous field agencies of the Government."[8] In its original conception, the core mission was the ten-person council itself, consisting the secretaries of key cabinet departments as well as the heads of the major independent agencies dealing with the Depression. The council would meet on a regular schedule, every other Tuesday. The meetings of these principals would be the venue to resolve such problems as lack of coordination, competition, duplication, or overlap of services and programs.[9]

Adding Information Activities

Roosevelt quickly began tinkering with NEC by expanding the mission of its staff. On December 6, 1933, only a few weeks after creating NEC, he directed that it create a field staff of state directors who would have a broad mandate to try to coordinate the local operations of the many New Deal agencies then in existence. He also ordered that NEC "set up in Washington a central information bureau for the purpose of conveying to the general public all factual information with reference to the various government agencies."[10] At a press conference, he explained:

> I think the time has come for us to try to consolidate information about the Federal agencies in the form of some kind of information that will tie everything in together, where any individual or group or corporation can go to find out all the

> intricacies of the new machinery . . . The main Council in Washington will sit as a central information bureau for the purpose of conveying any information with reference to various Government agencies and will send out that information, in simple, plain language, to the State Directors.[11]

Along with a follow-up statement later that month,[12] this was the birth of what led to the first presidential communications agency. It would grow and evolve to reflect FDR's desire to integrate information about the multiplicity of related activities of various federal programs and then disseminate the information so that the work of the federal government could be more easily understood. Some essential operating principles were enunciated by FDR at this original announcement. They were to guide the work of his experiment with a presidential communications agency throughout its existence:

- It would not be a propaganda agency, trying overtly to persuade and convince people about how well the administration was performing
- It would not be a censorship agency vis-à-vis the work of reporters
- It would not take over or replace the existing mechanisms for dealing with the White House press corps and other Washington-based reporters
- It would mostly deal with the public-at-large, not reporters
- It would serve as a central clearing house, not a substitute for the public-information offices of individual federal agencies
- It would largely be limited to disseminating information upon individual request
- Its informational activities were intended to have a tangible and pragmatic effect; by helping individual citizens as well as businesses identify federal programs and services that they could benefit from
- Its scope for disseminating information would be national, including through a network of state offices, rather than just releasing information in Washington.

Interestingly, when FDR talked in private about the rationale for NEC's information activities, he did not rely on the *pragmatic* justification for these programs, such as increasing participation in

New Deal relief programs. Rather, he emphasized the democratic rationale for disseminating information, so that the public-at-large would understand the policies and reasons for the administration's initiatives and then be able to make a judgment on their merits. A few years later, at a closed-door NEC meeting in December 1935 he said:

> it seems to me that the whole fate of what the government is trying to do at the present time depends, regardless of the election, on an understanding of the program by the mass of the people in the country. And, again, quite aside from politics, the continuation of the broad program successfully is dependent upon the approval of the people, which, again, is depending upon their understanding of it.[13]

So, Roosevelt's privately stated rationale for NEC's information programs reflected the theory of public reporting that public administration literature had been developing since the early years of the twentieth century. In Roosevelt's mind, it was a legitimate purpose of an administration to explain to the citizenry what it was doing and why—and then letting the democratic process take it from there.

However, other views of this new role for government were largely driven by political, partisan, and institutional reasons. For example, conservative voices in and out of Congress viewed NEC's information activities as pure political propaganda and wholly inappropriate for a tax-funded agency. The *Saturday Evening Post* said NEC was the "eyes and ears for the President" as part of his vast, expensive, overwhelming, and out-of-control publicity machine.[14]

In 1933, NEC's executive director, Frank Walker, had to create from scratch this new information apparatus. Lacking much precedent (besides CPI, which Roosevelt disdained), he was largely working with a blank slate. At that time, most information-related work was viewed as women's jobs, such as telephone operator, librarian, and typing. Therefore, Walker turned to Mary Dewson, head of the Democratic National Committee's Women's Division, and who was also familiar with the work of the New York Welfare Council's Information Service. On December 9, she wrote Walker thanking him "for believing the women can put this over."[15] Dewson recommended an initial staff of seven full-time employees and several support staff.[16]

NEC, like all the New Deal relief agencies, moved fast to implement its mandate. Using an allocation of $10,000 made by the president from general-relief appropriations,[17] Walker quickly began appointing state directors (all men) and information-service staff in Washington (mostly women). The new information staff proposed creating a publication that would help reduce confusion about all the relief programs then in operation. They suggested a loose-leaf binder that would provide authoritative and up-to-date information on the activities and programs of all federal agencies, with particular attention to the many recently created New Deal relief organizations. On January 23, 1934, NEC approved the idea[18] and a few months later issued its new publication, with the rather cumbersome title of *Daily Revised Manual of Emergency Recovery Agencies and Facilities Provided by the United States Government: A Simplified Textbook of Federal Activities which Enables Every Citizen to Use Effectively, Speedily, and Directly the Emergency Service which the Government Has Established.* This publication eventually metamorphosed into the *United States Government Manual,* a federal publication that continues to this day.[19]

In early February 1934, the newly appointed state directors were assembled in Washington to be briefed on their responsibilities and the expectations of them. President Roosevelt met with them briefly. In his comments to them, he identified two specific tasks that he expected of them. First, they were to engage in "disseminating information." Second, he wanted them to submit to him the "kind of reports that will keep us in touch with the broad picture in every one of the forty-eight States."[20] In other words, their information duties would be not only distributing information out to the public, but also reporting information to help keep the administration informed of the situation in every state. This was a clear commitment to two-way communication, often identified as the basic definition of authentic communication.

In March 1934, NEC's information staff was formally constituted into the United States Information Service (USIS)[21] with the goal:

> to aid persons seeking contact with some particular phase of governmental activity. With thousands of visitors constantly coming to Washington, many of them for the first time, this agency will act as a directing point through which the stranger may find the branch of government with which his particular problem is concerned. It will be the function of the United States Information Service to relieve the public visiting Washington from needless waste of time and effort in locating the desired department.[22]

The *New York Times* described USIS as "a sort of Federal Traveler's Aid." The headline in the *Washington Post* was more blunt, "New Bureau's Job Is to Make Going Rough for Lobbyists."[23] That was a reference to newspaper reports that some citizens and businessmen had been coming to Washington and were paying lobbyists for basic information or for services such as setting up appointments. The USIS would provide such basic information and services for free. The New Deal was indeed shaking up traditional Washington. If information was power, then under FDR information was free, to all people, not just the economic elite.

The last major initial component of NEC's information activities was the Division of Press Intelligence. The main function of the division was to clip articles from major newspapers that dealt with the New Deal and then compile a summary of news coverage and editorial commentary about the administration. The summary was sent to major officials in the White House and cabinet departments.[24] The division had first been created within the National Recovery Administration (NRA) in July 1933. But, after the US Supreme Court ruled that key parts of NRA's statutory powers were unconstitutional, the agency was slowly dismembered. In July 1935, the Division of Press Intelligence was transferred to NEC.[25]

By 1935 all four major components of NEC's information program—state offices, the precursor to the *US Government Manual,* USIS, and the Division of Press Intelligence—were in place. Three years later, NEC's information activities were expanded to "round out to the fullest the coordinating facilities of the council" by creating a Radio Division and the US Film Service.[26] With these information-related activities and other responsibilities, NEC's budget and staffing grew quickly. Even after peaking in fiscal year 1936, it continued to be a substantial agency after that. As table 2.1 shows, after its first year of operation, NEC's budget was never less than about $700,000 and staffing never less than 232. This was a extensive administrative effort, largely dedicated to information reporting.

Table 2.1
Budget and Staffing of the National Emergency Council

Fiscal Year	*Budget (actual)*	*Staffing (actual)*
1934	$460,000	88
1935	$692,687	346
1936	$1,471,395	431
1937	$1,061,796	389
1938	$693,763	232
1939	$850,000	340
1940	$850,000 (appropriated)	NA

Sources: House Appropriations Committee, *Work Relief and Relief for Fiscal Year 1940: Hearings,* 349; 52 Stat. 810; 53 Stat. 931; *Budget of the US, 1936,* 76; *Budget, 1937,* 59; *Budget, 1938,* 58–9; *Budget, 1939,* 61; and *Budget, 1940,* 68.

Here, indeed, was the precursor to an institutionalized presidential communications agency. However, since Congress never authorized NEC, it cannot be considered as the first *permanent* White House communications entity.

Field Service

NEC's state offices were a key component of the agency's overall mission, both information and non-information related. These latter responsibilities of the state directors included working with state government to pass legislation so that the state would be eligible for each New Deal program enacted by Congress—often each program had different eligibility requirements. The state directors were also expected to try to coordinate the substantive work of each federal agency in their state to maximize cooperation and minimize duplication or even competition. However, lack of explicit power over the state directors of New Deal agencies at times prevented the NEC representative from much leverage to accomplish better coordination. The president had written all cabinet officers and agency heads a few times requesting that they direct their field staff to work closely with NEC state directors, but bureaucratic politics and conflicting personalities often negated the effect of these instructions.[27]

The public-relations activities that state directors were involved in were categorized by NEC into six functions: press activities, radio programs, public speaking, personal contact, contacts with associations, and use of informative questionnaires and letters.[28] When President Roosevelt traveled, NEC would arrange for the appropriate state directors to meet his train and give him a report on their assessment of how the New Deal was faring in their state.[29]

One of the regular responsibilities of state directors was to submit periodic reports on public opinion and political developments in their state. The NEC headquarters in Washington would then try to discern any possible trends occurring nationally. Generally, these reports were submitted to the president on a monthly basis. At times, reports were requested on specific topics independent of the regular monthly submissions. For example, NEC asked all state directors to submit their analysis of the work of the Federal Housing Authority in their state, including "progress, shortcomings, community relations, etc."[30] At a press conference, FDR explicitly referred to these NEC reports and praised their utility to him and the administration:

> Red Leggett [NEC Acting Executive Director] has been getting out a very interesting statement once a month ever since he has been in, a sort of report or general picture of conditions in each state relating to needs, employment, public works,—all forms of Government activity—and recommendations as to how things can be better coordinated. Now, these reports have been coming to me every month and then going out to the different agencies affected by the report, so they have been very helpful.[31]

NEC sought to have at least one office in each of the forty-eight states and largely met that goal in 1934 and 1935. Depending on its budget, this was not always possible. For example, in mid-1936, it had thirty-six state directors in place.[32] At its funding trough in the winter of 1937–38, NEC had to briefly abandon its longstanding goal of forty-eight state offices, closing eleven offices, and began shifting to a new structure of regional offices.[33] But, its budget situation improved after that and it resumed its effort to have as many state offices as its budget would permit. By mid-1939, it had thirty-nine state offices.[34]

Appointing field staff on a state-by-state basis, rather than a regional basis, certainly had advantages, such as working on harmonizing every state's laws with New Deal programs. On the other hand, Fesler noted, "where the 48 states are made field service areas by an agency the requirements of political clearance for area directors are most insistent."[35] That, indeed, occurred from time to time with appointments of NEC state directors. For example, when NEC's budget cuts in 1937 necessitated closing several state offices, but the director of the Connecticut office had been endorsed by both of the state's US Senators. Taking care not to bash a political beehive, the NEC acting director consulted in advance with FDR about the political implications of closing that state office.[36] The political delicacy of appointing and firing state directors was even more politicized once Congress passed a law that required, indirectly, Senate confirmation of all appointments to NEC state director positions.

The Division of Field Operations was the largest administrative unit within NEC, consisting of roughly a third its budget and staffing. Most of the state offices were located in the largest city of the state rather than the state capital.[37] For some of the larger states—and depending on NEC's budget—there sometimes were some additional offices. Each office was usually staffed by three to four people: a state director, his (since they were all men) executive assistant, and one or two clerical employees.

United States Information Service

After the founding of USIS in March 1934, there was some concern within NEC about how successful it would be. There were three specific issues: whether the volume of inquires would justify USIS's existence, if the inquiries would be trivial, and if the inquiries would be so dominated by the unemployed seeking work that USIS would be little different from a job service. After three months of operations however, it was becoming clear that none of these concerns had materialized. In fact, one of the most surprising developments was that the inquiries—whether in person, by phone and by mail—were not only from individual citizens living outside Washington, but also from members of Congress and even other departments and agencies.[38]

After nearly one full year of operations, USIS had received 41,000 inquiries: 25,000 from citizens, 14,000 from federal agencies, and 2,000 from Congress. The inquiries often focused on the new structure of the executive branch with all the New Deal agencies being created and the missions of those new agencies. In response, besides what eventually became the *US Government Manual*, USIS created two other printed materials that clearly filled a need: a chart of the executive branch and a *Digest of Purposes of Current Federal Agencies*. Both were free and their distribution indicated how much of a need they were filling. In USIS's first year, 20,000 charts and 12,000 *Digests* were mailed out.[39] Slowly, the work of the service became routinized. The staff developed a comprehensive reference catalog of 15,000 cards with answers to questions that had previously been researched. Some of the most frequently asked questions were about locating federal employees and offices in the Washington area.

USIS's seventeen person staff was divided into three groups. The "front-office" handled all walk-in and phone inquiries, averaging about 150 every day. The Correspondence Section responded to all inquiries arriving in the mail. Every day about 250 to 300 letters were delivered. A third group, called the Congressional Information Section, had specialized researchers who focused on keeping track of developments in Congress and the Supreme Court. The pattern of inquiries was about 40 percent from citizens and from federal agencies and 20 percent from Congress; with about one-third of inquiries handled solely by USIS and two-thirds referred to the appropriate federal office for a more detailed response. The service's total budget was about $32,000 a year.[40]

A mirror image of the all-male corps of NEC state directors, USIS was entirely staffed by women, including its director. The only exception was an "office boy." The *New York Times* explained this women-only pattern thusly:

> First, they seem better fitted than men for the kind of work required—patient research, attention to minute details and delving into government documents and so on. Second, at the price he pays, Uncle Sam can get better-qualified women than men. Most of the salaries run from $1,440 to $1,600.[41]

By 1936, USIS had responded in two years to about a quarter a million inquiries and had opened its only branch office, in Rockefeller Center in New York City with a staff of two women. That office, too, quickly came to be used by a wide variety of inquirers, including advertising agencies, businesses, government agencies, and reporters.[42] In 1938, the New York office had handled about 7,500 inquires.[43] That same year, one academic researcher was so impressed with the work of NEC's information service—in contrast to counterpart activities at the state level—that he recommended all state governments should create centralized public-information agencies patterned after USIS.[44]

United States Government Manual and Other Publications

The publication in 1934 of NEC's *Daily Revised Digest* directory of federal programs and agencies had been a success. It was distributed to 1,300 Red Cross offices throughout the country, to the mayors of the 300 largest cities and to major federal offices that engaged in direct contact with citizens.[45] The next edition, issued on January 1, 1935, was renamed the *United States Government Manual; Revised Currently; A Simplified Textbook Designed to Inform Every Citizen as to Government Procedure and to Make Effectively Available All Federal Services.* This, the first *US Government Manual,* was also a loose-leaf, permitting updated pages to be inserted as appropriate. Five thousand copies were initially printed, but demand was so great that eventually 16,222 were distributed. About 4,000 copies were sold for $2.00 each—indicating that the new publication was meeting a real need. The purchase price included receipt of updated pages for the remainder of the calendar year. Other copies were distributed gratis to federal agencies, newspapers and magazines, NEC state directors and members of Congress.[46]

Besides the *Manual,* NEC published a small number of free publications. USIS created a free serial called *Digest of Purposes of Current Federal Agencies.* It contained a brief description of every agency of the executive branch including the legal authority under which it operated, its purpose, internal structure, and the address of the agency's information office for readers seeking additional information. A new, updated version was printed at least once a year. For example, the

1938 issue listed sixty-two agencies in its forty-five pages.[47] Given the almost revolutionary change in the scope and size of the federal government during the New Deal, this popular publication filled a need for basic information about the executive branch.

Other NEC publications included *Report on Economic Conditions in the South* (August, 1938); *Detailed State Report of Federal Expenditures, 1933–38; Informational Handbook;* and *Activities of the Federal Emergency Agencies, 1933–1938.* Every state office also issued several standard publications (often linked to the national compilations issued by NEC in Washington), including *Directory of Federal and State Departments and Agencies; Consolidated State Report of Federal Expenditures, 1933–1938; County Reports of Federal Expenditures, 1933–1938; A Narrative View of Agency Operations, 1933–1938;* and *Work Accomplishment Report, 1933–1938.*[48]

Division of Press Intelligence

Although the formal origins of the Division of Press Intelligence in the federal government dated to July 1933 when it was established within

Figure 2.1. Display of information distributed by the US Information Service, while it was part of the National Emergency Council (1933–39). Note loose leaf version of *United States Government Manual* on both sides of USIS sign. Credit: National Archives, Record Group 44, Box 996.

the National Recovery Administration (NRA), its de facto origins extend earlier than that. During Roosevelt's tenure as New York governor, his chief aide Louis Howe began systematically tracking newspaper coverage and then summarizing the results for FDR.[49] However, the basic concept of a governmental clipping service was not original to Howe and Roosevelt. Following the Mississippi River floods in 1927, Commerce Secretary Herbert Hoover directed his staff to clip all articles about the flood and forward them to his field headquarters where he was coordinating the federal response. These clippings gave him a detailed sense of the "spin" of the coverage, of editorial opinion, and of problems that were beginning to get the attention of reporters. Hoover often based his actions and statements on the information he had gained from the news summaries.[50]

Roosevelt's and Howe's active monitoring of press coverage continued during the 1932 presidential race. The Democratic National Committee created a research bureau for the campaign. It supplied the party's campaigners with accurate information about the federal government and its operations. The office also engaged in some press clipping and summarizing activities. They hired Katherine C. Blackburn, who had been the Secretary of the Woodrow Wilson Foundation since 1921, to run it.[51]

After Roosevelt's election victory, Howe wanted to establish a formal and official newspaper tracking and clipping system.[52] He asked Blackburn to create and run the office. But, there was no precedent for such an office in a presidential administration. A few weeks after Roosevelt took office, the White House formally requested the Civil Service Commission to approve a new civil service position in the office of Assistant Secretary of State Raymond Moley to be dedicated to "special work for the President . . . involving duties as a reference librarian."[53] The commissioners rejected the request, saying she was not qualified according to their requirements for such a position. However, given that "the Whie [sic] House desires immediate action" they found a loophole. Since the president "desires to avail himself of her services," the new slot could be exempted from merit-based competition and appointment since it fit in the category of "persons appointed by the President without confirmation by the Senate."[54] This awkward set-up led to some strange outcomes. For example, in spring 1935, the State Department's Board of Appeals and Review was conducting annual efficiency ratings for departmental employees. However, according to the department's acting chief clerk, "there is no one in the Department qualified to rate" Blackburn.[55] Louis Howe, secretary to the president, obliged by filling out the form.[56]

Upon her hiring by the Department of State, Blackburn had to create an operation from scratch. "I started with a chair, a desk and a stack of newspapers," she said of the beginnings of the office.[57] She established the "Division of Press Intelligence for the United States Government" with offices in the Department of Commerce building. Even though the division was officially part of NRA beginning in July 1933, the office kept using its original title, as though it was unaffiliated with any federal agency.

The division quickly developed a system for its operations. For newspaper coverage, it printed a *Daily Bulletin* (sometimes called the *Press Intelligence Bulletin*) based on articles in 400–450 daily newspapers, just about all the papers published in cities with a population over 50,000. Every day the newspapers arriving in the mail would be clipped for any articles that related to national issues. The articles would then be sorted based on subject and then listed in the daily digest according to these standard subject headings. Sometimes the daily summary was ninety pages long and contained between 6,000 to 8,500 items. The summaries were distributed not only to the president, but also to about 450 to 500 senior administration officials and to any senator or congressman requesting it. When readers would see the listing of an article of interest, the division would send over the full article. The office retained all the clippings in a master file with cross-listing notations so that previous coverage of a particular subject or by a specific columnist could quickly be accessed.

The division also distributed a weekly *Magazine Abstracts* that reviewed relevant articles in thirty-six weekly and monthly magazines. Unlike the daily summary that merely listed the articles, this review included a brief summary of the contents of each article. Its distribution list was almost 1,000. Besides these two basic publications, the division also had a Service Unit to respond to requests for specific articles or articles on a particular topic. In 1938, for example, it received requests for 1.2 million articles. Finally, the office had a small research office to respond to requests for *analysis* of coverage of a specific topic as opposed to merely a compilation. In spring 1939, it had fulfilled about 530 requests over the previous nine months.

To read and clip the newspapers and magazines, the division employed about sixty people and had an annual budget of about $125,000. The division also required a large amount of office space to permit not only the physical clipping activity, but also to store all previously clipped articles. By early 1939, the collection had over 4.5 million items.[58]

Blackburn was always seeking to improve her services to the president. For example, in October 1933, she asked Howe if the daily bulletin summarizing news clippings should have a section on announcements of new hirings found in the papers.[59] At the depths of the depression, such "good news" would be valuable to the administration about the success of its economic program. Howe liked her idea.[60] Another time, she asked if the division should create a recurring report on "News and Editorial Discussions of Coming Session of Congress."[61] FDR's secretary responded that the president "asks me to tell you that he thinks it is 'quite interesting.' "[62] FDR personally valued the work of the Division. When NEC was going through a budget retrenchment in early 1937, the acting executive director made a point of first checking with the president before imposing a proportionate budget cut on the Division of Press Intelligence. Roosevelt, as usual careful about putting certain things in writing, responded by dictating a note: "Will you speak to me about this at your convenience?"[63]

Radio Division

In the 1930s and 40s, radio was the sole alternative news medium to print. It was a relatively new technology that the administration quickly zeroed in on to bypass a hostile press controlled by conservative publishers. For example, Roosevelt's famous "fireside chats" were live radio broadcasts. NEC's major involvement in radio was triggered in 1936 by political considerations. Ever since the beginning of the New Deal, federal agencies and high-ranking officials had routinely asked radio stations for airtime to present information about the work of their agencies. In some cases, these requests were for more than a onetime appearance, involving proposals for weekly informational or dramatic programs. Since 1936 was a presidential election year, the White House was concerned that any political tint to these programs or any sharp increase in requests for air time could be seen as political and campaign-related, leading radio stations and networks to a shut off this broadcasting opportunity.

On March 12, 1936, Presidential Press Secretary Stephen Early directed NEC Acting Executive Director Lyle Alverson to assume a coordinating role for agency-radio contacts. NEC was to become the sole source of requests to radio companies for air time from government agencies. Conversely, it was to be the one-stop location for radio networks and stations seeking a government official to speak on a specific topic. Early wanted to be sure to keep federal agencies on the radio throughout the presidential campaign, under the assumption that maximum dissemination of information about the programs and activities of executive branch agencies—while strictly presented as neutral reporting—would redound to the president's political benefit.[64] (This central coordinating role for radio was a precursor to the identical later work of OGR regarding movies and donated advertising for public-service campaigns. See chapter 10.)

Later, newly appointed Executive Director Lowell Mellett formalized NEC's coordinating radio role by officially establishing a Radio Division within NEC on July 1, 1938. Its purposes were to promote informational programming about federal programs and agencies on local radio stations (in contradistinction to national radio networks) and to coordinate all radio activities in the executive branch. The Radio Division staff was small, consisting of three professionals (the assistant director was a woman) and two clerical workers with a budget for fiscal year 1939 of $20,000.[65]

The radio broadcasts were part of a series called "United States Government Reports" and were the radio version of such traditional reporting vehicles as printed annual reports. Generally, the Washington staff would prepare a basic script of questions and answers that would summarize the work and role of a particular federal agency. The scripts would be sent to all of NEC's state directors who would then invite the local representative of the agency to participate in the colloquy. The amount of such programs in each state was dependent on the number of radio stations willing to participate voluntarily and donate the airtime for the series as well as the initiative of each state office. In August 1939, the assistant director of the Radio Division reported that there was no consistent level of participation. It varied from "extremely desultory" in Alabama to "excellent" in the state of Washington.[66] Clearly, the degree of usage by local radio stations was solely dependent on the initiative and voluntary cooperation of each state director. In some cases, they were enthusiastic about the opportunity, whereas others disregarded it almost totally.

In the second half of 1938, after the first six months of the Radio Division's existence, about forty of the states had radio stations participating in the series with an average of 2.25 programs per week in every state. The Division had provided fifty-one scripts about the programs of thirty-seven federal agencies. By mid-1939, the weekly "US Government Reports" series was being consistently broadcast on 175 stations.[67] (In May 1939, President Roosevelt was the guest on one of the programs of NEC's Radio Division. See chapter 3.)

United States Film Service

During Roosevelt's first term, the Resettlement Administration, headed by Rexford Tugwell, had created a small film unit to document the difficult conditions in the dustbowl that prompted the creation of the agency. Called *The Plow That Broke the Plains,* the thirty-minute documentary vividly presented the harsh life of farmers in the plains. It was implicitly both a call to action and an effort to persuade the viewer of the rightness of the administration's efforts to deal with the problem. Released in 1936, New Deal opponents quickly labeled it propaganda, free advertising for the administration and a waste of taxpayer dollars. A follow-up documentary, *The River,* showed the flooding caused by the Mississippi. Again, the implicit message of the movie was the need for government action to prevent future flooding of people's homes and farms.[68]

However, the president was generally pleased with the movies and believed that such productions should be institutionalized in the federal government. So, he decided to transfer the documentary film unit from the Farm Security Administration (which the Resettlement Administration had been merged into) to NEC.[69] The United States Film Service was established on August 13, 1938, based on a presidential directive to NEC Director Mellett. Regarding the two movies already produced, "I desire that in the future the distribution and exhibition of these films be coordinated by the National Emergency Council in order that they may most effectively and economically serve the purposes for which they were produced." Second, he directed NEC to assume the production and distribution of a new documentary on unemployment that three New Deal agencies were involved in.[70]

By prearrangement, on that same day Mellett appointed Pare Lorentz, who had produced and directed the two previous documentaries, as head of the new US Film Service. Besides the two missions mentioned in the president's letter, Mellett added two other more general and coordinative duties. The Film Service was to coordinate the activities of the departments and agencies that were involved in the production or distribution of motion pictures and maintain a library of government films for use by educational and civic groups.[71] The next month, President Roosevelt further expanded the responsibilities of NEC's Film Service, including to

1. develop minimal standards for all motion picture contracts signed by federal agencies;

2. review any such proposed contracts, before they are signed, to ascertain that they meet these minimum standards;

3. review the proposed scripts for all movies produced by federal agencies for purpose of providing "constructive and technical criticism";

4. clearance (i.e., approval) of all proposed movies by federal agencies to "improve the pictures, prevent wastage, and effect very real economies in production";

5. review all requests from all private movie companies for use of federal property and/or personnel in the production of their movies.

The service "should examine the parts of the scenarios [i.e., screenplays] that involve Government participation and give motion picture producers the benefit of expert Government consultation."[72]

The Film Service started with twelve employees and quickly grew to twenty-three employees as well as some consultants who were paid on a per-diem basis. Its budget, based on transfers from other agencies, was $265,000 for fiscal year 1939 with a requested appropriation of $335,840 for fiscal year 1940.[73] By the end of the year, the staff had conducted a thorough survey of the documentaries made and held by all executive branch agencies. Twenty-six departments, bureaus, and agencies were identified as having about 400 films. It then produced a seventeen-page *Directory of U.S. Government Films* that were available for borrowing, and distributed 4,000 copies of the directory to educational and civic groups. Films could be obtained by contacting each agency directly or by working through the Film Service. By May 1939, it had received and responded to almost 2,000 requests for federal films.[74] Other Film Service activities included distributing *The Plow That Broke the Plains* and *The River* for showing in commercial theaters, some preliminary production work and filming of several proposed new documentaries, working with federal agencies planning films, preparing a standard contract to be used by agencies when signing contracts for production of movies, and surveying all federal production facilities in order to create a comprehensive plan to improve federal film facilities.

However, the Film Service never reached its potential during its brief existence at NEC. Its funding was dependent on transfers from other agencies, which made it vulnerable to decisions by many other administrators. Lorentz was sometimes difficult to work with and did not operate within the normal strictures of federal agencies. A White House aide wrote that the "genius of Lorentz is outweighed by his temperament."[75] Most importantly, the conservative coalition in Congress viewed the Film Service as a prime example of New Deal propaganda, a waste of money, and an activity that government should not be involved in.[76]

Waiting for Implementation of the Brownlow Committee Report, 1937–39

NEC slowly petered out as a cabinet-like body. It met infrequently in 1935 and for the last time in April 1936. Nonetheless, Roosevelt signed several executive orders to extend the council's life to continue its core information activities.[77] However, during this time, NEC had been shrinking in size and role. Then, events in 1938 led to a reinvigoration of its role. First, Congress defeated FDR's reorganization plan, which would have moved NEC's information activities to the Bureau of the Budget (BOB). Second, Roosevelt had thought the worst of the depression was over and decided to balance the budget by cutting spending. Yet, the economy was not rebounding and, if anything, cuts in "pump-priming" spending were making things worse. He then abandoned the effort to balance the budget and in late spring of 1938 resumed requesting large relief and public works appropriations funded through deficit spending.

As part of that new spending policy, he announced that he intended "to go back and reconstitute the N.E.C. the way it was working about two years ago. In other words, with a larger relief program . . . we have to have coordination in the different states . . . now it has to be stepped up again. The system worked exceedingly well."[78] He requested, and Congress approved, $850,000 for NEC for fiscal year 1939.[79] Also, in late April 1938, he named Lowell Mellett, who had just resigned from the Scripps-Howard News Service (which in Washington published the *Daily News*) due to his disagreement with its anti-New Deal stance, to be NEC's new executive director.[80]

Behind the scenes, there was frank discussion in the White House about the reasons for reviving NEC. Interior Secretary Harold Ickes always expressed his views to the president repeatedly and forcefully on matters connected to his responsibilities as well as on broader issues. In spring 1938, he kept telling Roosevelt that the administration needed to have a more vigorous propaganda program to respond to its emboldened critics and help shape public opinion. When Roosevelt responded that he had decided to appoint Mellett to head a reinvigorated NEC, Ickes wrote delightedly in his diary:

> The President has at last agreed to set up a propaganda unit. On Monday, Lowell Mellett, to whom I offered a position recently, will take over the National Emergency Council, which will be revived, and he will run propaganda from that vantage point.[81]

(For a discussion of whether NEC and then OGR indeed engaged in propaganda, see "A Propaganda Agency?" section of chapter 6.)

Roosevelt never convened a meeting of his "reconstitute[d]" NEC. Mellett's professional background was a tip off, an indication of how far NEC had moved from its original focus of coordinating relief.

Whether Congress would approve the Brownlow reorganization plan or not, FDR was going to have a robust informational staff within his presidential office.

In summary, from 1933 to 1939, Roosevelt had created an unprecedented formal and extensive presidential communications apparatus under the aegis of NEC. From the first year of his administration, he took personal steps to establish, maintain, expand, and fund this unique systematic attempt by the White House to report to the public on executive-branch activities as well as listen to public opinion regarding the administration's record. But, he wasn't satisfied with this temporary jerry-rigged set-up. The next three chapters describe FDR's persistent efforts to recreate NEC's information functions as a permanent and congressionally-authorized presidential communications agency.

Chapter 3

Planning a Presidential Communications Agency, 1936–39

Roosevelt's diminishing interest in convening any meetings of the National Emergency Council (NEC) did not affect his view of the value of its staff. Despite the word "council" in the agency's name, it had slowly morphed into a more conventional government organization, with an active and permanent staff pursuing the agency's mission. The lack of council meetings became increasingly meaningless. The problem for the president was how to institutionalize NEC's information activities, since funding it from relief appropriations could not be counted on permanently. Furthermore, with the conservative coalition in Congress opposing so much of his nontraditional federal initiatives and the general congressional antipathy to funding publicity staff in the executive branch, this was going to be tough to accomplish.

The Brownlow Committee

In early 1936, Roosevelt initiated a major effort to reorganize the executive branch of government. The changes he had in mind were significant and could not be adopted by executive orders. Major changes would require changes in federal law, hence approval by Congress. In March he appointed a three-member committee, consisting of Charles E. Merriman, Luther Gulick, and as chair, Louis Brownlow. Its formal title was President's Committee on Administrative Management, although it is often referred to as the Brownlow Committee.[1]

In terms of the political calendar, FDR thought the timing would be perfect. The commission would do its work during 1936, while he was running for reelection. Then, assuming he was reelected, the committee's recommendations would be the kickoff for his second term beginning in 1937, strengthening his ability to manage the federal government.

Although only a minor piece of the puzzle, the committee would need to make a recommendation about the future and fate of NEC, just as it would for practically every other federal agency. First, an initial survey of NEC's work was conducted by a staff member of the Bureau of the Budget (BOB) at the request of the committee. It was quite negative about most of NEC. It recommended shutting down most of the key activities of the agency including the Press Intelligence Division and the United States Information Service (USIS). The remaining parts, consisting of the *Government Manual* and a much reduced field service should be transferred to BOB.[2] From the perspective of a central budgeting agency, these recommendations made sense. BOB's mission of coordinating the budgets of federal agencies could logically be extended to coordinating field activities and reports of federal agencies. Also, the *Government Manual* was a useful reference book to people in government. On the other hand, press clippings and answering public requests for information were wholly unrelated to BOB's work and therefore viewed as not particularly important or worth preserving. But, this was just one staffer's opinion.

Second, during the summer of 1936, several of the committee's temporary staff fanned out to prepare reports on specific topics. Newly-minted Harvard Ph.D. James Fesler was assigned to research federal field services, a topic related to his just-completed dissertation.[3] Although Fesler's assignment covered the entire executive branch, given the coordinating role of NEC's state directors, he focused almost exclusively on NEC's field service. His visits to some NEC field offices caused anxiety in the agency.[4] NEC officials then obtained a copy of Fesler's preliminary report and drafted a defensive and detailed in-house critique.[5]

Third, the committee's research director, Joseph Harris, conducted his own brief investigation into NEC as a whole to complement Fesler's limited focus on NEC's field staff. Harris noted that "at the present time the activities of the staff are almost wholly related to the field service," with 249 of its 475 employees dedicated to that mission.[6] In his opinion USIS and Press Intelligence Division were "separate and distinct from the general activities of the N.E.C.," implying that since he conceived of no logic to their placement within the agency, he needn't even comment on their utility. In general, his report was negative about NEC.[7]

When the three members of the committee began assimilating all the staff reports in the fall of 1936, they had now three reports that were negative about NEC. Two reports—BOB's and Harris's—expressed no support for NEC's Washington-based activities (USIS and the Press Intelligence Division), and the third report, Fesler's, recommended terminating NEC's field service, a service which had informational responsibilities as well as coordinating ones. So, going into the crucial stage of developing preliminary recommendations, the weight of the staff recommendations to the committee members would suggest that both NEC's informational activities and field service should be terminated. Yet, that logical conclusion did not emerge in the committee's recommendation. In fact it recommended exactly the opposite. The committee's final report recommended retaining all of NEC's information activities and transferring them to BOB—the reverse of the recommendation in BOB's own report.[8] Something had happened to turn around the staff recommendations: FDR had intervened. According to Budget Director Smith, "the President had first proposed" the recommendation of transferring all of NEC's information services to BOB.[9]

To implement the president's express wishes, an early draft in the fall of 1936 of the committee's final recommendation about NEC was: "The informational, coordinating, and legislative clearance functions of the National Emergency Council should be transferred to the Bureau of the Budget."[10] That wording essentially preserved all of NEC's current activities, transferring it en masse to BOB. However, given the ongoing criticism of NEC by the conservative coalition in Congress, this explicit reference to retaining all of NEC's functions could revive that conflict. Therefore the next draft, dated December 18, 1936, totally revamped the wording of the recommendation:[11]

> The information~~al, coordinating, and legislative clearance~~ function~~s~~ of the ~~National Emergency Council should be transferred to the~~ Bureau of the Budget *should be developed and improved. The United States Information Service should be transferred to it, as should other appropriate activities in the coordination of the field services of the Government.*[12]

Despite the rewording, the substantive content was largely unchanged. It stated essentially the same thing, but in blander and softer terms. NEC was not mentioned at all. USIS, less controversial than NEC in toto and widely used by members of Congress, was named instead.

By directly referring to the coordination of federal field services (performed by the unnamed NEC), the recommendation provided a more logical connection to BOB's current mission, thus giving some "cover" to the part of the recommendation relating to information activities. The wording of the recommendation was now virtually done. It would only change in minor stylistic ways between this draft and its publication in January.[13]

However, the wording of the rationale for the recommendation was still in flux and went through several versions.[14] The drafts gradually strengthened the justification for an information function of the institutionalized presidency. Instead of an information function of BOB that "could" be created, it "should be established." Instead of a Division of Information and Coordination, it would be called the Division of Information. Such changes convey that BOB field and other coordinating activities would be conducted as part of its new information function, rather than as a parallel, separate and largely unrelated activity. Finally, the addition of an open-ended clause referring to other "related duties" permitted adding more information activities in the future, beyond those already specifically enumerated. For example, both the wording of the committee's reasons and its specific recommendation explicitly named only one of NEC's information-related divisions, USIS. There was no reference to NEC's more controversial Division of Press Intelligence. However, this vague wording in the report could later be claimed to have (implicitly) intended to include transferring the press-clipping operation to BOB as well as USIS. The final version of the committee's report, released on January 12, 1937, explained the rationale for the recommendation of transferring NEC's information functions to BOB thusly:

> A division of information should be established to serve as a central clearing house for the correlation and coordination of the administrative policies of the several departments in the operation of their own informational services, and to perform related duties. The United States Information Service might well be transferred to this division. It might also develop into a service which would supervise and foster regional associations of executive officers of the Government and other activities for coordination of the field services. The Director of the Bureau has been authorized by law to approve the use of printing and binding appropriations for the periodicals and journals published by Government agencies; the chief of the division of information could assist him in carrying out this duty.[15]

Based on the committee's final report and published staff papers, this discussion of information activities and related recommendation would seem to have been somewhat immaculately conceived. Fesler's report could not have served as the rationale for the recommendation to transfer NEC's information activities to BOB.[16] After all, Fesler's purpose was to analyze the coordination of the field activities of federal agencies. That was his orientation when he studied the work of NEC's state directors. He was not interested in NEC's central-information activities and, therefore, did not study USIS or the Division of Press Intelligence. The only overlap between his assignment and NEC's information activities was in the context of the information responsibilities of state directors. Fesler's final key recommendation to the committee was to abolish NEC's field service and replace it with a new small staff agency to promote coordination of federal-field administration. In the interest of being comprehensive and not leaving any loose ends, he also addressed the state directors' information responsibilities, suggesting transferring them to local post offices. Fesler's report didn't even mention USIS.[17] Yet, Fesler's background research paper was the sole staff report that contained any discussion whatsoever about NEC. So, publicly, only it could serve as the platform for a committee recommendation to transfer NEC's field service and *central information activities* to BOB. In reality, Fesler's study only justified a committee recommendation about federal-field coordination, along with tangential consideration of the information activities conducted in the field by NEC's state directors. But, the Committee used the tail to wag the dog. The recommendation to transfer NEC's field service *and* central information activities to a new BOB *Information* Division, indicates the sleight of hand that was quietly accomplished in the committee report. It was pure Roosevelt.

Implementing the Brownlow Committee Report, 1938

Now overwhelmingly reelected, Roosevelt was ready to release the committee's report. On Sunday, January 10, 1937, he briefed congressional leaders for two hours at the White House about the recommendations contained in the report, two days before publicly sending it to Capitol Hill. He discussed the need to strengthen the president's managerial agencies and briefly, but pointedly, mentioned the report's recommendation that BOB's scope be expanded "to perform certain services on coordination of informational activities."[18] Roosevelt was being careful. Knowing how controversial NEC's information programs were with the conservative coalition on Capitol Hill, he wanted to be sure that the congressional leaders couldn't later say they had been blindsided if and when this recommendation became controversial. He'd be able to remind them that he had explicitly included it when he had briefed them on the entire report. None of the congressional leaders raised questions or concerns about assigning information activities to BOB.

Roosevelt's legislative proposal to Congress to implement the Brownlow Committee report ran into a buzz saw on Capitol Hill. The coalition of Republicans and conservative Democrats sensed that Roosevelt might be vulnerable politically on some issues despite his reelection. They were joined by two other groups: members who feared that as a result of the reorganization the executive branch would become even more dominant over Congress and members seeking to protect "their" agency. The congressional and editorial rhetoric got so heated and hyperbolic that Roosevelt felt compelled to issue a public letter in March 1938, saying, "I am as much opposed to American Dictatorship as you are."[19] Nonetheless, the bill to implement the Brownlow Report was defeated in the House on April 8, 1938.

The Brownlow Committee's recommendation to create a Division of Information in BOB was a minor item in a report dealing with very major and contentious issues of control, power, the future relationship between the executive and legislative branches, and ideological politics. Congressional debate focused on those broader themes. Nonetheless, the information recommendation in the report did attract the attention and criticism of Arthur Krock. Krock was one of the most prominent and quoted reporters of his day. He was chief of the *New York Times'* Washington Bureau and authored a regular column analyzing political subjects. Politically, he was a conservative southern Democrat and his writings consistently had "an undercoating of acid between the lines, particularly when Krock was writing about the New Deal and Franklin Roosevelt."[20] In early 1937, the editors of the new journal *Public Opinion Quarterly* invited him to contribute a piece to its second issue.[21] Krock harkened back to the establishment of NEC's information activities in late 1933 and early 1934. He remembered writing about the administration's original plan for NEC to function as a central-information bureau, replacing the public-information offices of all the executive-branch agencies. However, the Roosevelt White House had quickly killed that plan for fear it would taint all of NEC's information activities as propaganda.[22] Krock's article was published in April 1937, while Congress was in the midst of debating the Brownlow reorganization plan. He specifically attacked the committee's information recommendation, analogizing its role to that of a funnel:

> there is a real menace to the legitimate flow of news to the public in the proposal of a Central Information Bureau by the Brownlow-Gulick-Merriman committee to reorganize the government. . . . this funnel could easily be turned outward, requiring news correspondents in Washington to apply to one agency for all the facts about the largest Federal establishment in history.[23]

Krock proceeded to imply that the new information office could, somehow, become the basis for censorship of the press. This inflammatory accusation, once put into the public domain, would not go away. For years later, congressional attacks on the Office of Government Reports (OGR) kept insinuating that the agency would become a censor and harm freedom of the press. When defenders of OGR would demand the proof that the agency had such legal powers, OGR critics could not cite it — but that didn't stop them from repeating the allegation (see chapter 5). In politics, if any (baseless) accusation is repeated enough, it would come to be believed, following the maxim "if there's smoke, there's fire."

Implementing the Brownlow Committee Report, 1939

The eventual defeat of the reorganization bill in April 1938, proved only to be a temporary obstacle. Roosevelt's political status had changed within a year and a new bill was submitted to Congress with some of its key controversial features stripped out. This time the bill passed and with little major controversy.[24] Roosevelt signed it on April 3, 1939. Now, a president was free to prepare any reorganization plan, as long as it did not affect a handful of politically popular agencies that Congress had excluded from the scope of the law, and then would submit the plan to Congress. If neither house objected to the plan by majority vote, then it would automatically go into effect.[25]

Roosevelt didn't waste any time. On April 25, he sent Reorganization Plan No. 1 to Congress. It included creating Executive Office of the President (EOP) and some of the agencies within EOP, but contained nothing about NEC.[26] It would go into effect on July 1, 1939. The next day, Roosevelt was ready to keep going. He met over lunch with Brownlow and BOB Director Smith for almost three hours to start deciding the details for Plan No. 2. This plan would, among many other items, cover NEC. At this point, the expectation was that the plan would propose a literal implementation of the Brownlow Committee report, namely that NEC would be transferred to BOB.

During the April 26 meeting, Roosevelt mentioned, in an aside to Smith, that he was leaning to changing his funding recommendation for NEC for the next fiscal year. He had already approved requesting $1 million for NEC for fiscal year 1940 in the message he was about to send to Congress with his proposal for the annual Relief Act. Now, he told Smith, he was beginning to think that he probably should recommend $1.5 million. That would give NEC's replacement a more solid start budgetarily.[27]

That brief comment was an example of Roosevelt's mastery of government in general and his intense personal interest in executive-branch information activities in particular. He realized the connection between the timing of the implementation of the reorganization plan that would include NEC's successor entity and his impending annual message to Congress requesting work relief appropriations for next fiscal year, including for NEC. He knew that by the beginning of that next fiscal year, NEC would no longer exist. So, whatever appropriation he obtained from Congress for NEC as part of the Work Relief Act of fiscal year 1940, that funding would become the base budget for the replacement information entity.

Another, subtler, detail about government was also involved. In the politics of the budgetary process, it's easier to obtain approval for the continuation of something than to enact a new funded activity. Last year's decisions have a momentum of continuation: "We've already looked this over before, we don't need to start from scratch all over again. That would not be a wise use of our time. We assume that the same factors that led to last year's outcome are still valid. Do we want to re-open every decision we make every year?"[28] On the other hand, a new proposal faces intense scrutiny; since this is the first time the legislative body is considering it. Congress was already familiar with NEC. Its existence, while still controversial with the conservative coalition, was nonetheless becoming a permanent feature of the federal executive-branch spending. Since most decisions in government are incremental ones, NEC was likely to continue being funded by Congress at the general level it had been funded up to now. So, trying to get Congress to increase funding for NEC from $1 million to $1.5 million would cause a stir, but it would still be within the normal course of business. It was do-able.

On the other hand, FDR could envision what Congress's reaction would likely be to a proposal to create and fund, for the first time, a new information program within the presidential office. As a de novo proposal, it would face much more intense scrutiny, certainly trigger the usual congressional outcries about executive-branch propaganda and, if approved at all, would be given an extremely limited budget. An appropriation of $1.5 million, even $1 million, was practically unimaginable. So, for the president, the perfect political scenario would be to get Congress to approve an increase from $1 million to $1.5 million appropriation for NEC for fiscal year 1940 and then, presto, recreate NEC as a new organization that would begin its life with this satisfactory budget level. Indeed, when the White House released the relief message to Congress, it included a request for $1.5 million request for NEC.[29]

Reorganization Plan Number 2

The work on the reorganization plan continued. During that process, Smith was getting increasingly concerned about the literal implementation of the Brownlow Committee recommendation about transferring NEC's staff and responsibilities to BOB in toto.[30] He wasn't sure there was a harmonious fit between BOB's mission and NEC, especially USIS and the Press Intelligence Division. And a BOB Film Service?! Certainly, he could see BOB having a stronger role in coordinating the field work of all federal agencies with a modest new BOB field service. That would be a good fit for the bureau. But the rest of NEC's activities would not. Yet, despite his concerns, Smith viewed his role as larger than that of a self-interested and parochial agency head. He and his agency had the institutional duty to implement the president's—any president's—decisions. They were part of his "official family." They were the *president's* staff. It was not their place to argue with the president about relatively minor matters. Smith felt he was on the horns of a dilemma and was not sure how to resolve it.

The final decisions about the second reorganization plan were decided on May 3, 1939 during a working luncheon the president had with Brownlow, Merriam, Smith, and Judge Townsend (a senior career attorney at the Department of Justice who handled legal issues relating to presidential documents and who had the president's confidence). NEC came up again. This time, the president suggested handling the transfer of NEC's responsibilities differently from the recommendation in the Brownlow Committee report. Perhaps NEC's US Film Service should be transferred to the Office of Education and the remaining parts of NEC be reconstituted as a separate unit within EOP? Smith, immensely relieved, quickly endorsed the president's idea. With no other concerns raised by the other three at the meeting, that issue was done.[31] So was born OGR—from an idea volunteered by President Roosevelt.

Creating a freestanding agency within EOP dedicated to public reporting went well beyond the Brownlow Committee's recommendation. Later, when speaking publicly about the rationale for OGR's creation, FDR blandly said it was one of a few new agencies he was compelled to create, by "providing a father for certain fatherless children."[32] On another occasion he said:

> Well, somebody has to coordinate these things and the principal users of Government reports are the members of the Senate and House. Anybody who wants a report, wants to get information about any subject, get hold of that office and you will get it inside of twenty-four hours. They may send a truckload of information.[33]

Six days after the May 3 meeting that decided the details of NEC's reincarnation, Reorganization Plan Number 2 was sent to Congress. One of its many items abolished NEC, transferred its Radio Division and the US Film Service the Office of Education and the remainder of NEC was "transferred to the Executive Office of the President and shall be administered under the direction and supervision of the President."[34] That wording was vague and lacked specificity. A presidential message accompanied the plan. Relating to NEC, it gave potential opponents little to object to. The message enumerated and described some of NEC's different activities, namely the Press Intelligence Division, USIS, *US Government Manual*, and the coordinating and reporting activities of the field offices. In a typical Rooseveltian flourish, he displayed his well-known talent for communicating complex concepts in an understandable and memorable way. He described USIS as:

> a post office address—"Uncle Sam, Post Office Box No. 1, Washington, D.C."—to which persons who want information about the Government but do not know the exact division or agency of the Government to which to apply, may write with confidence that their questions will be answered or else sent on to the proper agency for direct reply.[35]

The message was only slightly more specific than the text of the plan regarding NEC. Activities "transferred to the White House would be administered in the manner best designed to give the President the information he requires from all parts of the country."[36] This put the emphasis on collecting and reporting information to the president, rather than disseminating information to the public. Like the wording of the plan itself, the message did not refer to the creation of a freestanding presidential agency to handle NEC's information and field activities.

A crucial detail was only lightly mentioned in the message. The information activities being transferred to the White House would be "Subject to appropriations by the Congress."[37] On one hand, this merely stated the obvious, practically a tautology. In the US constitutional system, only Congress has the power to appropriate funds to the executive branch. Nonetheless, the reminder was an effective way to placate potential congressional opponents to the proposed transfer of information activities to the White House. "I'll only be able to do this," the president seemed to be saying, "if you'll fund it. So, if you don't like it, you don't have to kill this reorganization plan, just don't appropriate any funding subsequently." The brief mention in the president's message of the vital role of congressional appropriations regarding NEC's successor eerily presaged OGR's eventual fate in 1948. The comment also helps explain why he was so emphatic about getting appropriations for NEC's successor for fiscal year 1940 approved through a relatively routine appropriation to NEC in the fiscal year 1940 relief bill already being considered by Congress.

On May 9, 1939, the same day Roosevelt sent Reorganization Plan Number 2 to Congress, he also recorded a fifteen-minute radio interview with Lowell Mellett. NEC (and later OGR) had been providing radio programs to local stations as part of a general series of weekly interviews called "United States Government Reports." The purpose was to provide information to the radio audience about the activities of the federal government. The interview with the president was the kick-off of a new series of thirty-two radio programs. According to Lowell Mellett, Roosevelt had suggested taping interviews with the heads of all departments in a "Cabinet Series" after Mellett had told him about some of the "United States Government Reports" programs on local radio stations hosted by NEC's state directors. FDR thought that a new series of programs covering topics of nation-wide interest, rather than limited to one state, would be a good idea. He said that each interview should be intended to describe what each major agency of the federal executive branch did. NEC implemented the president's suggestion by first recording a "Cabinet Series" with the secretaries of the ten departments and then another twenty-one programs in the "Agency Series" with the heads of other independent federal agencies. Mellett felt "the thing of importance in the President's talk was his emphasis on the Government's duty to inform the people."[38] The interviews were not broadcast live over a network, rather they were—in the term of the day—electronically transcribed. This was akin to pressing vinyl records for a phonograph or, in a more contemporary example, making copies of cassette tapes or CDs to mail to radio stations. These copies were then sent to about 150 radio stations.[39] (For more information on the work of NEC's Radio Division, see previous chapter.) In the interview, Roosevelt emphasized his support for efforts by NEC to inform the public of its programs and activities:

> It seems to me important that before the people pass on the size of, or the question of continuing, these functions [i.e., new government programs] they should have an opportunity to obtain some factual information about them. The people, through Congress, have the right, at any time, to end any individual function, to increase it, or to add new functions. That is why knowledge of what Government does today is of such great importance.[40]

It surely is no coincidence that the same day Roosevelt sent a reorganization plan to Congress to institutionalize NEC's information programs, he also recorded a radio interview on the value of government reporting to the people. He was demonstrating his personal commitment to the activity and its value. And the rationale he used was almost a perfect restatement of the theory of public reporting that had been developed in public administration literature.

Prospective Funding for the New Agency

While Congress was considering Reorganization Plan Number 2, the fiscal year 1940 relief bill was slowly working its way through the legislative process as well. On May 25, the Deficiencies Subcommittee of the House Appropriations Committee held a hearing on the part of the bill relating to the president's request of $1.5 million for NEC. The effect of the reorganization on NEC came up during the questioning. Mellett tried to convey a "business as usual" message to implement Roosevelt's decision to secure funding for NEC's successor for fiscal year 1940 by focusing on simply continuing funding NEC as Congress had done previously.

Congressman J. Buell Snyder (D-PA): Where do you go from here in this organization or reorganization? Where do you go?

Mellett: We will be right where we are.

Snyder: You are not transferred?

Mellett: Under the reorganization plan it has been transferred directly to the White House. That is the language of the act. Actually this agency is directly under the President and always has been. We will continue to report to the President.

Congressman John Taber (R-NY; ranking minority member on the subcommittee): You are not in the Executive Office?

Mellett: No, sir; our office is in the Commercial National Bank Building. We have always been there.[41]

Most of the critical questioning by members of the subcommittee focused on the US Film Service. The Republican members also continued their ongoing criticism of NEC and sought to create a record to justify abolishing NEC. When the full committee convened in executive session on June 14 to act on the bill, Congressman Everett Dirksen (R-IL) moved that the committee delete all funding for NEC. His motion lost on a party line vote of nineteen to eleven.[42] Nonetheless, the committee voted to cut the funding for NEC, from the $1.5 million requested by the president to $850,000, the same level of funding it had for fiscal year 1939. The Republican members of the committee were not satisfied with that funding cut and included in their Minority Report a criticism of NEC:

> Two items in this bill must be mentioned which have nothing whatever to do with relief: The National Emergency Council, and National Resources Committee. Provision is carried in this bill for their continuance. The first is designed to promote propaganda and the second to promote Government spending. Neither agency, in our opinion, should be continued.[43]

When the House debated the bill on June 16, 1939, Dirksen offered the same amendment he had proposed during the committee's executive session. He described NEC as "a propaganda agency pure and simple. Instead of reducing expenditures, it is reaching out for more money and more authority in order to carry on because we are up against an election year."[44] Uncharacteristically, several Democratic members stoutly defended NEC's information activities. Jerry Voorhis[45] (D-CA) said sarcastically, "Is it not a 'terrible' thing that the people of this country should be informed about flood control, unemployment, and the problems of rural electrification, and all those things? And is it not just 'awful' for any government to give the people information on those important subjects?" Similarly Clifton Woodrum (D-VA) said, "many Members on the minority side of the House called upon the National Emergency Council for statistical information and for information they had to furnish. . . . I hope very much that the gentleman's amendment will not prevail, but that this agency will be permitted to go ahead."[46] The amendment was defeated on a party-line vote of 83 to 111. The bill passed as recommended by the committee, with $850,000 for NEC.

Playing its traditional role as an appeals body,[47] Mellett turned to the Senate Appropriations Committee to increase the appropriation in the bill from the House-approved level to the president's original request of $1.5 million. In particular he was concerned that the House-funding level would mean that the US Film Service would have no funding for fiscal year 1940 when it would be transferred to the Office of Education on the first day of the new fiscal year.[48] The committee was unsympathetic and recommended keeping NEC at the level approved by the House.[49] The full Senate approved the recommendation.

President Roosevelt signed the relief appropriations bill into law on June 30, 1939, the last day of NEC's existence.[50] While the US Film Service was losing any direct appropriations, the rest of NEC's information functions were transferring into the new EOP with funding for the first fiscal year of their operations maintained at the current level. This wasn't as much as Roosevelt had wanted, but it was a "win." His last-minute decision to press for increased funding for NEC in the fiscal year 1940 relief bill had worked. Congress had focused more on the question of the increase over the fiscal year 1939 appropriation than on the rationale for even funding at all the post-reorganization agency. He had succeeded in avoiding any congressional debate about the specifics of NEC's successor agency, its functions and—especially—its funding. He had spared the new entity the need to obtain funding from Congress on a de novo basis. The previous year's funding was simply continued, with only a minor political dust-up in the process.[51]

First Steps

Meanwhile, Reorganization Plan Number 2 had not faced any serious opposition in either the Senate or House. It was scheduled to go into effect on Saturday, July 1, 1939, the same day that Reorganization Plan Number 1 creating EOP would also go into effect. Based on the last executive order relating to NEC, the agency had been abolished on Friday night at midnight. At the moment that NEC expired, Reorganization Plans Number 1 and 2 had gone into effect. Among many features in the two plans, EOP was established and NEC's responsibilities as well as its fiscal year 1940 funding were transferred to the president. However, on that weekend morning, no one knew exactly how that transfer would be operationalized or specifically what the president had in mind. Back in May, he had suggested to Smith and Brownlow that NEC's information activities would not become a division of the budget bureau—even though that's what the Brownlow Committee had recommended. He had proposed instead, and they had agreed, that it would be a separate entity in the president's office. But what exactly? And what would it be called?

Roosevelt was busy that morning in the Oval Office handling all the paperwork necessary to implement the reorganization of the government that had gone into effect at midnight. One of the many documents that were prepared for him was a directive (not an executive order) regarding NEC. But, no one knew exactly what he wanted. So, he was given a document with a blank in it. It read:

July 1, 1939

Memorandum to Mr. Mellett:

The National Emergency Council having been abolished as of June 30, 1939, in accordance with the provisions of reorganization plan II, approved by Public Resolution No. 20, 76th Congress . . . and its functions (with the exception of the Radio and Film Divisions) transferred to the Executive Office of the President, you are hereby appointed Director of the ______________ a part of the Executive Office of the President.[52]

When Roosevelt reached the blank space in the document, he wrote "Office of Government Reports" and then signed the letter. So was born the first presidential communications agency, with the president personally inventing its title at the very last minute. Later that same Saturday, Mellett notified all NEC employees that they were being transferred to the new agency.[53]

OGR and EOP continued to emerge and develop over the summer, but now at a much more gradual pace. Everything was new, unprecedented, unfamiliar. For example, regarding terminology, some early internal documents referred to all the entities within EOP as "the Management Agencies," echoing the Brownlow Committee's theme that an executive office of the president was needed so that the president could better manage the entire executive branch. Hence, the common mission of the agencies within EOP was, theoretically, to facilitate the president's management of the federal government.[54]

The new agency name didn't receive broad usage quickly. Eleven days after NEC ceased to exist, a reporter asked Roosevelt about the supposed political activities of an NEC staffer in New York.[55] Similarly, on July 17, a Congressman complained on the floor of the House about NEC's *current* activities.[56] Mangled variations of the new name included Office of Federal Reports,[57] Government Reporting Agency,[58] Bureau of Government Reports,[59] Office of Reports,[60] and Office of Information.[61]

However, Roosevelt's in-house administrative directives creating OGR and EOP did not have the formal legal status necessary to implement the reorganization plans. That would take an executive order. Through the summer, Roosevelt held back on triggering the official implementation of the reorganization plans by signing the necessary executive order. He very much was occupied by events in Europe and their possible impact on the United States. On Tuesday, August 29, the president invited Louis Brownlow to lunch. By this time, tensions in Europe were at a high point. Within the last year, Germany had persuaded Great Britain to sign the Munich Accord "appeasement," occupied the regions of Czechoslovakia that were dominated by ethnic Germans, violated the Munich agreement by occupying the rest of Czechoslovakia, signed a military alliance with Italy, and then signed a secret military treaty with the Soviet Union. All that month, Hitler had been making threats against Poland. In response, the previous Friday, August 25, Great Britain signed a defense treaty with Poland. It would not let Germany do to Poland what it had done to Czechoslovakia. Now, Great Britain and France were preparing for war. It appeared that war was imminent.

Roosevelt wanted to meet with Brownlow to think about the organization of the federal government in a time of war. He especially did not like the idea that some were talking about, of appointing a "war czar." Instead, he wanted a fluid structure, solely under his control through executive orders, not subject to congressional approval, with the ability to make changes whenever he wanted and, above all, structured so that the president was placed in the indispensable and central role.[62] The president specifically wanted to meet with Brownlow on August 29 because the next day he was scheduled to meet with the War Resources Board (WRB). The Army and Navy had created that Board earlier in August. Its members consisted mostly of "captains of industry" and big business including the CEOs of General Motors, US Steel, and AT&T. The purpose of the board, from the perspective of the military, was to push the president to approve the Industrial Mobilization Plan (IMP) and permit its implementation.

WRB, with its composition of business and corporate leaders, reflected the military's vision of wartime mobilization: the military and the business sector working together to control the economy in order to produce all the matériel the Army and Navy needed. The military saw no operating role for the president. Rather, IMP's centerpiece was the appointment of a single all-powerful civilian wartime administrator who would, theoretically, be accountable to the president, but in a relationship akin to that of a corporate CEO to the chair of the board of directors. The war czar would oversee five superagencies that would encompass the entire effort by the civilian economy to support of the military's needs. One of those five super-agencies would be called the Public Relations Administration. IMP had been in preparation by the military over more than a decade. Now, the whole planning effort was about to culminate with WRB presenting the latest version of IMP to the president. The Army and Navy thought the prestige of its membership could virtually force the president to sign it. Or, at least, that's what the military hoped would happen. But, Roosevelt—working with Brownlow—was developing some ideas of his own. The path to this climactic meeting between Roosevelt and WRB over IMP had been first set many years before, shortly after World War I had been won. The next chapter describes the events that led to this August 30, 1939, showdown meeting about the organization of the federal government for the next war and the relationship of this planning process to presidential public relations.

In this chapter we have seen the strong presence of all three analytical prisms related to the story of OGR. First, the strong opposition by Congress to the growing powers of the presidency vis-à-vis the legislative branch were manifested. The battle over the reorganization of the executive branch embodied that rivalry. Second, Roosevelt's specific interest in strengthening his communications capacities and willingness to fight to achieve them demonstrate the gradual emergence of the central role of modern communications in American government. Third, the planning for OGR showed the increasing acceptance within the administration of the importance of public reporting as part of modern governance.

Chapter 4

A Better Idea from the Military?

The Industrial Mobilization Plan for a Public Relations Administration, 1931–39

During World War I, the Committee on Public Information (CPI), headed by George Creel, had handled federal public relations related to the war. President Wilson had created it through an executive order in 1917. That agency had a tumultuous history, with claims of great success from participants and observers but also significant congressional criticism.[1] After World War I, the civilian and military leadership of the United States engaged in planning for a possible future war. One of the many questions they faced was the federal government's public-relations organization in the event of another war.

Initial Plan: 1931

As a result of dissatisfaction with the civilian mobilization for World War I, including incidents of war profiteering and the ostensible excessive power of the privately-owned munitions industry, in 1930 Congress created a War Policies Commission (WPC) to advise it how industrial mobilization should be handled in case of another major war.[2] The commission held public hearings in 1931 and received a wide range of testimony. Although most of the testimony related directly to purely industrial issues, the scope of the commission also covered wartime civilian morale and public support for total mobilization. One of the

Army officers working on early versions of the Army's industrial mobilization plan was an obscure staff officer, Major Dwight D. Eisenhower.[3] In a March 11, 1931, letter to Herbert Bayard Swope, a prominent reporter, Eisenhower explained the Army's rationale for a public relations "super agency"[4] as part of the nation's industrial mobilization:

> The idea is to *unify* our efforts in this field under the direction of an expert. Some means must be provided to keep our population informed of important happenings, but we must guard against a trend toward hysteria on one hand and pessimism and defeatism on the other. We want one hundred and twenty million people think alike, and along those lines that will make possible a unified and continuous military, economic, industrial, and moral effort.[5]

To accomplish that, the Army's plan recommended a "central publicity agency set up by the war-time President" and managed by an appointee directly under the president. Eisenhower personally preferred that the agency have both publicity and censorship powers, but that was not the Army's official position.[6]

A week later, Swope testified before the commission. He was the only witness who testified on the subject of public relations. With no regard for the First Amendment, he propounded total government control of the news media as part of a war mobilization effort. He suggested that the Commission's final report recommend creation of a propaganda department and a special cabinet-level Secretary of Information.[7] This office would have absolute powers to promote civilian morale and support for a war effort. While Koistinen characterized this testimony as "virtually dictatorial solutions for managing public opinion during hostilities,"[8] Swope's comments were simply in line with Eisenhower's letter.

The initial version of a proposed Industrial Mobilization Plan (IMP), the commission's raison d'être, was drafted by the War Department. General Douglas MacArthur, Army chief of staff, presented the plan to the commission at a hearing on May 13, 1931. In his opening statement, he addressed public information issues by noting that "public opinion is the most potent force in war"[9] and therefore the government should organize efforts to maintain high national morale. The Army's plan proposed that the nation's war effort be concentrated in a war cabinet, called the Advisory War Council that would be accountable to the president. It would consist of the Secretaries of War and Navy and the directors of four "superagencies" to be established upon mobilization: selective service (i.e., the draft), War Industry, Labor and Public Relations.[10] According to the plan:

> The director of public relations will have responsibilities of great importance. Public opinion, which can be sustained in the long run only if the methods employed for the conduct of the war are efficient and just, is nevertheless moulded [sic] by the presentation of proper information to the population. The director of public relations will necessarily be in constant contact with the other chief subordinates of the President, and will conduct his office so as to promote the confidence of the public in all parts of the governmental organization.[11]

A graphic representation of the centrality of the director of public relations is reflected in the "Proposed Plan for the Governmental Organization for War" as he is one of six chief subordinates to the president (see Figure 4.1).

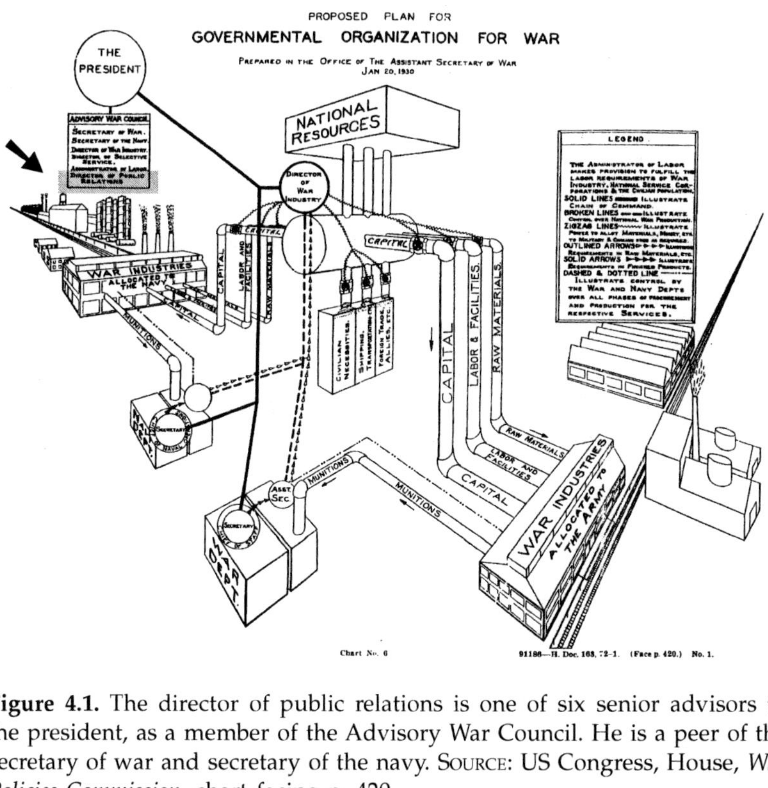

Figure 4.1. The director of public relations is one of six senior advisors to the president, as a member of the Advisory War Council. He is a peer of the secretary of war and secretary of the navy. SOURCE: US Congress, House, *War Policies Commission*, chart facing p. 420.

One of the appendices prepared by the Army provided the draft of a presidential proclamation to be issued to implement the plan. In it, the duties and powers of the director of public relations would be "to advise and assist the President in all matters relating to public information as to the progress, aims, and purposes of the Government of the United States in the present emergency."[12] Besides having a director of public relations as one of the six chief subordinates to the president, the plan also envisioned a robust public relations orientation by some of the other agencies directed by the director's five peers. For example, the table of organization of the Labor Administration included a director of a bureau of publicity who would report directly to the labor administrator.[13]

Koistinen criticized the role that the Army in general, and its general staff in particular, assigned itself for planning the Public Relations Administration. The central role of the military in developing the agency to mold public opinion, he suggested, "could be a hazard to national traditions."[14] Nonetheless, there was an informal agreement between the civilians of the War Department and the uniformed leadership of the Army that public relations and selective service were in the planning domain of the General Staff, not the Office of the Assistant Secretary of War.[15] The origins of this agreement dated back to the 1920s. At that time, a plan for wartime selective-service advertising was drafted by a cadre of reserve officers, "all of them of great prominence, in the fields of advertising, publicity, and radio, and several of whom had been associated with George Creel in various advertising endeavors during World War I."[16] Their plan anticipated that this selective service's public-relations campaign would be merged into the broader public-relations agency already contemplated by the general staff planners working on the Industrial Mobilization campaign. This proposal, when presented to the civilians in the Office of the Assistant Secretary of War, seemed logical and therefore they concurred in it. However, this act of assent was later interpreted by the general staff as the precedent that assigned exclusive responsibility for public-relations planning to the Army.[17]

WPC, which was chaired by the secretary of war, did not issue its own industrial mobilization plan. Rather, in March 1932, it forwarded the Army's plan to the president and Congress along with the full record of its hearings and documents.[18] The commission also recommended that the War and Navy departments should continue working jointly on an industrial mobilization plan and that Congress should review the revisions "at least every two years."[19] Indeed, the implementation of that recommendation led to further exploration of public relations as part of the nation's wartime industrial mobilization.

Revised Plan: 1933

As recommended by WPC, the first revision of the 1931 IMP was prepared by the Army and Navy and then submitted to Congress in 1933.[20] This iteration provided an extensive and detailed description of the role of public relations in a national war government. The introduction to the plan provided the rationale for its attentiveness to public relations, namely that "The support of public opinion is so essential that anything that may appear to the majority of the people as unnecessary, unfair, or unjust cannot be permitted to creep into the plans."[21] The head of the information effort was renamed the administrator of public relations.[22] In the body of the report, the purposes of the Administration of Public Relations (APR) were spelled out:

> The mission of this administration is to coordinate and direct the national publicity activities so as to insure that the purposes, views, and progress of the Government in prosecution of the war are properly and adequately presented to the people and that the aid of public opinion is enlisted to the fullest possible extent in behalf thereof.[23]

The mandate for the agency was very broad and ambitious. For example, it was expected to

1. coordinate and direct all publicity activities of the federal government;
2. combat disaffection at home;
3. combat enemy propaganda at home;
4. advise the President;
5. operate a Bureau of Information for "proper and reliable information concerning the aims and activities of the Government";
6. be a central clearinghouse for news announcements of all government agencies and to "require the viséing[24] of all press releases."

The administration's structure, besides a standard administrative division, had four line divisions: news, pictures, civic cooperation, and advertising. A graphic representation of APR's structure is reflected in an organization charge included in the report's appendix (see figure 4.2).

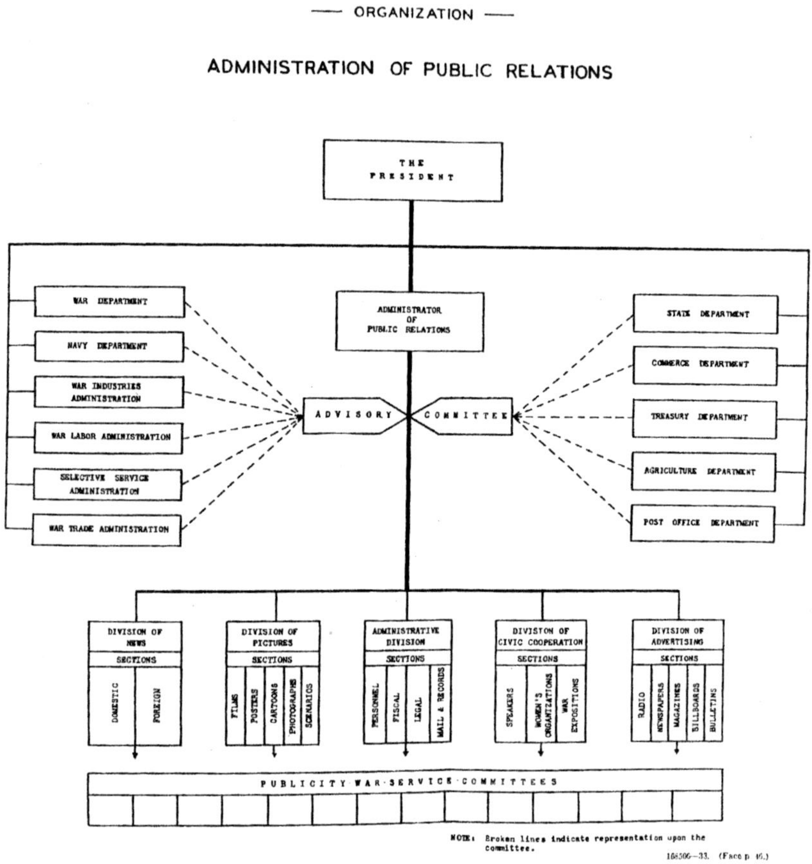

Figure 4.2. Administration of Public Relations Organization Table. SOURCE: US Congress, Senate, Special Committee Investigating the Munitions Industry, *Industrial Mobilization Plan: Revised—1933*, chart facing p. 46.

This organizational chart outlined an interesting method of categorizing discreet elements of public relations. It was not based on media outlets, such as newspaper, radio, periodicals, and film. Nor was it based on purposes, such as censorship, counter-propaganda and interdepartmental coordination. Rather it was based on outputs and products, i.e., print press releases, pictures (whether movies, stills or cartoons), and advertising. With this structure, a typical newspaper would likely receive materials from at least three different offices within APR: press releases from the news division, still pictures from the pictures division, and public service ads about the war effort from the advertising division.

The plan did not appear to envision a large staff that would take over the work previously conducted by individual cabinet departments. Instead, some of its work would focus on coordinating these other public-relations offices. That's why the plan expected that many committees would function under APR's rubric. This approach was pragmatic from the perspective of bureaucratic politics and the traditional turf wars of federal agencies. These problems would be finessed with the expectation that the new organization "need not disturb the public relations organizations or the personnel of the information collecting staffs within the various executive departments and independent agencies."[25] Harold Tobin and Percy Bidwell put a much more negative interpretation to this approach, stating "publicity men regularly in government employment were to be excluded from the war organization."[26] This observation implied that APR would not be staffed by civil-service mediocrities and instead would rely on top-quality talent borrowed temporarily from the private sector.

Finally, despite many similarities between the 1933 plan for APR and the Committee for Public Information (CPI),[27] the plan included one significant break with the precedent set by CPI. That agency had been formed by executive order of the president. This meant it lacked any formal congressional approval. This was often interpreted as one of the causes of the many congressional attacks on the work of the committee.[28] Therefore, trying to learn from history, the 1933 plan proposed that APR be established through an act of Congress, rather than executive order.

Revised Plan: 1936

The revised plan submitted to Congress in 1936 maintained the central role of public relations.[29] It slightly renamed the agency, from APR in the 1933 plan to Public Relations Administration (PRA). The agency was one of the eight agencies that consisted of what was called the Emergency Establishment.[30] PRA's general mission was unchanged from the 1933 plan. However, the detailed appendix contained in the previous version was deleted, with the explanation that "the organization, duties, and procedure for this Administration are being revised by appropriate agencies, and, when completed, will be included in the next revision of the industrial mobilization plan."

The disappearance of the detailed appendix dealing with PRA that had been included in the 1933 version was due to both civilian-military and Army–Navy turf wars. Generally, there was intense competition and rivalry between the uniformed officers of the Army and the civilians who staffed the War Department. In this case, the rivalry was between two principle offices working on IMP, the Army's general staff and the Office of the Assistant Secretary of War. As noted previously, for the 1931 plan, there was an informal understanding between the two that the general staff would have lead responsibility for the sections on public relations and selective service. When the civilians under the assistant secretary of war prepared a redraft of the appendix on selective service for the 1936 plan, the military fought back fiercely to protect "its" turf. It insisted that a joint Army–Navy panel (i.e., uniformed military officers) be explicitly assigned the responsibility for drafting the sections on "public relations, publicity, censorship, and the Selective Service system."[31] In return, the military agreed that it would no longer review the industrial sections of the plan.

Furthermore, the general staff was also concerned about the Navy becoming involved in public relations. Its close examination of the plans for the initial transitional phase of mobilization discovered a section stating that until PRA would come into being, all responsibility for conducting public relations including "censorship, propaganda, and publicity" would be controlled by the joint Army and Navy Munitions Board.[32] This would give the Navy a larger role in public relations than the Army had desired. Eventually, the Army's deputy chief of staff and the assistant secretary of war worked out these concerns. They agreed, amongst other items in contention, to shift responsibility for drafting the section on PRA to the Special Joint Army and Navy Public Relations Committee. However, the reworked public-relations plan wasn't ready when the 1936 plan went to print, so the appendix dealing with PRA was left blank with the brief explanatory note cited above. It was finally completed and approved in August 1937.[33]

Paul Koistinen noted that during these turf wars, the basic issue of "why public relations belonged to the General Staff remained unaddressed."[34] He considered this a "weak spot" of the entire plan, suggesting that civilians, rather than military, should be involved in issues of public opinion and the free press.

Final Plan: 1939

Notwithstanding the commitment in the 1936 plan to provide a detailed appendix on PRA in the next version, that promise was not fulfilled. In October 1939, the Army and Navy submitted to Congress their revised and updated version of IMP.[35] The central focus of the revisions was on establishing a War Resources Administration, headed by the Administrator of War Resources. This one person would have sole control over all industrial activity, including facilities, commodities, power, fuel, transportation, trade, labor, price control and finance. He, essentially, would be the civilian war czar, accountable to the president and Congress. Only two of the six emergency administrations would not be under the direct supervision of the Administrator of War Resources, PRA and the Selective Service Administration. Both were expected to work closely with the War Resources Administration and serve on its advisory committee, but, formally, they were independent agencies reporting directly to the president. PRA's assigned mission would be:

> the coordination of the dissemination of information for the public. This information should insure adequate presentation to the people of the purposes, views, and progress of the Government in the prosecution of the war. . . . The maintenance of a high national morale is a continuing function of this administration.[36]

Although the 1939 plan did not contain much detail about PRA, a study by the influential New York–based Council on Foreign Relations did. Tobin and Bidwell speculated on the "probable organization"[37] of PRA by focusing first on the changes in the federal government since World War I. For example, most federal agencies in the 1910s did not have publicity officers, while, by 1940, most did. Therefore, there would be no need for PRA to have as large a publicity staff as the Committee on Public Information had. At most, they suggested, there might be a need for PRA to perform an accuracy check of press releases drafted by all agencies before those agencies could release them. Similarly, by then the Army and Navy had "a much keener appreciation of the importance of publicity than they had in 1918." Both had since developed specialized publicity and broadcasting staffs, although Tobin and Bidwell observed that the Army had done less well than the Navy in that regard, "partly because its activities are less easily dramatized, and partly because its publicity work is decentralized." Should mobilization require additional staffing, Tobin and Bidwell suggested handling those needs within each military service, not by PRA. They suggested that each service had in its specialized reserve-officer-corps civilians with the needed professional backgrounds. Nonetheless, they emphasized the importance of the Army and Navy public-relations staffs working closely with PRA.

Also, during IMP's many iterations, the federal government meanwhile had created several specialized agencies providing communication services that hadn't existed in the 1910s. Writing after the creation of OGR, Tobin and Bidwell suggested that the merger of OGR's Division of Press Intelligence, the US Film Service and the Federal Security Agency's film and radio offices could create the core of the new PRA. This would obviate the need to create a new agency from scratch.

During this long IMP development process, President Roosevelt neither played a major role nor taken a position regarding its adoption and implementation. Generally, he had an aversion to irrevocable delegation of authority. He preferred administrative structures that assured that all major problems and interagency conflicts would by necessity be brought to him for decision. Furthermore, he viscerally opposed the underlying principles of IMP, described by Harris as

> a supergovernment, separate and distinct from the regular departments, and manned by businessmen drawn in for the purpose, aided by military personnel, would have charge of all administration affecting the conduct of the war.[38]

Given his experience during the Great Depression and the New Deal, Roosevelt would not permit big business to run the federal government. He also wouldn't compromise on the principle of civilian control over the military. And that control must be exercised by the president as commander-in-chief, not by civilians hand-picked by the military.

That's why, in early August 1939, the Army and Navy had created the War Resources Board (WRB). They hoped a high-level and prestigious group could put Roosevelt in a public position where he had to make a decision about IMP, ideally accepting it in toto. In such a scenario, the military saw WRB morphing into the organizational core for the implementation of IMP. All that was needed was FDR's OK. But, President Roosevelt had other ideas in mind regarding organizing the civilian war effort in general and organizing the wartime domestic public-information program in particular. The next chapter describes how Roosevelt deflected IMP and its public-relations recommendations so that it would not interfere with his desire to create the first permanent presidential communications agency, a goal he had already begun working towards (as summarized in chapter 3).

Chapter 5

Congress Authorizes a Presidential Communications Agency, 1939–41

Chapter 3 had concluded with President Roosevelt inviting Louis Brownlow to the White House for lunch on August 29, 1939, so that he could prepare for his meeting with the War Resources Board (WRB) about the Industrial Mobilization Plan (IMP) the next day. As part of the larger controversy over federal organization in time of war, the meeting with WRB would also be the moment where the conflict about two very different approaches to executive branch public relations (especially in wartime) would be joined. Roosevelt's preference for a permanent civilian agency tentatively called the Office of Government Reports (OGR) and located within his "official family" was described in chapter 3. Chapter 4 presented the military's parallel effort to create an all-powerful civilian wartime czar to control the economy and whose domain would include a public relations superagency.

Roosevelt Outfoxes WRB and the Military

Roosevelt and Brownlow's lunch lasted almost three hours.[1] They had a detailed discussion about Roosevelt's general preferences regarding presidential management and organization of the federal government, as well as the lessons of the organization of the federal war effort in World War I, when Roosevelt had been assistant secretary of the Navy.[2]

Finally, they discussed the president's new options based on the powers just granted him by the 1939 Reorganization Act. Roosevelt and Brownlow talked through the afternoon until after five o'clock. The president said he didn't like the premise of IMP, certainly didn't like turning over to big business the power to run the civilian economy. He specifically referred to IMP's recommendations in the area of public relations as the ultimate example of why he opposed the plan:

> If I were to set up a scheme such as recommended by this report, turning over the sole administration of the economy of the country, *even the public relations of the White House*, to a single war administrator—even though he were appointed by me—I would simply be abdicating the presidency to some other person. I might choose that person, but I would be expected to select him for a small group of big businessmen whose names were submitted to me by a committee.[3]

Roosevelt's singling out the function of public relations in that private conversation with Brownlow indicated not only the general importance he attached to that activity, but also his awareness of the connection between IMP's public-relations recommendations and his own preference for OGR as the fulcrum of federal public-relations activities in wartime.

Brownlow agreed with Roosevelt's negative assessment of IMP and its premises, particularly about the need to preserve the management principle of the president being the top manager of the federal government, not a figurehead. The two talked about alternatives to IMP. Brownlow suggested using the power of the Reorganization Act to create—whenever Roosevelt chose to formally establish the Executive Office of the President (EOP) by executive order—another unit in EOP responsible for wartime civilian needs. Roosevelt enthusiastically endorsed that approach. He directed Brownlow to begin drafting such an executive order and to include Brownlow's idea about an EOP entity as an alternative to WRB and IMP. Roosevelt was now ready to meet with WRB.

The next day, August 30, he finally met with the board. Unlike his three-hour meeting with Brownlow the day before, he permitted this one to last only fifteen minutes. He used up most of that time talking. The president made clear that he could only accept an organizational structure where the heads of the various agencies would report directly to him, rather than to a wartime "czar." He would not permit a single, wartime administrator to displace his presidential prerogative. FDR promised he would carefully study whatever report they eventually issued, "but at the same time he intimated that he might have some different ideas."[4] The meeting was over with the WRB members "hardly having uttered a word."[5]

Two days later, September 1, 1939, Hitler invaded Poland. Based on the pact they had signed just the previous month, the Soviet Union also invaded Poland from the east. Having signed mutual assistance pacts with Poland, Great Britain and France were now obligated to declare war on Germany. London went into blackout conditions as the sun began setting on that first day of the war. In the midst of those crises that day, FDR again summoned Brownlow. He wanted to seize the initiative and create a wartime administrative structure to his liking. Roosevelt directed Brownlow to finish drafting as quickly as possible the executive order formally establishing the executive office of the president and that it should include a provision implementing their discussion about presidential control of wartime civilian administration, not the IMP approach. On Friday, September 8, Roosevelt signed and issued Executive Order 8248. It established EOP and included five agencies within it: the White House Office, Bureau of the Budget (BOB), National Resources Planning Board, Liaison Office for Personnel Management, and OGR. The order also included a sixth potential EOP entity, "such office for emergency management as the President shall determine."[6] The executive order defined OGR's functions and duties broadly:

1. To provide a central clearing house through which individual citizens, organizations of citizens, State or Local governmental bodies, and, where appropriate, agencies of the Federal Government may transmit inquiries and complaints and receive advice and information.

2. To assist the President in dealing with special problems requiring the clearance of information between the Federal Government and State and local Governments, and private institutions.

3. To collect and distribute information concerning the purposes and activities of executive departments and agencies for the use of the Congress, administrative officials, and the public.

4. To keep the President currently informed of the opinions, desires, and complaints of citizens and groups of citizens and of State and local Governments with respect to the work of Federal agencies.

5. To report to the President on the basis of the information it has obtained possible ways and means for reducing the cost of the operation of the Government.[7]

By signing the executive order, Roosevelt's idea of a permanent presidential communications agency had just moved a quantum leap forward. Its legal basis was now an executive order based on the authority Congress gave the president when it approved Reorganization Plan Number 2. In the executive order, OGR received an extremely comprehensive and open-ended mandate. Its duties encompassed two-way communication, disseminating information to the public (through USIS and state field office) and reporting back to the president on public opinion. It also was to maintain its field offices for purposes of providing information and coordination with state and local governments as well as direct contact with the public.

It was the most comprehensive federal information agency ever created, with broad and flexible mandate for both direct services as well as coordinative activities throughout the federal government. The president was seeking to institutionalize the activities that NEC had been performing since 1933. Roosevelt and Brownlow thought it was very helpful that OGR was the organizational successor to the depression-era NEC, since that would make the agency "particularly suited to crises, economic or military."[8] OGR was to be a permanent agency in the executive branch and part of the president's official family. It was to help him manage the information needs of the government in the same way that BOB was to handle budgeting, the Liaison Office for Personnel Management was to handle human-resources administration, and the National Resources Planning Board was to planning.

The Public Relations Plan of the War Resources Board

Roosevelt's September 8 executive order had created a fait accompli regarding the task of WRB. The creation of EOP with a stand-by entity for emergency management certainly signaled his desired approach to management of the civilian economy during wartime. The specific creation of OGR in the executive order also expressed the way he wanted to handle the information needs of the nation in the coming emergency. Nonetheless, WRB continued meeting and preparing a report. About a month after the executive order, on October 12, 1939, the board submitted its report directly to the president. In one respect, the board members had gotten one of the messages that the president had conveyed to them. Notwithstanding the military's continuing interest in a single wartime civilian administrator, the board surrendered to political reality and stated, "We therefore do not recommend centralization of power in a new superagency."[9] WRB recommended instead establishing seven new and independent wartime agencies, each reporting directly to the president. One of the seven agencies WRB envisioned would be PRA, with the mission of the "the creation and maintenance of a high national morale. It should present to the people the purposes, views and progress of the government in the prosecution of the war."[10]

Yet, it was all for naught. Upon submission of its report, FDR treated WRB as though the report concluded the board's business and implied that it was now dissolved.[11] Also, he arranged for the report to be classified top secret, thereby preventing others from using it as the basis for wartime industrial mobilization.[12] Even with the board conceding the issue of a single wartime super-administrator, he still didn't want Congress to be able to attempt to use WRB's "son of IMP" as the basis of a statutory wartime organizational structure. FDR wanted to do things his own way and wanted to achieve his goals by exercising his inherent executive powers.

With that died IMP and its recommended PRA. But for Roosevelt's opposition, it most likely would have come into existence. OGR was now in operation and any other plans to supersede it with PRA had been nixed by Roosevelt. He had gotten his way regarding wartime civilian organization overall, including information and public relations.

The Military Tries Again and Again

The military remained tone deaf to FDR's subtle hints and overt actions in the fall of 1939 regarding IMP, WRB, and their respective public-relations recommendations. Around the same time that Roosevelt was dispatching WRB's recommendations, the military was putting finishing touches on a "Basic Plan for Public Relations Administration." Its envisioned PRA would encompass both publicity activities and censorship. The agency's mission would be "(1) The necessity for maintaining national morale, and (2) Denying information to the enemy."[13] The plan included a draft legislative proposal for the president to submit to Congress to obtain explicit statutory authorization for PRA, thereby overcoming one of the congressional objections to the Committee on Public Information during World War I.[14]

Army and Navy public-relations staff would be so closely integrated into the operations of the agency that it was hard to differentiate between PRA and the military. In a sense, PRA was constructed to provide the appearance of a civilian agency, when it was—de facto—part of the uniformed military services. While Secretary of War Harry Woodring signed the proposal on October 24 his Navy counterpart,

Acting Secretary Charles Edison,[15] was more sensitive to Roosevelt's signals over the last few months. He provided only a quasi-endorsement of the plan and cautioned, "The President has a plan of his own with which the subject Plan is not in entire harmony."[16]

Woodring disregarded Edison's caution. On November 14, about two months after the creation of OGR and about a month after WRB's report had disappeared into the void, he submitted the plan for PRA to Roosevelt to approve it for implementation. Roosevelt treated it casually. He let a month go by before sending copies to Budget Director Smith and to Brownlow on December 14 asking, "What do you think?"[17] On January 2, Roosevelt blandly sent the plan back to Secretary Woodring with a five-word cover note "To speak to me about" it.[18] However, Budget Director Smith, ever conscientious and well organized, wanted to be sure that nothing fell between the cracks. Therefore, when he met with FDR on February 10, 1940, his list of items to discuss included the joint board's public-relations plan. It was the second-to-last subject he brought up during the meeting. Did the president have any instructions for BOB regarding the military proposal? FDR waved him off. Smith's dictated summary of that part of the conversation was that "The President has ideas on this subject that are in conflict with the Joint Army and Navy Board, but indicated that he was not disposed to go into the matter at this time by way of suggesting changes in the Board program."[19] In other words, FDR knew what he wanted, didn't like the military plan, and was unwilling to use the plan as a baseline document for modifying it into what he wanted. Similarly, he was unwilling to act based on timing that was propitious to anyone but himself. Smith dropped the subject and never raised it again.

Unbelievably, the military still hadn't gotten the message. It was tone deaf to the president's rather heavy-handed hints. On June 10, 1940, the War and Navy secretaries re-submitted to FDR their approved plan for PRA. They wrote that the reason for the resubmission was "in order that we may be advised of the features that are not in harmony with your own ideas; to the end that a complete plan, meeting with your approval, may be prepared."[20] FDR never responded.[21]

By now, Roosevelt was already well on his way to constructing his own version of IMP, including a public-relations component. Eight months after signing the executive order creating EOP, on May 25, 1940, Roosevelt signed an administrative order activating the Office for Emergency Management (OEM), the sixth of EOP's agencies.[22] For the duration of World War II, OEM then provided a thin administrative cloak covering the alphabet soup of wartime agencies FDR established, abolished and merged under OEM's umbrella. Some of those agencies had public-relations responsibilities and information staffs.

For example, OEM itself had a large and semi-autonomous Division of Information led by Robert Horton,[23] as did the civil defense agency.[24] Roosevelt did things his way. And he usually got his way. As a result of his maneuvering, timing, and mastery of the government, OGR had been created and was becoming a fact of life in Washington, a permanent one if FDR could accomplish that.

Seeking Permanent Appropriations Through the Back Door

When FDR created OGR, it was funded by a Congressional appropriation of $850,000 for fiscal year 1940 for NEC from a relief bill. Now, in late fall 1939, it was time to focus on the beginning of the fiscal year 1941 budget cycle. This would be the first time that OGR would come before Congress for an appropriation. The first step was to finalize the president's budget message to Congress. BOB Director Smith met with Roosevelt on December 14 to review budget requests for all EOP agencies. Regarding OGR's budget, FDR decided not to approve the largest of the options BOB had prepared and instead cut their budget to BOB's second alternative, $1,055,000. Even though this was a "cut" from the highest option, it was—nonetheless—a significant increase in OGR's budget over fiscal year 1940, by about one quarter over its previous base of $850,000.[25] With that funding level, OGR was estimated to have about 360 full-time permanent staff in fiscal year 1941, compared to about 300 in the current year.[26]

Although the budget wasn't officially released until early January, the House Appropriations Subcommittee that had jurisdiction over EOP wanted to get an early start. This was the Independent Offices Subcommittee, which handled one bill—the annual Independent Offices Appropriation Bill. The bill was somewhat of a grab-bag, covering all civilian executive-branch expenditures that did not go to cabinet departments, including the budget for the White House and the newly created EOP. The two ranking minority members of the subcommittee, Richard Wigglesworth (R-MA) and Everett Dirksen (R-IL), had tried to defund NEC in toto the previous year. Now, NEC was back by another name and to be funded by a different bill.

The first sign of trouble for OGR came when Budget Director Smith testified on December 19. Subcommittee Chairman Clifton A. Woodrum (D-VA) raised a question about the possible lack of jurisdiction by the subcommittee to fund OGR and another agency transferred to EOP, the National Resources Planning Board (NRPB). Wasn't it true, he asked, that Congress could only appropriate funding to federal agencies it had formally established and authorized to receive funding? Smith and his staff tepidly tried a few arguments: that congressional approval was implicit when it earmarked funding to NEC the previous year, that the act of appropriating funding this year would be a de facto authorization, and that an agency created by presidential executive order under a congressional delegation of power to the president could be seen as indirect congressional approval.[27] Another argument, that Congress had approved the creation of the agency when it permitted Reorganization Plan Number 2 to go into effect was also a weak argument that the House Parliamentarian said would not do.[28] The subcommittee members, both Democrats and Republicans, would have none of it. Unless OGR was explicitly authorized by Congress to receive appropriations, it could not be funded in the regular annual appropriations bills that funded routine agency operations.[29]

Later that day, it was OGR's turn. Because of the early timing of the hearing, Lowell Mellett was not available to testify since he was away on a Christmas vacation. Filling in for him were Assistant Director Blackburn, Executive Officer Addison Foster, and Philip Hamblet, special assistant to the director. They were taken through the regular paces by the subcommittee members, asked about the mission of the agency, budget request versus current budget, staffing, publications, temporary employees, printing, and cars. No subcommittee members asked them about the issue raised with Smith, whether OGR was properly in the bill itself.[30]

Chairman Woodrum later telephoned Foster and said he didn't think that the House Committee would appropriate anything to OGR due to the legal point he himself had raised at the hearing. Oddly, he suggested that OGR try to have its appropriation reinstated into the bill by the Senate Appropriations Committee. Apparently what he meant was that any point of order on funding OGR raised by House Republicans during floor debate would most likely have to be upheld, but that such a ruling would not bind the Senate. That exact scenario had happened several years earlier regarding a different agency and, after the Senate had approved the funding, the House accepted the Senate version of the bill. Barring that scenario, he later told Budget Director Smith, OGR would have to continue to be funded through allocations from relief bills.[31]

Indeed, when the House Appropriations Committee reported out the bill on January 16, it had deleted all funding for OGR and NRPB because "an investigation of the legislative history . . . fails to disclose any basic law authorizing its existence."[32] Later that day, the House debated the bill. Even though OGR was not in it, several minority party members discussed it. Subcommittee member Dirksen said OGR is "better known as 'ogre' " and that Foster's testimony "was so unconclusive [sic] that it was almost pathetic." He called OGR "nothing but a political bureau" and even criticized the consolidated list of federal relief recipients NEC had created in West Virginia to prevent duplicative assistance.[33] Congressman John Taber (R-NY), the ranking minority member on the full committee (but not a member of the subcommittee) described OGR as

> a propaganda outfit, designed to embark the Government on all kinds of programs which have never been regarded as Federal functions; to embark the Government upon all sorts of things that will bankrupt the Government of the United States.[34]

These Republican leaders had drawn the line in the sand with OGR's first appearance before Congress. If they had their way, they would defund it and—barring that—would do whatever they could to hamper, impede, and harass it. OGR was be to, in the neutral lingo of reporters, a "controversial" agency.

When President Roosevelt was asked about the House action on OGR and NRPB at two press conferences, he acted unruffled. If it turned out that a specific act of Congress would be needed to fund the agencies, fine, he would pursue that.[35] But the *New York Times* quoted Capitol Hills sources saying "that the chances of Congress approving such requests were slight" for either agency.[36] Still, the president wasn't ready to submit separate legislation right away. First, he wrote the House leadership how disappointed he was with what happened. These small agencies, he wrote, were part of his official office and he felt he needed them. They had helped him save money, more than their budget totals. Since he had never tinkered with congressional and Supreme Court budget requests, he thought the same comity to be reciprocated.[37] Second, he strategized about how to get the funding for the agencies back into the bill when the Senate took it up. Budget Director Smith described FDR as "very anxious" to preserve the agencies and "going after this matter hammer and tongs as he does not want to lose the appropriation" for NRPB and OGR. Third, Roosevelt directed Smith to personally testify on the issue before the Senate Appropriations Committee as a way of signaling the Senators the importance he attached to the subject.[38]

In late January, Smith and Mellett testified before the Senate Appropriations Committee's Subcommittee for the Independent Offices bill. Mellett gave a broad overview of the work of the agency and elicited a surprising endorsement of the rationale for the agency from one of the members of the Senate's "economy group." Senator Alva

Adams (D-CO) said, "I think one of the weaknesses of our Government is the shortage of means of information to our people as to what the Government is doing."[39] Smith emphasized that the press clipping services of OGR to all executive branch agencies was a money-saving device, because now all other departments and agencies could cancel their own clipping services which were, due to lack of economies of scale, more expensive.[40] For a while things looked good. The subcommittee, in principle, decided to include some funding for OGR and NRPB[41] with the *New York Times* reporting that "the subcommittee found a means for saving three executive agencies close to the heart of the New Deal."[42] But, when the committee's report was issued, it contained no funding for OGR.[43] A member of the subcommittee explained that the lack of congressional authorization for OGR and NRPB was as compelling to the Senate as to the House.[44]

With the option of having the Senate restore funding to the Independent Offices Appropriation Bill gone, the administration shifted its efforts to funding OGR for the upcoming fiscal year through the annual relief bill (as NEC had been funded) and then, during that year, to seek legislation authorizing funding for OGR. The Deficiencies Subcommittee of the House Appropriations Committee held hearings on the Work Relief and Relief bill for the next fiscal year in March. As usual, Mellett was closely and critically questioned.[45] In mid-May, the House Appropriations Committee recommended $500,000 for OGR, about half of what the president had requested for it for fiscal year 1941 and a cut of about forty percent in what Congress had earmarked for NEC/OGR in the previous year's relief bill. The text of the report explained that the underlying reason for the cut was the agency's lack of statutory status.[46]

Yet that major cut did not satisfy the agency's critics. When the bill was debated on the floor of the House, Dirksen offered an amendment to delete all funding for OGR. The *New York Times* characterized his effort as "one of the most important fights" in the floor debate on the entire bill.[47] (This heated debate was occurring as the German surprise attack on Western Europe was inexorably pushing back French and British troops towards Dunkirk.) The debate on the amendment showed the political equation that OGR was up against. The Republican critics of the agency repeatedly depicted OGR's information activities as unnecessary, political, useless, propaganda generating, vanity serving, and wasteful. One member went so far as to describe OGR as "a personal OGPU for the President."[48] OGPU was the then acronym of the feared political secret police in the Soviet Union, later renamed KGB. It was notorious for torture, arbitrary arrests, assassinations, massacres, concentration camps, and other forms of extreme official terrorism. The use of this appalling hyperbole signaled the lengths Republicans would go to attack OGR. They had declared all-out war on it. On the other hand, the Democratic debaters largely confined themselves to the argument that the president had said he benefited from the work of the agency and therefore the majority members should support it. None of the Democratic speakers attempted to defend the agency and its mission. Eventually, on a party-line vote, the amendment was defeated, 93–145.[49] This was hardly a victory for OGR. First, its budget was still substantially cut based on the committee's recommendation, whether from its current funding or from the president's request. Second, no one was willing to defend it on the merits.

Now it was the Senate's turn. Again, the Senate Appropriations Committee would serve as an appeals body for the administration to seek to reverse decisions made in the House. On May 27, 1940, it held a hearing on the OGR budget. Mellett asked it to approve funding for OGR based on the president's request of $1,055,000. The tone of questioning was much more sympathetic and the parochial political interests of each member dominated a lot of their questions. Each senator wanted to know if there was an OGR field office in his state, if not why not, how much the state director was paid compared to other state directors, etc. Their focus was on protecting their state.[50] Since most House members do not represent a whole state (except those from the lowest population ones), this perspective was always absent from House hearings. When the Committee released its recommendations, it was indeed sympathetic to OGR's request, but not beyond the status quo. It recommended $830,000 for OGR for fiscal year 1941, the same amount NEC had for the previous two fiscal years.[51] Unlike the House floor debate, OGR was not an issue during the Senate floor debate. In the conference committee, the two houses compromised between the House level of $500,000 and the Senate's of $830,000. However, they did not equally split the difference, agreeing to $750,000, a sum closer to the Senate's figure.[52] Without any further floor fights on the OGR appropriation, President Roosevelt signed the relief appropriation bill into law on June 26, 1940, only four days before the beginning of the new fiscal year.[53]

But Roosevelt wasn't going to give up that easily on funding OGR at the level he desired. If Congress wouldn't cooperate, well, there were other ways. He knew how to make the complexity of government accounting work in his favor. The Military Appropriation Act of 1941 and the Naval Appropriation Act of 1941 had included discretionary presidential funds that he could use for any purpose he would deem in writing as relating to the national defense. In November 1940, FDR authorized an additional $230,000 for OGR for fiscal year 1941 from those discretionary funds so that it could deal with the increased press of business on USIS, the Press Intelligence Division, and the state offices caused by the war in Europe.[54] In May 1941 he approved another $70,000 for OGR for the remaining two months of fiscal year 1941.[55] This gave OGR a total spending budget for fiscal year 1941 that was very close to the $1,055,000 that the president had recommended to Congress for OGR for fiscal year 1941. With the additional money, amongst other things, OGR would be able to have a state director and office in each of the forty-eight states. However, while FDR got what he wanted in the short run, these transfers raised the ire of his political opponents in Congress. They suggested he was undermining the institutional prerogatives of the legislative branch's exclusive power of the purse. This was a separation-of-powers argument crafted to appeal to all members of Congress, including those generally supportive of Roosevelt. The effect of the transfers was to become a running issue that would return again and again in the fight over OGR's fate, in particular regarding spending caps for the agency.

Seeking Authorizing Legislation: House of Representatives

Although fiscal year 1941 wasn't even half over, it was already time to make final decisions for the president's January 1941 budget message to Congress for fiscal year 1942. He decided to ask for $1,444,333 for OGR, about double what Congress had appropriated for the current year, and $300,000 more than it had to spend that year including the transfer from the discretionary presidential account.[56] OGR was growing fast. But it still did not have congressional authorization. Without that, it could not be institutionalized as a permanent part of the government. Instead, every year, it would need to receive indirect funding, such as from relief bills or discretionary presidential national-defense accounts. No agency could last forever in those circumstances.

Roosevelt had no choice but to seek enactment of a law that would provide a statutory basis for OGR and permit appropriations to it in the annual Independent Offices Appropriation bill. Roosevelt approved pursuing such legislation at a meeting with Budget Director Smith on December 18, 1940.[57] It was a hurry-up plan. The goal was to pass the authorizing legislation as early as possible in the spring, before the fiscal year 1942 appropriations process would be over. Then, assuming the bill passed, OGR could still receive its fiscal year 1942 appropriation in the 1942 Independent Offices bill. The timing was tight. Everything would have to happen and at the right time for the plan to work. But the political landscape did not look favorable. The

New York Times had earlier reported that, according to its Capitol Hill sources, congressional approval of such a bill was considered "slight."[58] Roosevelt was facing quite a legislative hurdle. And his opponents on Capitol Hill knew it, too.

The bills were introduced in the House and Senate in mid-February, 1941, by the chairmen of both Committees on Expenditures in the Executive Departments, Senator Lister Hill (D-AL) and Congressman James O'Leary (D-NY).[59] These two committees would have jurisdiction over any legislation to authorize OGR. So, the introduction of the bills by the committee chairmen was a good sign about the prospects of the proposal, since a committee chairman can control the fate of bills in his committee. It would be highly unlikely for a bill to become law with the active opposition of the chairmen of the relevant committees. HR 3368 and S 887 were very short:

> There is hereby authorized to be appropriated annually to the Office of Government Reports in the Executive Office of the President a sum not exceeding $1,500,000 in order to:
>
> a. provide a central clearing house through which individual citizens, organizations of citizens, and State or local governmental bodies may transmit inquiries and complaints and receive advice and information;
>
> b. assist the President in dealing with special problems requiring the clearance of information between the Federal Government and State and local governments and private institutions;
>
> c. collect and distribute information concerning the purposes and activities of executive departments and agencies for the use of the Congress, administrative officials, and the public; and
>
> d. keep the President currently informed of the opinions, desires, and complaints of citizens and groups of citizens and of State and local governments with respect to the work of Federal agencies.

The wording of OGR's four missions was identical with the language of the executive order creating OGR.[60]

However, that same week, the latest issue of *Collier's* magazine had a long story about Mellett. It claimed a plan for censorship of the news media, radio, and Hollywood had already been prepared in Washington, that Mellett was going to be the head of the censorship office, that this new centralized Office of Public Information would include not only censorship but also propaganda in support of the New Deal and President Roosevelt—a continuation of what it claimed Mellett was doing already, first at NEC and now at OGR.[61] The article could not have been more damaging, not only in terms of content but also its timing. First, it revived Arthur Krock's April 1937, contention that OGR was a censorship-in-waiting agency (see chapter 3). The shrewdness of this attack line was that it would trigger automatic sympathy not only from the working press and newspaper publishers, but also from academics and intellectuals—all influential groups in affecting public opinion. Second, it seemingly confirmed what congressional Republicans had been asserting for many years about NEC and now OGR, that it engaged in pro-administration propaganda. Third, it depicted Mellett as an ominous, threatening, and scary official, describing him as mysterious, feared, quiet, wire pulling, and deeply embedded in the president's confidence. Here was someone, it seemed to say, who ought to be brought down sooner rather than later—before any more damage is done to freedom of the press. The article provided a brief against OGR for all the congressmen and senators just weeks before the consideration of the bill authorizing its permanent existence. Is this the monster you really want to unleash, it seemed to be asking its Capitol Hill readers?

A foreshadowing of the floor debate about the bill occurred when Senator Joel Clark (D-MO) sought to insert the *Collier's* article in the *Congressional Record*. He said the article described "the operation of a system to be set up in the country under the Hill censorship bill. . . . I think the article itself will sufficiently explain the purport of the censorship proposal."[62] Senator Lister Hill (D-AL) promptly began debating Clark about the bill. He said, "I desire most emphatically to deny that there is any censorship about the bill, or any idea, any thought, or any intention of censorship." Several other senators promptly jumped in to the debate, described by the *New York Times* as "a half-hour's impromptu and acrimonious argument."[63] It was just the beginning. Coverage in other publications followed *Colliers'* spin. *Editor & Publisher* wrote about the criticisms of the bill, with nothing from the other side. The headline said it all: "Says Permanent OGR Ideal Method for Censorship."[64] "The cries of the free press may soon be stilled," claimed an editorial in *America*.[65] Other negative editorials were published by the *New York Herald Tribune* and the *Hartford [CT] Courant*.[66]

The first hearing on the bill was scheduled for February 26, 1941, in the House. The Sunday *New York Times* that appeared only three days before the hearing set the stage and laid out one of the lines of attack that would put proponents of the bill on the defensive right from the start. The article described the Hill-O'Leary bill as the next major administration battle on Capitol Hill, now that the Lend-Lease bill was on its way to passage. Considering the importance of Lend-Lease to the history of World War II, this comparison conveyed the intensity of hostility to OGR by the conservative coalition. In the eyes of Roosevelt's legislative opponents, OGR was in the same category of importance and magnitude as Lend-Lease. The criticism of the bill was that it would authorize a propaganda agency for the administration. Their proof? According to the *Times*, "some critics of the administration think they discern written between its [the bill's] lines provision for a propaganda bureau."[67] At that time, Hitler's coming to power in Germany was widely viewed as an example of the power of propaganda. Propaganda was thought of as a kind of highly powerful brainwashing technique that no one exposed to it could withstand. It could seemingly convince anyone to believe anything. The novels *1984* and *Animal Farm*, written in the gloom of the post World War II era, help capture and depict these powers attributed to propaganda in that era. From the perspective of the 1940s, propaganda was an inherently antidemocratic activity. Accusing someone in government of using propaganda raised the specter that the propagandist was seeking to undermine the very essence of American democracy itself.

After banging the February 26 hearing to order, Chairman O'Leary read a statement from Roosevelt giving the rationale for OGR, namely that "the President may at all times have information concerning the progress of the Nation's business, and that the Congress, the departments and agencies of the executive branch and the public may have a channel through which is available an over-all picture of the Government's program and activities."[68] Mellett was the only witness at the hearing. Chairman O'Leary's second question to him went to the heart of the controversy that the *Collier's* article had kicked off. Would the bill give OGR the legal authority to engage in censorship? No, Mellett answered. The ranking minority member on the Committee, Charles Gifford (R-MA) agreed. "There is nothing in the bill that has anything to do with that," he said. Instead, he focused on *Collier's* other accusation about the bill: "We dread this bill as a propaganda machine." Mellett responded later that the materials prepared by the Press Intelligence Division were of clippings on a subject and were not colored by whether they supported or opposed the administration. Similarly, he said, the information released by USIS to an inquiry was limited to factual information, not opinion. Generally, the Democratic members posed sympathetic and helpful questions to Mellett and the Republican members asked him critical questions. A reporter characterized the two-hour hearing as "stormy."[69] As soon as the hearing was over, the Committee went into executive session and voted twelve to five, on a party line vote, to report the bill out with a positive recommendation.

Arthur Krock's next column in the *New York Times* was about the bill and did everything it could to kill OGR. He wrote that the bill would permit OGR to engage in both propaganda and censorship, that it duplicated services already provided by other units of the federal government and that it was a waste of money. Most devastatingly, he associated OGR with the propaganda activities of the Axis nations: "If Congress passes H.R. 3368 it will be simple to synthesize the effort in the pattern of Berlin, Rome and Moscow."[70]

When the Committee report on the bill was issued on March 3, 1941, it was brief and bland, dedicating about as much space to the president's letter to Chairman O'Leary as to the committee's views. The key endorsement tepidly stated, "There is a real necessity for this Office which has demonstrated its usefulness while operating at a moderate expense according to the President."[71] However, the report also contained a minority report longer than the majority's. Its harshest focus was on the intangible accusations about OGR, claiming it would establish "a bureau of propaganda" and "would provide an ideal method for imposing a complete and rigid censorship of every kind of news, military and civilian alike."[72] The House debated the bill on March 25, 1941. It was a fierce and extensive two-hour debate, covering twenty-five pages of dense text in the *Congressional Record*.[73] Republicans used every plausible and implausible argument to oppose the bill while Democrats usually responded with milder statements. When the time allotted for the debate expired, the bill passed on a party line vote of 202 to 144 (and 83 not voting).

Seeking Authorizing Legislation: Senate and Conference Committee

The Senate Committee on Expenditures in the Executive Departments held its hearing on the bill on April 1, 1941, about a week after it had passed the House. Mellett used his prepared remarks to rebut the allegations made by opponents of the bill in the House. No, the bill did not give OGR any new authority beyond the executive order. No, federal agencies were not now compelled by OGR to "canalize" their public information to OGR.[74] No, the Division of Press Intelligence does not interpret information and does not release clippings to the public, only federal officials. It was neither a propaganda, censorship, nor political agency. As in the House hearing, Republican members asked critical questions and Democratic members posed supportive ones. Senator James Davis (R-PA) said that the act of collecting press clippings and seeing negative coverage could "be so distasteful to them, if I may put it that way, that it would cause them to begin to look around and to work for censorship." Senator Theodore Francis Green (D-RI) retorted that even if OGR wanted to engage in censorship due to a possible dislike of coverage, it would still have to have the legal authority to do that. And the bill didn't give them the power to engage in censorship, he said. Senator George Aiken (R-VT) suggested that the bill could lead to "censorship through usage." He meant that OGR, on behalf of the president, could take over release of information from the departments and then color all released information to fit the administration's political positions. Green, again, retorted that in Aiken's scenario there was misinterpretation of information, but not censorship. Nonetheless, Aiken said, he opposed the bill.

The day after the Senate hearing, Arthur Krock again dedicated his column of news analysis to the OGR bill. He gave many arguments against the bill including that OGR should not be funded at a time when all nondefense spending was being closely scrutinized; that OGR could control information coming from all executive-branch departments to be sure everything "fitted into a single, authoritatively controlled groove of Administration propaganda" and that since OGR "does not provide a missing function, it is suspect for the new restrictions in information it could impose."[75] Nonetheless, on April 17, the Senate committee voted the bill out favorably.[76] The report provided a new rationale justifying OGR's USIS activities: "It is apparent that the public and its representatives in dealing with these 243 branches [i.e., agencies] of the Federal Government are in great need of the continuance of the service which the Office of Government Reports has been so efficiently rendering."[77] Senator Davis, as the ranking Republican member of the committee, added a minority report that was five times the length of the majority report. It summarized all the objections to the bill and provided a new rationale for calling the bill a censorship proposal by claiming that "*The best way to censor is not to forbid but to flood the country with material one wishes the public to accept.* Out-and-out censorship would not be necessary. The objective can be attained in many different ways which look innocent enough on the surface."[78]

The bill came up for debate on the Senate floor on May 20 and it was longer than the House debate, covering thirty pages of dense text in the *Congressional Record* compared to twenty-five for the House.[79] Given that the House membership was about four and a half times that of the Senate, the length of the debate reflects the political intensity of the subject. As in the House, the critics attacked OGR with pointed and sometimes hyperbolic accusations. Senate Democrats responded mildly, at times defending the bill without defending the substantive work of the agency, such as: this is nothing new, it's been going on for seven years, this is only an authorization—you can always oppose appropriations, the president has asked for it, etc. During the debate, opponents submitted many amendments to the bill, including deleting OGR's power to answer inquiries from the public, halving the maximum authorization from $1.5 million to $750,000, sunseting OGR within two years and abolishing all field offices. All amendments except one were rejected.[80] On the final roll-call vote, the bill passed forty to eighteen, with thirty-seven senators absent. The vote was, generally, along partly lines, although both conservative Democratic Senators from Virginia, Harry Byrd and Carter Glass, voted with the Republicans.[81]

A conference committee was necessary because of the minor amendment that was adopted in the Senate. This gave opponents another chance to try to block the bill and air their concerns about OGR. However, eventually, the House approved the conference committee report (which rejected the Senate amendment) on June 3 by a party-line vote and the Senate accepted it by unanimous consent.[82] On June 9, 1941, President Roosevelt had the pleasure of signing the bill into law. It became Public Law 107 of the Seventy-Seventh Congress.[83] Now, OGR had statutory status. It was a permanent and legally sanctioned agency of EOP. It now qualified for routine annual appropriations in the Independent Offices Appropriation Bill and was authorized to received funding as high as $1.5 million a year from congressional appropriations.

Given the opposition to OGR from the congressional conservative coalition, passage of the bill was an extraordinary political and legislative accomplishment. That Roosevelt would succeed in getting Congress to approve this bill should not be considered an a priori assumption. Skilled politician that he was, he didn't always succeed. Consider the fates of several other initiatives that he cherished, including the National Resources Planning Board (OGR's peer in EOP and, therefore, also needing authorizing legislation), the US Film Service, the National Youth Administration and the Federal Theater Project. Congress killed all these programs, notwithstanding FDR's support. These examples indicate the magnitude of FDR's achievement in obtaining congressional authorization for OGR. It wasn't easy and it hadn't been a forgone conclusion.

The events of this chapter provide a strong illustration of the three analytic prisms for understanding the historical significance of OGR. Roosevelt saw IMP as a threat to his expansive interpretation of his constitutional role. Despite the Democratic majorities in both houses of Congress, Roosevelt had to fight repeatedly to protect his plans for

OGR, especially for passage of authorizing legislation. Democrats tepidly went along, but had little enthusiasm for the project. Nonetheless, Roosevelt was ready to battle Congress, the military, and the economic elite of the country to assure that he would control communications. He understood the strategic importance of controlling communications and keeping it under his purview. Ultimately, Congress passed a federal law institutionalizing the duty of the federal government to engage in public reporting and to do so on a centralized basis. Public reporting had come of age.

Chapter 6

In Operation, 1939–41

Mission and Overview

The creation of a federal agency in 1939 dedicated solely to government reporting, as one of the original five agencies in the newly established EOP, demonstrated the importance that Roosevelt attributed to this function. OGR was also the tangible implementation of public reporting as advocated at the time by public administration theory. Here, clearly, was an effort to institutionalize the obligation of the executive branch to have a permanent mechanism for reporting to the citizenry about the activities of federal administrative agencies in order to contribute to an informed public.

Under FDR, the federal executive branch had grown in size and importance. He transformed the federal executive branch by expanding activities of existing cabinet agencies, creating temporary and permanent new agencies, increasing the coherence of a centrally directed executive branch over previously semiautonomous federal agencies, and expanding the scope of federal programs. These changes made necessary an effort of the executive branch to engage in public reporting directly to the citizenry, rather than through the legislative branch. Here, in full flowering, was the implementation of the theory of public reporting as had developed up to that time in public administration literature (see chapter 1). Yet, citing academic literature in political debate was hardly persuasive. How to describe and explain the Office of Government Reports's (OGR) raison d'être in terms that were both understandable and convincing to political and lay audiences? There was an a priori hostility in Congress to agency spending on publicity, public relations and press officers (see chapter 11). One of OGR's senior officials came up with a concise and lay-oriented formulation that captured the agency's work. She wrote that OGR's mission was to bring "the people in closer touch with the President and the President in closer touch with the people."[1] Yet that description still wasn't informative about how OGR sought to bring about such closer relations. During the many times that Lowell Mellett testified before Congress about OGR from 1939 to 1942, he gradually developed a series of nonacademic descriptions of the rationale for an agency assigned to conduct public reporting:

- "the Government has a duty to inform the people . . . [and] the Government has the duty to keep itself informed."[2]
- OGR "has attempted to register public opinion, [and] to report public opinion" to the president.[3]
- OGR's "state offices are used by the general public as a point to which they can go to get information on the activities of any Federal agency in the field, or in Washington."[4]
- State offices also "follow the local opinion concerning the work that is being done and the response to the Federal operations in the State, and they report to us; we report [it] to the President."[5]
- Newspaper clipping "enables us to understand to some extent how well the people of the county understand what is being done by the Government."[6]
- The widespread distribution of news summaries throughout the Administration "keep[s] the Government informed of what is being published, what is being thought in the county, and what is being desired by the country."[7]
- On disseminating speeches of cabinet secretaries, but not speeches of individual members of Congress: "we take Cabinet officials as accepted responsible spokesmen for the administration and the Government, and when they make a declaration of policy we feel that is information to be given to the public."[8]
- On disseminating information about new laws: "we felt sure that after Congress had enacted this law you gentlemen would want people to know what it was about."[9]

In more contemporary terms, the purpose of the Office of Government Reports (OGR) was two-way communication, reporting to the president about public opinion and reporting to the public about government activities and programs. OGR Director Mellett emphasized that the agency was in the information business, not the propaganda business.[10] Its role was providing information about federal programs in response to citizen inquiries and keeping the federal government informed of the views of the public. He viewed the two missions as equal in importance.[11] This focus on two-way reporting, continued from NEC, parallels the classic definition that effective communication requires, as an absolute, two-way communication.[12] Edward Shils's contemporaneous overview of OGR's operations viewed its raison d'être

> as a channel for the two-way communication between the government and the governed. It supplies information, upon request, to persons who are outside the government and who are desirous of learning about the operation of particular government agencies. It also maintains a continuous service for reporting to the president and to the appropriate agencies the state of public opinion regarding a large variety of topics.[13]

Richard Steele's historical perspective confirmed the role of the agency as more than distributing information to the public, but also of reporting to the president on trends in public opinion.[14] A dynamic definition of public reporting was emerging from how it was practiced by OGR, entailing distributing information from the government to the public to enhance democratic accountability and simultaneously improving the capability of listening to the public to improve the responsiveness of the government to the needs of the country.[15]

During its existence as a free-standing agency from 1939 to 1942, OGR's annual appropriations were in the range of $830,000 to $1.7 million and its staffing between 304 to 439 employees.[16] One of five (later six) agencies within the Executive Office of the President (EOP), OGR's expenditures were about twenty-eight percent of all EOP spending.[17] OGR's internal structure consisted of three divisions: Field Operations, United States Information Service (USIS), and Press Intelligence.[18]

OGR senior leadership consisted of six to seven senior officials[19] and that management team was very stable. There was no turnover in the senior staffing of the agency from its creation in September 1939 through to June 1942, when it merged with other agencies to create the Office of War Information (OWI). Regarding the role of women,

OGR was an agency with less of a glass ceiling than the norm for that era, when public administration was a predominantly male occupation. Upon its creation in September 1939, two of its senior officers were women, including the assistant director. In mid-1940, a leadership position that had been vacant since 1939 was filled with another female appointee, thus making women about half of OGR's six to seven senior officials. This pattern continued through to June 1942.

OGR's status was strengthened in September 1940, when President Roosevelt appointed OGR Director Mellett to be one of his White House administrative assistants.[20] Mellett had increasingly gained FDR's trust since being appointed to head NEC in April 1938. The *New York Times* wrote that "few men in Washington officialdom today enjoy the President's confidence to a greater extent than he."[21] By wearing both hats simultaneously, Mellett was enhancing the perceived importance of OGR and, since his White House duties included some communications responsibilities, could assure a role for OGR in all relevant administration communications activities. FDR even joked about how OGR would fare with Mellett in the White House: "I guess he will keep—what do they call it?—a motherly eye over it—a fatherly eye, I should say."[22]

OGR's daily operations during 1939 and 1942 were a continuation of NEC's programming and activities (chapter 2). The need to change stationary letterhead and the like were just about the only changes in the routine work of its three major operating divisions. In fact, the lack of change was used as a major selling point to Congress whenever OGR faced authorization and appropriation committees. Their mantra was "we're now doing exactly what we've been doing since 1933." However, in the run-up to World War II, OGR's defense-related activities were the driving force for new products and services and a larger agency. However, these new activities were indeed closely related to pre-war activities and were simply a logical extension to meet changing circumstances. Thus, the depictions of continuity were, at their core, correct representations.

Division of Field Operations

The Division of Field Operations sought to have at least one office in every state.[23] During the budget trough in the late 1930s, NEC was on the verge of abandoning that goal and instead shifting to a structure of regional offices. However, with the appointment of Mellett to head the agency and the presidential decision to expand OGR, the goal of a forty-eight-office field service was revived. Nonetheless, during this time, its budget did not permit attaining that goal. In the 1939 to 1941 period, it operated thirty-four field offices.[24] The states without a field office were "supervised" by an office in an adjacent state.

Each state office tended to be small, usually a state director, another professional, and one or two secretarial staff. They served as the central information clearinghouse for residents of each state vis-à-vis the federal government.[25] The duties of the state office were to engage in two-way communication. On one hand, state directors were viewed as the president's "eyes and ears" throughout the country. They were to report to Washington on developments in their area. In the other direction, they were to disseminate information about government activities and programs. State offices were viewed as the field counterpart to the United States Information Services (USIS) activities in Washington.[26] Generally, each office distributed all OGR publications throughout the state and also published some state-specific reports, such as compilations of defense spending in each state. Also, like USIS, state offices often received inquiries from businessmen seeking contracts to supply goods and services to the federal government. Seeking to assist these businessmen and save them a trip to Washington, state offices and the Division's Washington office would make inquiries to locate the correct official for that particular businessman's needs. In 1941, 5,000 such cases were handled.[27]

The mission of each office was to provide comprehensive information on federal government programs in each state, to head committees of representatives of all major federal agencies operating in that state in order to enhance cooperation and coordination, to liaise with state government to promote state legislation and administration that would mesh with federal activities, and to submit reports to Washington on local public opinion and needs regarding the federal government.[28] The field offices provided local radio stations with tapes of an ongoing feature called "US Government Reports." Each program consisted of a fifteen-minute discussion about a particular federal agency or program and an interview with a senior administrator from the featured agency or activity.[29] The Division's Washington headquarters published two reports for use by the field staff, the *Information Digest* summarizing the preceding day's events and *This Week in Defense* summarizing defense news. For example, the *Information Digest* for June 11, 1942, was a six-page summary of all information released from official sources in the previous twenty-four-hour period. It included sections on relations with Russia, rubber for the armed forces, the war front, oil and copper, rationing, re-registration of loyal aliens, and exchange of nationals.[30]

Mellett was frequently hearing from governors, senators and other major politicians about their views on the appointment of a state director in "their" state.[31] A senior Congressman recommended someone to head the Massachusetts office while the mayor of Boston nominated someone else. The president responded that OGR's budget did not permit reopening that office.[32] The senator from Utah wondered why OGR didn't have a state office in his state and, by the way, he had the perfect candidate for the job.[33] Indiana's senator protested the person selected to head the state office. Mellett responded that earlier the senator had "assured me in so many words that any person I would choose to appoint would be satisfactory to you," but held the appointment in abeyance nonetheless.[34] Several North Carolina congressmen protested the closing of the Raleigh office and shifting the responsibility for their state to OGR's Virginia office. Mellett confidentially briefed Roosevelt that the incumbent had been appointed at the insistence of the state's Senator, but "he has not revealed any real capacity for the job."[35] So, FDR responded that budget cuts necessitated the closing of the North Carolina office and those in several other states; "I wish it were possible to meet your request, but I can see no way to do it at this time."[36]

For OGR's reporting function, Mellett put the emphasis more on reporting to the president about public opinion than reporting to the public.[37] For example, in October 1939, he reported to FDR on the employment situation, noting "An increase in private employment is reported in 33 out of 40 States covered in this survey, but in only three States—Montana, New Hampshire and Virginia—has there been any reduction in the necessity for Federal and State assistance to those in need."[38] Two years later regarding foreign affairs his summary noted, "repeal or modification of the Neutrality Act is supported by a majority of the general public in twenty States and by most of the press in thirty-four States surveyed."[39] It will be recalled that President Roosevelt had stated at a press conference about how valuable he found the reports he was getting from the agency, then called NEC (see chapter 2).

At times, Mellett also sent copies of a report submitted to the president to the heads of the agencies involved. For example, a review of conditions in defense areas was shared with the heads of the housing, civil defense, and budget agencies.[40] At other times, he submitted portions of reports from state directors directly to the head of an agency, as he did in September 1941, when he sent to Fiorello LaGuardia, head of the Office of Civilian Defense, a summary of state reports regarding public attitude toward the civil defense program.[41] Sometimes, reports and surveys were requested. First Lady Eleanor Roosevelt, who served as assistant director of the civil defense agency, asked him for a report on the effect of the war on the average citizen. He responded a few weeks later with a detailed report from the state directors.[42] During

1941, five agencies asked the field staff to conduct surveys on particular topics, including administrative and coordination problems of vocational-training programs, effectiveness of Army public relations, and implementation of the president's proclamation on increasing employment opportunities for minorities.[43]

United States Information Service

USIS was the Washington-based counterpart to the informational activities of OGR's field offices. Its formal mission was to assist "the public by furnishing, on request, factual information on the structure, functions, and operations of Federal departments and agencies. It [also] directs persons desiring appointments or interviews to offices where they may be arranged."[44] USIS's activities involved answering mail, phone calls, and in-person inquiries as well as distributing packets of information based on requests. It had a staff of about twenty-seven people, not counting the *Government Manual* and New York employees.[45]

The Post Office delivered to USIS all mail that was not specifically addressed to a particular federal agency. In fact, Roosevelt even invited citizens to write to "Uncle Sam, P.O. Box 1, Washington DC."[46] Once opened, if a letter dealt largely with one agency, USIS would forward it to the appropriate office. However, if it concerned several federal agencies or was more in the nature of a request for general information, then USIS staff handled the responses. For example, when the Richmond (VA) Public Library asked its local Congressman for 113 federal publications, the congressional office forwarded the letter sequentially to twenty-five federal agencies and each sent those publications on the list that it had published. Seven months later the letter was still making the rounds. When the letter eventually reached USIS, it was able to respond regarding the remaining publications. An OGR official wrote the congressman that had he forwarded the letter immediately to USIS, the Richmond librarian would have received all extant publications on his list within about a week.[47]

In calendar year 1941, USIS's Washington center received and answered about 44,000 letters, averaging about 175 letters a day. Before the construction of the US Information Center on Pennsylvania Avenue, USIS was located on the fifth floor of an office building in downtown Washington. Despite that relatively inaccessible location, it had about 3,800 in-person inquiries in 1941, an average of about fifteen walk-ins every day. In terms of phone calls, in 1941 it received about 60,000 incoming calls, averaging about 265 a day—or about once every two minutes.[48] At its offices, USIS had a long rectangular

Figure 6.1. Data bank, US Information Service, Office of Government Reports. (Photo taken at office suite used before moving to the US Information Center in late April 1942). Credit: National Archives, Record Group 44, Box 996.

room for its files. Along one of the long walls were cabinets containing thousands of cards on pullout trays with information on frequently requested subjects. Staffers would sit on wheeled chairs and slide down the wall to reach the tray with the information they were seeking.

One of the main repositories of information at USIS was its reference library. It accumulated all major executive branch and congres-

Figure 6.2. Data bank, US Information Service, Office of Government Reports. (Photo taken at office suite used before moving to the US Information Center in April 1942). Credit: National Archives, Record Group 44, Box 996.

sional documents, executive orders, proclamations, Supreme Court decisions, current membership of federal regulatory commissions, annual reports of all federal agencies, etc. At that time, this was a unique collection that existed nowhere else in Washington, including the Library of Congress. Reporters, congressional offices and other federal agencies were among the prime users of the library. The library also maintained a listing of about 2,500 associations, organizations, and nonprofit agencies that were interested in public affairs, largely created by compiling the sources of inquiries USIS received. This list was used by other federal agencies seeking to reach out to organizations that might be particularly interested in a new program or service of the agency. USIS also maintained a centralized list of federal employees to help when someone was trying to locate a specific person. This was the only locale in Washington of such a list, which was constantly updated and revised.[49]

USIS also had one branch office, in New York City. It was located in midtown Manhattan, in the concourse of the RCA Building in

Rockefeller Center, and had a staff of five, all women.[50] They wore a uniform that included a badge displaying the US shield with "U.S. Information" embroidered on it. The office handled mail, walk-ins, and phone calls like the main USIS office in Washington. In 1941, it received about 69,000 phone calls—10,000 more than the Washington office—and about 25,000 walk-ins, more than six times the DC office.[51] USIS staffed the two information booths at the federal government's pavilion at the 1939–40 World's Fair in New York City, receiving about 350,000 requests for information and distributing about 650,000 pamphlets and brochures.[52]

In the run-up to World War II, USIS began a new service of sending out packets of information to libraries. It would assemble a monthly packet of timely federal publications that the libraries could loan to readers, important government announcements for the libraries' reference service, posters, and bibliographies providing sources of additional relevant information.[53] Other mailings were sent to teachers and schools, upon request. They included *Navy Communiqués*, the semiweekly *Bibliography on National Defense* (published by the Library of Congress), *Training within Industry Abstracts* and the Press Intelligence Division's *Information Digest*.[54] USIS also created information packets on specific issues that it would loan, upon request, to civic groups, program directors of women's clubs, local volunteer civil defense units, etc. The packets included mimeographed materials and government publications. Subjects of the packets included the National Defense Program, the Armed Forces and Related Services, Selling to the Government, Nursing, Nutrition, Women in Defense, and Citizenship. Although most USIS distributions were intended for domestic audiences, the national defense emergencies in the late 1930s and early 1940s (and then the state of war after Pearl Harbor) prompted it to disseminate some information abroad as well. At the request of the Department of State, USIS assembled basic information packets about the United States for distribution by American diplomats stationed in South America to local schools and libraries.[55]

United States Government Manual

A staff of five produced the *United States Government Manual*.[56] The first edition of the manual that was published by OGR rather than NEC was released in October 1939. Instead of continuing with the loose-leaf format used by NEC, OGR decided to publish it in a bound volume and to make it available for sale in paperback and hardcover versions.[57] The bound format of the manual, first instituted by OGR, continues to be the format to this day (2005).[58] When OGR took over the manual and turned it into a bound volume, it decided to issue it tri-annually. This, indeed, was the manual's publication schedule in 1940. However, that schedule proved unrealistic, especially due to the constraints in the run-up to World War II. OGR published it semi-annually in 1941 and 1942 (although, by the time the fall 1942 issue was published, OGR had already been merged into OWI). OGR also expanded the scope of the manual to include information about Congress, the Supreme Court, and the District of Columbia government, comparable to the details it had been providing about executive branch agencies. The circulation and size of the manual were consistently increasing when it was published by OGR (see table 6.1).

For the federal government, the manual always turned a profit. However, because sales by the Government Printing Office did not accrue to OGR, it never appeared as such in its budget and appropriations documents.[59]

Other Publications

Besides the *Manual*, OGR generally did not view its mission as that of a significant *publisher* of government documents, brochures, pamphlets, and other written materials, focusing mostly on *distributing* publications of other agencies. The items it published either were of

Table 6.1
***United States Government Manual* Size and Circulation**

	Oct. 1939	*Feb. 1940*	*July 1940*	*Oct. 1940*	*March 1941*	*Sept. 1941*	*Spring 1942*
No. of Pages	551	552	653	680	694	705	708
Bought by Federal Agencies	1,255	1,332	2,049	2,106	2,624	3,099	4,610
Distributed free to Congress, etc.	2,500	2,025	1,025	1,750	1,750	2,000	2,000
Sold by the Government Printing Office	2,704	3,415	4,675	6,509	10,091	12,401	20,000 (est.)
Total Copies	6,459	6,772	7,749	10,365	15,159	17,500	26,610

Source: "US Government Manual, 3/11/42," briefing book for Mellett for Congressional testimony, March 1942, Box 898, RG 44.

a "general information" nature or compilations of government-wide information that weren't available elsewhere in printed form. OGR annually published several directories and summaries generally aimed for use by the public, including an *Informational Handbook* (Publication No. 6) containing data and tables on subjects of general interest such as public debt, national income, and employment rates; *Activities of Selected Federal Agencies, 1933–1939* (Publication No. 7); *County Reports of Federal Expenditures* (Vol. I), and *Consolidated State Reports* (Vol. II, Publication No. 10) containing cumulative agency-by-agency and county-by-county information on spending by federal agencies; and the president's *Annual Report to Congress on Emergency Relief Expenditures.*

USIS also mimeographed several other more specialized directories and lists, more often for internal use by federal agencies than for the public-at-large. For example, it created and maintained several mimeograph lists of contact persons in federal agencies for chief clerks, executive officers, exhibit officers, information and publication offices, laboratories, legal divisions, libraries, personnel officers, telephones and traffic managers. In the years just before World War II, OGR began publishing some reports relating to defense expenditures and other defense-related subjects, including the *National Defense Program Contracts and Expenditures,* which was issued twice a month, by state and within each state, by federal contracting agency, and *This Week in Defense* (re-titled after Pearl Harbor as *A Week of the War*) which summarized major developments and was mailed to about 9,000 weekly and country newspapers by request of the National Editorial Association.

However, these OGR publications were much more the exception than the rule for the agency, especially when contrasted to the gusher of publications issued by federal agencies through the Government Printing Office. Despite the above list, it mostly distributed the brochures and pamphlets of other executive-branch agencies.[60]

Press Intelligence Division

The premise of the Press Intelligence Division was that *how* an issue was covered by American newspapers and magazines provided a basic sense of public opinion: what was important or not, what was controversial or not, what was of local interest or not. By monitoring news coverage as well as editorials, senior administration officials would obtain a rough sense of citizen reaction to, and interest in, federal programs. Mellett said it "attempted to register pubic opinion, to report public opinion."[61]

The division subscribed to about 350 daily newspapers. Every morning, Division staff would read all the newspapers that had arrived in the mail in the previous twenty-four hours, note any story relating to public affairs and mark it for clipping. By mid-morning, it would produce its *Daily Bulletin* and distribute it to about 900 federal officials. The *Bulletin* was typically about eighty pages and was essentially an index, listing by subject areas all articles that had been published regarding that topic. Then, when a reader saw articles listed in an area he or she was interested in, the Division would deliver copies of those articles. In 1941, the division distributed nearly 300,000 clippings to fulfill such requests.[62] The clipping service also responded to standing orders for clippings on a specific topic. Operating like a commercial clipping service, agencies would request that they receive copies of any article that was published on a subject of interest to the agency. In 1941, it filled these standing orders by distributing nearly two million articles. OGR's clipping service gradually became the sole centralized service for the entire federal government, with BOB and Congress cutting funding for individual clipping services maintained by each agency. In this particular activity, the economies of scale of OGR's press clipping service were permitting reduced expenditures throughout the federal establishment.[63]

The division also retained copies of all articles it had clipped in a master file, accumulating a collection of about six million clippings by mid-1941. This collection was also available when an agency sought to review press coverage of a specific topic or in a specific region of the country. In one case, a senator had asked for all clippings on the subject of unemployment and technological development. OGR had to ask if he wanted all clippings, which would have been a carload, or just a sampling. He asked for a sampling.[64]

Besides daily newspapers, the division monitored coverage in weekly and monthly magazines. It subscribed to about sixty journals and issued *Magazine Abstracts*, a summary of both news and editorial coverage of public-affairs topics. In 1941, *Magazine Abstracts* was sent to about 1,700 government officials every week and covered about 15,000 items from those magazines. Unlike the index-orientation of the *Daily Bulletin*, *Magazine Abstracts* included a concise summary of the contents of each article and editorial. Some referred to it as the *Reader's Digest* of federal news because it provided readers with a comprehensive review of news developments in the prior week. For that reason, the Department of State had a standing request for 300 copies that it distributed to all its posts overseas.[65]

In mid-1941, Mellett asked Roosevelt if he would like a weekly summary of editorials in daily newspapers as a compilation from the

Daily Bulletin. FDR said yes.[66] Generally, the summaries included quantitative information as well as narratives. For example, the last weekly summary before Pearl Harbor began with the observation that "Labor problems and the Japanese-American crisis continued to occupy major attention of editorial writers during the period covered by this week's analysis."[67] The summaries included negative coverage of the administration. For example, a report on March 19, 1942, noted that "Of the 32 editorials, only 5 supported the President's position and these only mildly so."[68] In late 1941, the division began subscribing to "26 Negro weeklies" in order to monitor public opinion specifically in the African-American community.[69]

A research staff prepared special reports on press coverage of specific topics. In 1940, about 2,000 requests for such reports on specific subjects were requested from throughout the federal government, prepared and submitted. As a result of the run-up to World War II, a year later requests had jumped fifty percent to 3,000.[70] In general, the division had about 100 employees and functioned in the fast-paced atmosphere of a newsroom. At times, it had trouble retaining readers, clippers, tabbers, and stencil cutters. For example, in fall 1941, the division had lost about one third of its staff, most because they "disliked the pressure under which it was necessary to work" and the hours of the overnight shifts necessary to have the *Daily Bulletin* ready for distribution in the morning.[71]

Radio Division

In the 1939 reorganization that abolished NEC and created OGR, the NEC Radio Division was transferred to the US Office of Education with an allocation of $20,000 from the congressional appropriation of $850,000 for fiscal year 1940. Ostensibly, this meant that the newly established OGR was no longer involved in radio in any way. That was incorrect. When the reorganization went into effect in mid-1939, OGR/NEC was in the midst of completing two special series for its ongoing radio programs called "United States Government Reports," interviews with cabinet members and conversations with heads of other major agencies. This continued until November 1939—well into fiscal year 1940.[72] For fiscal year 1941, OGR was allocated $20,000, to maintain some radio production activities.[73] So, the reorganization and the transfer of the radio division from NEC to the Office of Education did not affect its in-house production of radio programs. OGR's production of radio programs actually increased in frequency. During 1941, it had released fifty radio programs, essentially one a week, each on a particular federal program or bureau. During 1941, many of the programs dealt with defense related topics, such as recruiting defense workers, selling war bonds, merchant marine activities, etc.[74] Typically, fifty to sixty radio stations broadcast each program.[75] Also, in September 1939, President Roosevelt had recalled that the Interior Department had a fully equipped radio studio. He dictated a short note to Mellett suggesting that OGR take over the studio to clean up one of the loose ends that hadn't been taken care of in the reorganization.[76] Mellett and Budget Director Smith were leery of hasty action for fear of triggering a major turf battle among agencies, especially considering OGR's role (or non-role, really) in radio since the reorganization. They suggested to the president that perhaps appointing an interdepartmental study committee chaired by Mellett would move the issue forward less precipitously. Roosevelt approved the suggestion.[77] Mellett then arranged for the president to send a letter on this to the secretary of Interior and the administrator of the Federal Works Administration creating the committee.[78] The Committee on Radio Programs met at least once, on December 12, 1939.[79]

OGR eventually created a Radio Consultant office with a staff of four employees. Its responsibilities included working with other agencies to arrange for production of their radio programs, assist in making arrangements for presidential radio broadcasts, production of OGR radio programs and represent OGR on the Defense Communications Board.[80] Generally, through these actions OGR had succeeded in establishing relatively centralized control of federal agency radio activities. When FDR asked Milton Eisenhower in late 1941 to evaluate all federal war-related information activities, Eisenhower's report described OGR's centralization of federal radio activities as "the most successful thing of its kind now functioning."[81]

Film

Like the radio division, NEC's US Film Service had been transferred to the Office of Education as part of the reorganization plan that created OGR. So, theoretically, OGR should not have had any role in film. However, as with radio, OGR continued some vestigial involvement. On August 3, 1939 Mellett and Education Commission John Studebaker signed an agreement that even though the Film Service was now part of the Office of Education, OGR would continue to be responsible for the contents and the completion of two film productions then underway, on unemployment and on health.[82] However, there were ongoing difficulties working with Pare Lorentz, the head of the Film Service and the director of the films[83] (see chapter 2). Also, there were problems with Studebaker himself. In the first half of 1940, several White House aides tried to straighten out the problems with Lorentz and Studebaker, but to no avail.[84] A year later, dealing with another problem about Studebaker, exasperated aide James Rowe wrote FDR:

> Of course there is no solution to this problem until Studebaker is removed. Studebaker is incapable, anti-Roosevelt, and has done nothing in terms of education ever since he has been there, except to intrench (sic) himself as deeply as he can. He would make an excellent model for a statue of The Bureaucrat.[85]

In response, Roosevelt dictated a note to Rowe: "Will you and Lowell find a job for Studebaker?"[86] Mellett had tried to find a college presidency for Studebaker, but "unfortunately, the educators are on to him just as much as the Administration and there is no chance of that."[87] Finally, opposition in Congress by the conservative coalition to funding federal films succeeded in choking off the money for the Film Service that had previously been allocated through other relief agencies. The Film Service was formally discontinued on June 29, 1940.[88]

However, even after that, OGR continued having a role regarding film. During 1941, OGR gradually emerged as the central contact point for Hollywood producers seeking the cooperation of federal agencies in the filming of movies. According to Mellett, "The motion-picture industry itself desires, as nearly as possible, to deal through one agency here."[89] In March 1941, Mellett reported to the president that "The motion picture industry is pretty well living up to its offers of cooperation."[90] This informal role grew throughout 1941. It was later codified after Pearl Harbor when Roosevelt designated Mellett as the Coordinator of Government Film and OGR opened an office in Hollywood (see chapter 7).

Posters

In early 1941, Mellett assigned OGR's Arch Mercey to look in to the quality of government posters. In the run-up to World War II, federal agencies were increasingly using posters to convey messages about desired civic cooperation, agency needs, etc. Mercey reported that federal posters were "not as good as the taxpayers have a right to expect. Poster work can be greatly improved without additional expenditures in terms of personnel and printing costs."[91] Just as he had been gradually assuming a central coordinating role in radio and movies, Mellett then inquired of the president if he should do the same with posters.[92] Roosevelt responded with a dictated note of authorization. "I think you had better exercise a certain amount of coordination or supervision over posters. We are beginning to get into that period of art!"[93]

Armed with that presidential charge, Mellett moved quickly to create an Interdepartmental Poster Committee. Its initial areas of work would be to focus on design improvements, production facilities in and out of government and recommendations of a central clearinghouse for poster matters.[94] By April, Mellett was corresponding with heads of all major agencies regarding coordinating and improving federal posters, "especially with reference to the defense material."[95] As with radio, Milton Eisenhower's 1942 study for the president of war-related information activities agreed with and generally approved of the success of Mellett's effort to centralize poster work.[96]

A Propaganda Agency?

The conservative coalition in Congress and hostile reporters and publishers often attacked OGR (and its predecessor NEC) as a propaganda agency. For example, *American Mercury* described NEC as part of "Dr. Roosevelt's Propaganda Trust."[97] During the congressional debate over the legislation to authorize funding for OGR, an opponent of the agency described its as a "potential Ministry of Propaganda."[98] Yet a political accusation is not the same as a factual confirmation. Similarly, just because a contemporary author described FDR as "one of propaganda's great packagers"[99] doesn't automatically make OGR a propaganda agency. Indeed, was it? Based on the preceding summary of its internal structure and operations, it is now timely to examine this question.

Of course, what is propaganda? Walton suggested in 1997 that a modern definition should involve a checklist of ten factors.[100] Without repeating all the details here, propaganda generally involves a deliberate use of communications mechanisms to persuade a mass audience of the correctness of a political position, irrespective of facts, rationality, fairness, and openness to opposing views.

Certainly, some aspects of OGR can immediately be ruled out as part of a propaganda operation. For example, the *Government Manual* could not be so classified. The book was a factual summary of the agencies of the federal government. It contained no other information other than names, addresses, summary of programs, and contact information. Similarly, other factual OGR publications, such as state-by-state tabulations of federal relief expenditures would not be propaganda. Also, the individualized responses to individual inquiries received by the USIS—whether received by mail, phone, or in person—could not be propaganda since these activities did not reach a mass audience simultaneously. Generally, OGR did not issue press releases, eliminating that as a potential for propaganda. It sometimes forwarded information from other federal agencies, but not in a wholesale and systematic effort to qualify as propaganda. Similarly, much of the work of OGR related to the incoming side of two-way communication, such as the work of the Division of Press Intelligence to clip newspapers and the reports by OGR field staff of public opinion and major developments in their states. That such information would be used by other political actors to frame outgoing propaganda messages is, of course, possible. But, strictly speaking, the incoming communications could not, by definition, be part of a propaganda effort.

What does this leave? The greatest potential for propaganda by OGR would seem to be connected with its radio, film, and poster responsibilities. They were all connected to mass media and mass audiences, often with messages that went beyond mere information with efforts at persuasion and even efforts to affect behavior. For example, radio programs featuring interviews with cabinet secretaries could have the potential for propaganda. When the political appointee heading an agency describes the problems facing the agency (say, unemployment as a challenge to the Department of Labor) and then summarizes agency initiatives to deal with that program—is this reporting or propaganda? At the very least, providing factual information to the public about government programs can have the consequence of mobilizing public opinion to support that program. Yet, if the speaker refrained from overtly calling for support, is it still propaganda? A political scientist, writing at the time of these events, concluded that propaganda (i.e. persuasive communications) had become an inevitable instrumentality of activist public administration, undermining the traditional role of Congress as the setter of the nation's policy agenda. He concluded that this new phenomenon "ought not be subjected to moral judgment. . . . As in the case of every other political power, experience may show that it is both beneficial and dangerous."[101]

A more apt illustration would be OGR's involvement in films. It distributed (but did not produce) documentaries such as *The River* and *The Plow That Broke the Plains*. These short movies were about flooding and soil erosion, respectively. They were powerful visual images of human suffering that inexorably led the viewer to cry out, "we need to do something about this." Yet, is this propaganda or merely information?

What is the empirical boundary between information and propaganda? Or, like pornography, is it in the eye of the beholder: "I'll know it when I see it"? Here is where the overheated rhetoric of the 1930s through 50s about propaganda loses any seemingly social science rooting. If it is an empirical concept, then defining something as propaganda does not make it objectionable. If OGR's outbound communications were propaganda, then what of it? Persuasive messages from government to the public are almost universal: "buckle your seat belt," "don't skip school," etc. Therefore, the power of the concept derives from its negative connotation, which requires a value-laden definition. Yet, more often then not, propaganda is what someone who disagrees with the content of the message labels it as.

Mellett insisted that OGR was not a propaganda agency, that it merely disseminated information, mostly upon request. In fact, he played an obstructionist role regarding proposals to President Roosevelt in the late 1930s to create a propaganda agency that would seek to raise public morale in response to world developments.[102] He said there could be no national propaganda policy until there was an accepted national policy enacted by Congress as well as the president.[103] In an article in late 1941 in *Atlantic Monthly* with the provocative title of "Government Propaganda," Mellett publicly drew the line in the sand. "It would be wrong for the President to use funds voted by Congress to set up an agency designed to whip Congress into line with his thinking. And the President has not done so."[104] The subject was considered so important that the *New York Times* published a news article summarizing Mellett's essay.[105]

However, OGR was not pure as the driven snow. Archival records document occasions when its activities were slanted to reflect the administration's political policies. For example, in 1936 (while still called NEC), Acting Executive Director Lyle Alverson was working on a report that would be released to the public summarizing all administration relief activities since 1933. He shared a draft with White House press secretary Early and got back a response which included some clear political directives:

> The President is insistent that the low point in the depression be fixed as March, 1933 or early in the year 1933—this for obvious reasons. . . . I must leave you with the responsibility of making absolutely certain that no agencies reporting their activities for this summary are permitted to say anything at cross purposes with each other.[106]

NEC was expected to crunch the numbers in its report to conform to the political needs of the administration as well as to coordinate the public statements of agencies to prevent any appearances of internal disagreements within the administration. This incident indicated a political slant to some of NEC's public statements, certainly at cross-purposes with the assurances that it would not engage in pro-administration propaganda.

Just months before the conversion from NEC to OGR, Mellett wanted to embark on a specific campaign relating to affecting public opinion on a pending national issue. He asked the president if he should instruct the state directors to promote the benefits of international trade agreements to the economy of each individual state. At that time, agreements with Canada and Great Britain were just going into effect. Each state director could work "to create more widespread understanding of the Trade Agreements." NEC's goal would be to "provide the public with adequate data, upon which an intelligent opinion of the program may be based."[107] Three days later, Roosevelt dictated a note of response, "I wholly approve the recommendation for further informational services in regard to the Trade Agreements program. Please do all you can."[108] Depending on the particular economy of each state, the NEC local director was to point out the specific benefits to farmers, businesses, manufacturing, etc., which would accrue from the agreements. So, for example, a publication issued by the Wisconsin office included how major local employers would benefit from international trade agreements, singling out livestock farmers, meat packers, manufacturers of chassis for cars and trucks, vegetable processors, and paper printers.[109]

Even before Pearl Harbor, OGR quietly worked with sympathetic Hollywood figures to promote the production of movies that were consonant with the administration's interventionist foreign policy. After Pearl Harbor, these efforts became overt and explicit (see section on "Adding Responsibility for Film" in chapter 7).

Although these are certainly examples of propaganda—in any commonly understood meaning of the term—such incidents seem to be more the exception than the rule. It appears to be unreasonable to brand OGR as a propaganda agency even though it occasionally did engage in such activities.

Back to Capitol Hill for Fiscal Year 1942 Appropriations

In June 1941 OGR had received statutory status (see chapter 5). It was now permanently authorized by Congress to receive and spend appropriated funds. The appropriations process would now require starting the lawmaking process all over again, this time with the two Appropriations Committees. But, the first day of the new fiscal year was less than a month away. It was too late for OGR to be added to the fiscal year 1942 Independent Offices Appropriation Bill. To have any money to spend in fiscal year 1942 OGR would have to be funded, again, as part of an omnibus special appropriation bill. And with the new fiscal year only weeks again, that would have to happen quickly.

The quickest legislative vehicle for such action was the Second Deficiency Appropriation Bill for 1941. Due to its focus on national-defense spending, the bill was on a fast track. With the by now familiar pattern of congressional treatment of OGR and NEC, Congress approved giving OGR $1,093,730 for the next fiscal year, a figure substantially closer to the House level ($1,015,000) than the president's original request of about $1.5 million that was also approved by the Senate. The Conference Committee report also maintained a provision passed in the House banning presidential funding transfers to OGR and a Senate provision requiring Senate confirmation of state directors.[110] The funding ban meant Roosevelt could not supplement the appropriation with transfers from discretionary funds under this control. The president signed the bill into law on July 3, 1941, just a few days into the new fiscal year.[111]

While the president and Mellett were disappointed with the funding level approved by Congress, the administration had nonetheless been a remarkably successful with Congress regarding this controversial agency that was strongly opposed by the conservative coalition. Over the previous six months, Congress had, first, permanently authorized funding for OGR, giving it statutory basis. Second, it had approved funding for fiscal year 1942 of about $1.1 million. That was much more than the $830,000 it had appropriated the previous year. This increase just about fully covered the amount Roosevelt had transferred to it ($300,000) during fiscal year 1941 from other sources. While OGR could not expand, it could operate during the new fiscal year at the same level it had operated the previous one, without needing any presidential transfers. However, the ban on additional funding from other sources, unique among all federal agencies, was an obstacle to expanding operations to the level anticipated by the president's request for about $1.5 million. Nonetheless, this was a relatively minor setback compared to what Congress had done. The president had reason to feel satisfaction at how far he had come in creating a permanent presidential communications agency. He had accomplished a lot since the beginning of his effort in late 1933 with an informational staff under NEC. After two years of operation, one observer viewed OGR as "a little publicized but vitally important branch of public relations work" of the administration.[112] Later that year, he described OGR as "of fundamental importance to the defense program."[113]

The events covered by this chapter have demonstrated the relevance of OGR to the fight between Congress and the president over primacy, the growing importance of communications in American government, and the increasing institutionalization of public reporting as part of modern public administration. Congress only grudgingly gave FDR what he wanted for OGR, fighting over every political yard. OGR was seen one of the factors that could tip the balance of power from the old form of congressional government to a new powerful presidency. OGR gave Roosevelt an organized and comprehensive communications apparatus to disseminate information about the work of his administration and to listen to public opinion.

Chapter 7

High Water Mark, Winter–Spring 1941–42

The defense buildup prior to World War II and then the declaration of war had a great impact on the Office of Government Records (OGR). The number of inquiries it received from the public, requests for clippings from federal agencies, requests for surveys by its state directors, etc., all contributed to an enlarged workload. In 1941, a senior official testified at a congressional hearing that OGR's "work has about trebled over the previous years."[1] According to the official history of federal administration during the war, OGR's activities "were greatly expanded after the attack on Pearl Harbor."[2] In response to the significant increase in demand for its services, after Pearl Harbor Roosevelt approved—and in some cases initiated—four major efforts to expand OGR's capacity: seeking to lift its statutory spending cap, expanding OGR's budget and staffing, adding film coordination to its mission and building the US Information Center in downtown Washington. This chapter describes the first three of these initiatives and the next chapter describes the US Information Center. In general, Roosevelt saw for OGR important roles vis-à-vis the war, even though he wanted it to be a permanent *civilian* agency. For example, during a public controversy about accurate defense production statistics, he said at a press conference that it was to "Lowell Mellett's Bureau" that citizens, reporters and Congress should turn for authoritative information.[3]

The wartime expansion of OGR implicitly highlighted a delicate balancing act that the agency tried to accomplish during this period.

On one hand, OGR was now an ongoing statutory civilian agency within the Executive Office of the President (EOP). Its duties and activities were in force irrespective of war. On the other hand, the war (and the national defense emergency before Pearl Harbor) played a major role in the demand for its services. Hostile congressmen who were opponents of the agency thought that OGR was using the war as an excuse to expand. From their perspective, it was a bureaucracy in search of a mission. For the administration, using the war as the justification for the essentialness of OGR was also a political trap. The more OGR emphasized its wartime relevance, the more it would be viewed as a wartime agency, a temporary entity that could be terminated—or at least sharply cut back—when the war was over. That delicate balancing act was particularly noticeable when, right after Pearl Harbor, Roosevelt ordered preparation of a plan to reorganize and integrate all wartime information programs, but explicitly directed that the plan should exclude OGR (except its film office). By doing that, he was emphasizing the agency's permanent role irrespective of its large role in responding to wartime information needs. Yet, when OGR was included at the very last minute into the new Office of War Information, that could be seen as confirming that its raison d'être was much more a wartime one than an ongoing civilian one. However, in mid-December 1941, right after Pearl Harbor, these were all issues that had not yet played out. Rather, these were silent factors in the background that gradually emerged in the course of events.

Lifting the Congressional Spending Cap

In the first two weeks after Pearl Harbor, FDR sent to Congress in rapid order eight requests for emergency wartime appropriations. One was about OGR. This, again, is an indication of FDR's strong commitment to the agency. It was a priority for him, fully consonant with the new war status. As will be recalled, OGR's funding for fiscal year 1942 had came from the Second Deficiency Appropriation Act of 1941. Congress had appropriated $1,075,000 to the agency for its operations.[4] However, Congress had attached a rider to that funding that banned the president from supplementing OGR's budget by transferring to it funds from discretionary accounts he controlled. Mellett approached the president and Budget Director Harold Smith about seeking to lift that legal barrier if, indeed, the demands for information services as a result of the war would necessitate some supplemental funding from the president's other funds. Only five days after Pearl Harbor, Mellett sent a formal letter to Smith outlining the request, the rationale for it and a draft of the statutory language he would need.[5] To get a sense of the chances of Congress lifting the ban, Lowell Mellett talked to House Majority Leader John McCormack (D-MA). McCormack wasn't sure it would pass and conferred with Appropriations Committee Chairman Clarence Cannon (D-MO). Cannon agreed with McCormack's political assessment, but promised nonetheless "he would do all he can" to help.[6]

On December 17, only ten days after Pearl Harbor, Roosevelt sent a message to Congress asking that it repeal the 1941 law prohibiting him from transferring to OGR any additional funds. The Bureau of Budget (BOB) statement accompanying the president's message noted that the statutory limitation was "seriously impairing the effectiveness of this agency."[7] Acting with unusual alacrity due to Pearl Harbor and military setbacks in the Philippines, Congress acted on this and the president's other seven urgent requests promptly. On the same day as the president's message regarding OGR, the House Appropriations Deficiencies Subcommittee held a hearing on all eight presidential requests. Mellett and Executive Office Phillip Hamblet testified on the president's OGR request. They said that the requests from the Army and Navy for clippings from the Division of Press Intelligence on specific topics had increased by 700 percent in the past year. In fact, Philip Hamblet said, "it is increasing so rapidly in recent days that we have been unable to make an accurate forecast."[8] Clifton Woodrum led off the questioning by pointing out that congressional refusal of the request would be, de facto, meaningless since if the ban were retained, the president could transfer money "to some other agency set up by law rather than the Office of Government Reports and call on that agency which would be to some extent duplicating your work."[9] However, war or no war, the conservative coalition in Congress still didn't like OGR. Richard Wigglesworth questioned the need for such a large growth in OGR, asserting that the $275,000 increase the Congress gave it for fiscal year 1941 over fiscal year 1940 was surely generous and should be adequate. William Lambertson (R-KS) could not understand why the Army and Navy would still have any need for press clippings. "War has been declared, and we want to know what the Army is going to do rather than gathering information about what the public thinks about it."[10]

Two days later, on December 19, the House Appropriations Committee reported out an omnibus appropriations bill responding to all the president's requests. It included a political compromise, evidence of conflict within the committee on what to do. Rather than a blanket repeal of the ban on in-transfers of funds from presidential discretionary accounts, the committee recommended creating a cap on such transfers, not more than $800,000 for fiscal year 1942. Added to the direct appropriation the previous summer, OGR would now be able to expend a total of $1,893,730 by the end of the fiscal year. The rationale for lifting the ban repeated Woodrum's point. The tangible demand for services "if not performed by the Office of Government Reports, would need to be met by creation of additional facilities in new or existing agencies at greater expense."[11] The bill was debated later that day on the floor of the House. Notwithstanding the national emergency, the traditional opposition by some in Congress to OGR persisted. Several congressmen zeroed in on the OGR section of the bill and denounced it forcefully. For example, Clare Hoffman (R-MI) said, "Let us get the tents for the boys, and the housing; the guns, the tanks, the bombers, whatever it may be, and all those other things that all know are necessary. Let us get those things, and then let us leave these newspaper clippings for some other time after the war is over."[12] However, some Congressmen were willing to defend OGR, even though it was politically disadvantageous to be seen as supporting public-relations spending. Especially unusual was for a Republican to speak well of the agency. George Bender (R-OH) said, "I have studied this department and watched it very carefully. I am pleased to testify that it is one of the most efficient departments in the Government." Wigglesworth then submitted a floor amendment to delete the Committee's $800,000 amendment. After a brief debate, his amendment was defeated fifty-two to seventy. The Senate made no changes in the OGR part of the bill and didn't debate the subject either.[13] So, even in the scary first weeks after Pearl Harbor, Roosevelt was not able to get the OGR spending restriction totally rescinded. This is an indication of the fierceness by which OGR's opponents fought the agency—war or no war. Nonetheless, substituting the ban on in-transfers to an $800,000 cap was a victory for Roosevelt, permitting a major expansion in OGR's size and budget.

Expanding in Size and Budget

The president signed the bill into law on December 23.[14] OGR could now spend about $1.8 million during the fiscal year. However, since the year was half over, and the additional funding was covering only 6 months worth of spending, the annualized budget for OGR at that spending *rate* would be about $2.6 million. Mellett lost no time after the December congressional vote. Even before the president signed the bill into law, Mellett had already submitted a formal request to BOB to have the president assign the full amount of $800,000 to OGR from his discretionary accounts.[15] BOB gave his request close scrutiny, suggesting that some salary estimates could probably be reduced due to the time lag caused by the recruitment process to fill slots. It recommended only $700,000.[16] Roosevelt approved BOB's recommendation and signed the necessary paperwork that day.[17] He wanted OGR to be able to move quickly in its expansion. Roosevelt's action now gave OGR about $1.7 million for fiscal year 1942.

Even with the preoccupation in December on expanding spending for fiscal year 1942, it was also the time of year when the appropriation process focused on the next fiscal year. On January 5, 1942, the president released his budget proposal for the fiscal year 1943 to Congress. Given the long lead times the Government Printing Office required for printing the annual budget document, the figures for OGR (and many other agencies) were already out-of-date since they had been finalized before Congress's December action. As such, the president's budgetary fiscal year 1943 recommendations reflected his choices, values and preferences regarding OGR independent of what happened in December. Roosevelt certainly demonstrated in that budget message his continuing commitment to OGR. He asked Congress to increase OGR's appropriations by almost fifty percent, from about $1 million in fiscal year 1941 (before Congress's December actions) to $1.5 million. He also asked for an increase in OGR staffing by about 20%.[18] Most of the new staff would be stationed in OGR's field offices. One of the leading Democratic members of the House Appropriations Committee personally attested to FDR's high level of interest in and commitment to OGR. During one floor debate on OGR, Woodrum noted, "the President does feel very keenly and very intensely that this agency furnishes him with valuable information."[19]

Three days after the release of the budget, Mellett and Hamblet were back on Capitol Hill. They were testifying before the Independent Offices Subcommittee of the House Appropriations Committee as part of the subcommittee's hearings on fiscal year 1943 funding for all the agencies covered by the annual Independent Offices appropriation bill. It will be recalled that as a result of the passage in 1941 of the legislation authorizing appropriations to OGR, the agency now qualified to be part of the routine appropriations process of the subcommittee (see chapter 5). This funding cycle on Capitol Hill was the first time that OGR could finally benefit from its "normal" status.

Mellett and Hamblet presented two sets of figures, the president's request in the Budget Message and additional expenditures permitted by Congress's action in December—which they assumed would be renewed for the next fiscal year. The figures they projected for fiscal year 1943, compared to the original amounts for fiscal year 1942 and the post-December 1941 budget for fiscal year 1942 gave a sense of the surge in the agency's size, budget, staffing, and operations. OGR's budget and staffing would more than double from its original fiscal year 1942 appropriation (see table 7.1).

The hearing was brief with most of the questioning factually oriented. Even minority members such as Wigglesworth largely refrained from baiting questions and criticisms. He did, however, highlight the sharp increases by converting them to percentages: "you are proposing to increase your departmental force from 330 to 642, or about 100 percent, and your field force from 109 to 294, almost 200 percent?"[20] These stark numbers could be used effectively as attention-getters in floor debate[21] and with the press.[22]

Two weeks after the hearing, the House Appropriations Committee released its report for the Independent Offices Appropriation Bill for fiscal year 1943. It recommended that OGR be appropriated $1.5 million, exactly the amount the president had requested in his original pre-December budget message. Regarding transfers, the committee recommended statutory language limiting transfers to OGR from the president's discretionary accounts to an additional $900,000 during the fiscal year, for a total of $2.4 million.[23] This, again, was what had been requested. Clearly, the majority party on the committee, especially Woodrum as the subcommittee chair and Cannon as committee chair, was giving FDR what he wanted for OGR.

That same day, the House debated the bill. Wigglesworth introduced an amendment to cut OGR appropriation to $760,000, with the purpose of eliminating OGR's field service.[24] The debate followed the, by now, typical choreography. Wigglesworth and several other Repub-

Table 7.1
OGR Budget and Staffing: Fiscal Years 1941–43

Fiscal Year	*1941 (actual)*	*1942 (as originally approved)*	*1942 (after Pearl Harbor, estimated)*	*1943 (pre-Pearl Harbor request)*	*1943 (after Pearl Harbor, incl. transfers)*
Budget	$1,033,600	$1,075,000	$1,821,872 (actual; annualized: $2,400,000	$1,500,000	$2,402,871
Staffing (FTE)	414	438	936	532	936

Sources: House Appropriations Committee, *Additional Appropriations Incident to the National Defense: Hearings;* and House Appropriations Committee, *Ind. Offices Appropriations Bill for 1943: Hearings.*

licans sharply criticized OGR and public-relations spending by the administration. When asked to compare OGR and the Nazi propaganda department headed by Joseph Goebbels, Wigglesworth said, "I am afraid that I am not sufficiently versed as to the set-up in Germany but the objectives sought would seem to be similar."[25] This appalling statement helps capture the tone and content of Republican and conservative attacks on Roosevelt and the New Deal. They used extreme and over-the-top public rhetoric to depict Roosevelt as a threat to democracy, to a republican form of government and the free-market economy of the United States. Here, Wigglesworth was saying that the goals of a propaganda ministry in a dictatorship that was in a state of war with the US were similar to that of OGR. Certainly, by January 1942, the brutalities, oppression and antidemocratic policies of the Nazi regime were well known. Nonetheless, he didn't hesitate to make the comparison.[26] Again, typically, Democrats tried to defend OGR without putting themselves in the political trap of defending supposedly wasteful spending on government propaganda and public relations such as Majority Leader McCormack's statement, "I would not vote for any reduction in any appropriations that the president of the United States had asked for insofar as the conduct of his own direct activities was concerned." Only Frank Hook (D-MI) was willing to venture slightly further by saying, "a well-informed public is the best defense of America."[27] The amendment was defeated. Hence, OGR appropriations emerged from the House in maximal condition, precisely what the president had recommended. This approval, halfway through the appropriations process, envisioned OGR with a budget of $2.4 million for fiscal year 1943 and staffing of approaching the 1,000 mark. When the House passed the bill on January 22, 1942, and sent it to the Senate, FDR's goal of a permanent and substantial information agency within the president's official family seemed well on its way to routinization.

Adding Responsibility for Film

The relationship between the federal government and the movie industry in the years between the beginning of World War II in mid-1939 and Pearl Harbor in December 1941 had been a touchy one. Although many in Hollywood were sympathetic to Roosevelt's internationalist and interventionist policies, isolationists dominated Congress.[28] Those senators and congressmen criticized movies that they suggested were covert propaganda for Roosevelt's views.[29] Nonetheless, when Hollywood established its National Defense Committee in the fall of 1940, consisting of producers (i.e., the Hollywood studios), distributors and theaters, OGR and others in the administration quietly began working with it.[30] For example, the movie *Dive Bomber,* released in August 1941, had been made with the full cooperation of the Navy and included in its credits the following opaque statement: "This picture produced under the auspices of the Motion Picture Committee, cooperating for National Defense."[31]

Pearl Harbor changed everything. With war having been declared, political pressures from isolationists in Congress disappeared. Now, Hollywood could openly cooperate with the federal government. This would be one way for the industry to demonstrate its patriotism and participation in the war effort. The National Defense Committee changed its name to the War Activities Committee of the Motion Picture Industry. Only five days after Pearl Harbor, its executive committee adopted a resolution requesting that the president designate an agency or individual in the federal government to serve as liaison between all executive branch agencies (with the possible exception of the military) and the movie industry. This would create a single channel to organize and systematize cooperation between the two.[32] Roosevelt quickly accepted the offer. He named Mellett, in his capacity as OGR Director, to serve also "as coordinator of Government Films for the duration of the war." The coordinator's authority would include:

1. representing the federal government to the motion picture industry;

2. coordinating requests from federal agencies to motion picture distributors and exhibitors to show documentaries and other films produced by the agencies for public educational purposes;

3. planning and coordinating production of films by federal agencies intended to "inform and instruct the public during the wartime crisis";

4. advising motion picture producers on "ways and means in which they can most usefully serve in the national effort."[33]

OGR moved quickly to plan a film coordination office.[34] By early February, it prepared a staffing and budget plan, anticipating about twenty-five full-time employees and an annual budget of about $100,000.[35] By mid-March OGR's new Division of the Coordinator of Films had a staff of ten, including a deputy coordinator; an educational section that focused on educational, training and information films; a film research, reports and information section that included a comprehensive film registry; and a Legal Advisor who dealt with issues arising from the industry's particular trade practices and laws.[36] The office continued growing quickly. One of the immediate goals was to open an office in Hollywood, formally called the US Government Movie-Radio Center. People in the movie industry called it the Hollywood White House.[37] Mellett appointed his friend, professional colleague and protégé Nelson Poynter to head the office and hire staff, with an approved budget for thirty-two employees. Poynter headed to California to establish the office there.[38]

Shortly after his appointment, Mellett had demonstrated to the movie industry how helpful he could be to them. At the request of the War Activities Committee, he wrote to General Lewis Hershey, head of the agency that drafted men into military service, to give consideration to the movie industry. He requested "that the motion picture industry be protected, as far as it is possible, against the disruption of its operation through the calling of such essential men into the armed services."[39] Hershey accepted the request and notified all selective service boards in California that "the continuance of motion picture production is in certain aspects essential to the national health, safety and interest and, in other phases, essential to war production."[40] The decision was controversial when it was announced because it implied that a high visibility industry that had no obvious or tangible role in war production was seeking to be exempted from the impact of the war and avoid the sacrifices that all other Americans were facing. A front page story in the *New York Times* quoted George J. Schaefer, chair of the War Activities Committee, as assuring the public that the exemption was not a blanket or categorical one and that the studios would only seek to apply the new policy based on whether a particular individual's absence "would cause a serious loss of effectiveness." But, a theatrical and film producer said the exemption was unjustified and had not been in place in World War I.[41] Sensitive to public image and not wanting to be viewed as cowards or snobs, the next day the Screen Actors Guild announced that it opposed the draft exemption policy because actors "should be subject to the same rules for the draft as the rest of the country."[42] This story had the possibility of turning into a controversial political issue. Majority Leader McCormack inquired about the deferment policy. Mellett quickly responded, defensively, that Hershey's pronouncement was only a suggestion, that it would not have blanket application but only to some aspects of motion picture production and that each decision would be made on a case-by-case basis focusing on the particular merits of that individual situation. He expected it would only apply in "a negligible number of cases, and in such cases it will be chiefly to prevent the stopping of a picture production already under way."[43] Mellett had learned his lesson.

He advised Poynter in the Hollywood office not to get anyone deferred from the draft. So, when Poynter was eventually asked about getting Clark Gable out of military duty, he refused. When the same request came up for leading man Robert Taylor, he agreed to intercede solely to postpone Taylor's induction by a few weeks to permit the completion of a film that included a theme fitting within OGR's film guidelines.[44]

In April, Mellett spent three days in Hollywood meeting with studio heads, independent producers and others in the movie industry. For example, one of his goals during that visit was to increase and improve the shorts related to the war that were being run in movie theaters.[45] The studio heads promised him that within six months they would provide twenty-six new shorts, with quotas assigned according to the size of the studio. Mellett gave them a list of thirty-five topics for movie shorts including "What Can I Do? This Is Your War," "Men of the Merchant Marine," "Workers and Soldiers," and "This Is Your Enemy."[46]

The Hollywood office opened for business on May 4, 1942.[47] The office was located in the heart of the movie industry district, at the fabled corner of Hollywood and Vine and had about 8,000 square feet of space. The responsibilities of the office included maintaining an up-to-date central file with information on all films currently in production, staff to work directly with federal agencies in Washington to procure the production assistance requested by the movie studios, and liaison officers to convey film ideas generated in Washington to the studios. They would also read proposed scripts and review completed films.[48] The size of the office—more staff than had originally been envisioned in February for the entire Film Coordinator's office—is an indication of the near-exponential expansion of all federal war-related offices since Pearl Harbor as well as the importance the administration attached to Hollywood's role in the war effort. By November 1942, the film office had 106 employees and an annualized budget for salaries of $349,860.[49] In June 1941, the Hollywood office distributed to movie producers a detailed binder entitled *Government Information Manual for the Motion Picture Industry.* It was unbound so that later additions supplied by OGR could be added to it. The purpose of the manual and the Hollywood office was "the supplying of current information and opinion from Washington . . . [and] to help the motion picture industry in its endeavor to inform the American people, via the screen, of the many problems attendant to the war program." The manual explicitly outlined the themes and content that the administration desired to be included in future movies.[50]

By late spring, OGR's Office of the Coordinator of Government Films was fully functioning. The Washington-based staff produced a comprehensive fifteen-page list of films and documentaries made by all federal agencies that were available for loaning and were free of charge.[51] OGR created a "Research Assignment Sheet" so that staff in Washington and the West Coast office could systematically coordinate, track and respond to all requests received from film companies.[52] During 1942, the Hollywood office reviewed 219 scripts for proposed movies and screened 248 completed movies.[53] In general, Clayton Koppes and Gregory Black concluded that Mellett and the studios had a realistic understanding of the basis for a mutually beneficial and cooperative relationship. "The government needed Hollywood, but too much propaganda could wreck the movies' entertainment appeal—the very thing that made the studios attractive to the propagandists. On the other hand, the film makers sincerely wanted to cooperate, but not at the risk of hurting their profits."[54] After Milton Eisenhower studied all of the government's information programs in 1942 at FDR's request, he was "fulsome in his praise"[55] of the OGR film office:

> The motion picture work of the Federal Government is clearly more centralized, more efficiently managed, and is getting more effective results in its field than is the Federal information work with any other media.[56]

With the outbreak of the war, Mellett and OGR had moved quickly and successfully to create a film coordination office. He had demonstrated that OGR could handle war-related responsibilities and could implement new tasks on short order.

In summary, this chapter has presented Roosevelt's actions to expand significantly OGR's mission and scope with the beginning of the US's role as a combatant in World War II. He pursued four initiatives. Three of them were congressional approval to lift a statutory restriction on OGR spending, increasing the agency's staffing and budget, and assigning it the new responsibility of liaising with Hollywood. He was successful in accomplishing all three. The fourth post-Pearl Harbor change in OGR's mission, the creation of a United States Information Center, is discussed in the next chapter.

Roosevelt's willingness to push Congress on OGR and Congress's willingness to push back—all while the smoke at Pearl Harbor had barely cleared—indicate the increasing intensity of the sense that OGR represented the struggle for predominance between the two branches of government. Both sides clearly understood the increasing importance of communications in government. The institution that controlled communication was likely to win the battle for public opinion. The growing fierceness of these political struggles reflected a basic disagreement about whether public reporting was indeed an integral part of modern public administration.

Chapter 8

Roosevelt Fights to Create the US Information Center, Spring 1942

Besides his post-Pearl Harbor efforts to repeal the congressional limitation on the Office of Government Reports (OGR) funding, expand its budget and staffing, and to assign it the responsibility for film coordination (described in chapter 7), FDR took one other action to strengthen OGR's role during the war. He wanted the US Information Service (USIS) to open a central walk-in information center in downtown Washington to handle the sharp increase in visitors to the capital who were seeking to participate in the national effort to win the war. This seemingly modest project ended up triggering a major political firestorm that had long-term implications for OGR's fate.

Genesis

In the months right after Pearl Harbor, Roosevelt began discussing with Lowell Mellett his idea to expand significantly the agency's ability to deal with the public's need for information in wartime. In particular, FDR felt USIS should have a new central location in the wartime capital where people could go to for any question they might have. For example, new employees were flocking to Washington and having trouble finding housing. Many servicemen were in town briefly on their way to new assignments. But, especially, small businessmen were descending on the city seeking to sell goods and services to the military. With the sudden sharp increase in war needs, business opportunities abounded—if the small businessmen could find the right contract officer in the right department. Sometimes, that was like seeking a needle in a haystack. There were stories about some of these businessmen being taken advantage of. Lobbyists, influence peddlers and lawyers helped them make such contacts and charged exorbitant fees, when the same information would be easily available free from government sources like OGR.[1] This particularly galled someone like FDR, whose economic policies were geared to opening up economic opportunities to all people rather than the previously closed economic system of the "old deal": economic royalists, big business and holding companies. Free government information services could create a level playing field for the small businessperson competing with large, well-connected corporations to provide the government with goods and services. Catton described the idea of the information center as "an honest attempt to meet a pressing public need—a whole series of pressing public needs, as a matter of fact."[2]

As the idea took shape, Roosevelt asked Mellett to put together a plan for a new USIS headquarters building in downtown Washington. Not a puny information booth, but a major structure. An entire building dedicated to free information, called the United States Information Center. It would be a tangible symbol of OGR's raison d'être, namely FDR's commitment that government should seek the broad dissemination and easy accessibility of information for the citizenry. USIS was currently located on the fifth floor of an office building in downtown Washington. This was not the kind of location that could successfully serve the throngs now coming to Washington. Roosevelt had been concerned about the location issue as far back as 1935. During one of the meetings of the National Emergency Council (NEC), when USIS was just one year old, a report was presented about its activities and operations during that first year. The president interjected only one question: "Do they all know how to reach the United States Information Service?"[3] Although he accepted the answer he was given then, by 1942 he was convinced it was no longer adequate. What was needed was a new building, a major structure, centrally located so everyone could find it easily. That new building would be the culmination of Roosevelt's thinking of the importance of public reporting, beginning with the creation of an information staff in NEC in December 1933.

Months later, FDR explained at a press conference his rationale for the information center using the folksy tone that was one of the ingredients of his successful communication style:

> Well, this particular illustration—the fellow who came down, he makes—well, I won't tell you exactly what he makes—what shall I call it?—tiles. You know what tiles are. What are tiles? Who are tiles used by in the Government? Probably 15 or 20 different departments or agencies. And at the end of one week he came up to me and his collar was wilted, shoes were worn out, and he said: "I have had one week of run-around. I have been given the run-around for one solid week." Well, actually, he hadn't been given the run-around, except that he had gone, in the course of that week, to 15 or 20 different departments to find out if—if they needed tiles. Well, tiles are a sort of thing that you can't centralize. You can procure, yes. But in time of war there are any number of persons on a very small scale—this fellow had a small plant—he only employed 25 men. . . . Why there are thousands of little business men who come down here—have worn out their shoes. All right. Now the idea is that a man coming down—little business—would go to a central place, and say to somebody at the desk, "I want to sell some tiles." Or, "I want to use my shop for making something that I can make, even if it isn't tiles, for the Government—for the war." And at the front desk the man looks it up and says, "All right. Tiles—Room 101." Well, that's practical.[4]

This explanation was nearly a repeat of the rationale used for establishing USIS as a division of NEC in 1934 (see chapter 2). Creating a larger and more accessible building to cope with the increased flow of such visitors to Washington in 1942 compared to 1934 was simply an extension of what USIS had been doing for the last eight years. Information was power, and the New Deal was about redistributing power—to those who were not in the economic elite and didn't previously have easy access to the corridors of power in Washington. Roosevelt personally nurtured the idea for the information center. He even had a hand in its architectural design.[5]

A few months later, when the proposal for the center had became controversial, Roosevelt—who was good at ducking things when he wanted to—went out of his way at a press conference to claim paternity of the idea and take responsibility for its political fallout:

Q: I understood that [the Information Center] was the brainchild of Mr. Mellett?

A: No.

Q: Nothing to do with it?

A: No. It was mine.[6]

By his own public words, the US Information Center was an initiative that President Roosevelt was personally involved in, including its conception, mission, location, and—when it became controversial with Congress and the press—defending it.

Implementation

The president had given Mellett his marching orders. It was time to move toward implementation. In late December 1941, Mellett wrote BOB about centralizing OGR operations from its scattered and cramped locations in Washington.[7] At the same time he directed his staff to begin thinking about expanding USIS to deal with the anticipated wartime increase in inquiries it will be handling. On January 7, a preliminary expansion plan included the need for a "Temporary building on [the federal] Triangle" in downtown Washington.[8] Over the next few weeks, OGR staff assessed in more detail the need for such an expansion and met with other information staffers in several departments.[9] By January 23, 1942, Mellett met with the Public Buildings Administration (PBA) about the idea and funding for it was earmarked on the twenty-eighth.[10]

On February 2, 1942, President Roosevelt signed a letter to Mellett directing on him to create the US Information Center.[11] The letter was made public immediately and carried in the *New York Times* the next day.[12] The plans for the new building and its site were well underway by the time the President had signed the letter. FDR had personally selected a small triangle of parkland on the south side of Pennsylvania Avenue, between fourteenth and fifteenth Streets NW. This site was at the heart of the federal government's "downtown" as well as Washington's central commercial area, on the street connecting the Capitol and the White House. It was between the Commerce Department and the Washington and Willard Hotels, within a stone's throw of many other buildings of major federal agencies, including the Treasury and Justice departments, as well as being near the Washington Press Club's building. The site was under the control of the Capitol Park and Planning Commission, which approved the location of the project. The building's design was approved, as required, by the Commission of Fine Arts.[13] This project was on a fast track, being personally supervised by the president.

PBA then began working with a contractor to construct the building. Based on the alphabetical identification system used for all the temporary wartime buildings that the service was constructing in the Washington area, this one was called "temp (or tempo) V," meaning that it was the twenty-second major building underway in the series of temporary wartime buildings.[14]

Senate Appropriations Committee

In preparation for staffing the new center, Mellett had a problem. OGR's appropriation for fiscal year 1942 contained statutory language limiting any additional funding for OGR from the president's discretionary funds to $800,000. He suggested to Bureau of the Budget (BOB) Director Harold Smith that the president request Congress to increase that ceiling by another $300,000.[15] FDR thought that request was too modest. Instead, FDR directed the budget director to send a message to Congress on February 10 asking that it wholly rescind the ceiling.[16]

The Senate Appropriations Committee quickly took up that presidential request as part of its hearings on the First Deficiency Appropriation Bill for 1942. The chair of the subcommittee handling deficiency appropriations was Kenneth McKellar (D-TN). McKellar was a major Senate power. A reporter described him as "shrewd, tricky, unscrupulous and ruthless."[17] Also, he was obsessed with expanding his patronage powers and carried major grudges when government officials declined to permit that to happen.[18] In 1942, Appropriations Committee Chair Carter Glass (D-VA) was in declining health. Although he refused to resign, he was absent for long stretches.[19] That meant McKellar, next in line in seniority, was increasingly the de facto chair of the full committee. And, inevitably, someday he would ascend to the chairmanship. Then he'd be in an even stronger position to help or hurt the administration. Although he had generally been a supporter of the New Deal—with some prominent exceptions—with the outbreak of the war he was increasingly breaking with the administration over what he considered to be spending not directly related to the military emergency.[20]

Mellett was invited to testify at a hearing right after the president's message requesting repealing the limit on transfers to OGR had been sent to Capitol Hill. Philip Hamblet, OGR's executive officer who was more familiar with budget and operational details, accompanied him. It quickly became clear that the hearing was on the concept of the information center as a whole, not limited to the president's repeal request. It also became a de facto hearing on the agency's fiscal year 1943 budget request, rather than conducting it separately as part of the committee's hearings on the Independent Offices Appropriation Bill, as would be customary.[21] Mellett and Hamblet estimated that OGR would need to hire 140 more employees to deal with staffing the new information center as well as its expanding wartime capacity in general. They expected needing $285,000 above the current spending ceiling to accomplish that. Subcommittee Chair McKellar and Senator Pat McCarran (D-NV) both expressed their opposition to a blanket repeal of the limitation, preferring instead to increase it by a specific amount. That approach would give them much more leverage to micromanage the agency. However, the fact that they discussed this alternative sum-certain approach did not mean they were substantively endorsing an increase in the ceiling, whether by a specific amount or an unlimited one. Mellett emphasized that no other federal agency had a similar statutory restriction on in-transfers of presidential discretionary funds.

The testimony included discussion of the new temporary building. Its construction cost was being funded, separately, from an appropriation of $25 million to PBA for temporary wartime buildings. That appropriation had no limits or earmarkings on its use. It was solely under the discretion of the executive branch. Mellett estimated that the new information center would cost $600,000. At one point, Hamblet unintentionally provided ammunition to the opponents of the president and OGR.

> Hamblet: . . . As far as advertising the service is concerned, the way we have thought of that was, for instance, all of the porters at Union Station, all of the taxi drivers in town, and all of the hotel clerks and bell boys are going to be told of the service so that anybody who asks them will be referred to this one central information spot. We do not anticipate any radio ballyhoo program advertising the service.
>
> McKellar: You certainly don't think we ought to set up a service like that, using bell boys at the hotels to refer inquiries? You are making it sound ridiculous, my dear sir. Do you want it to be handled at the hotels, among the bell boys, so that they can decide who should come to you or not?
>
> Hamblet: Senator, I simply meant to refer to those to whom any visitors might turn for information.
>
> McKellar: We have fan dancers and artists in some of the departments, and if you are going to add bell boys, you are going to make this the most ridiculous government in the world. I am opposed to that scheme.
>
> Mellett: I don't believe Mr. Hamblet said that, exactly, Senator.

> McKellar: I am just remarking on what I heard him say—and I take it he means what he says—that I, for one, don't want bell boys referring people to the Government.[22]

It was a political gaffe by Hamblet, but intended sincerely. What he had said was consistent both with logic as well as OGR's internal planning. Certainly, cab drivers and others in similar positions are frequently asked a wide range of questions by travelers. In fact, in modern times, when cities have tried to become more visitor-friendly, these efforts have often included training for taxicab drivers, hotel staff, and others who come in contact with travelers.[23] Also, back in January, when OGR staff was planning the launch of center, one of the four steps in the plan was, "Publicity—newspaper, radio, news reel, hotels, taxi drivers, station attendants."[24]

Two days later, Mellett and the president got the answer from the committee to their request about lifting the ceiling, whether totally or by a specific amount. The full committee did not include any change in OGR's appropriation ceiling when it reported the bill out on February 13. In fact, it did not even mention the subject of the president's message to Congress.[25] McKellar and the rest of the committee had just sent a clear negative message about the expansion of OGR, the president's use of discretionary funds to supplement its budget and the plan for the new information center. However, the report's silence also contained a minor advantage to the information center proposal. Legally, a congressional committee report is merely a summary of the views of that committee, certainly not the viewpoint of both houses of Congress. It does not have the force of law. Yet, generally, most federal agencies treat Appropriations Committee reports very seriously, virtually as de facto laws and explicit statements of legislative intent.[26] The report did not state any opinion about OGR's information center nor about the reason it was rejecting to act on the request the lift the ceiling. It was simply silent. From McKellar's perspective, this *implicitly* expressed disapproval of the entire concept of OGR expansion and the proposed information center as well as increases in funding to cover these activities. But, the report could have stated that, yet didn't.[27] Mellett and the president therefore could reasonably interpret the identical situation differently. The committee had decided not to change either OGR's funding or transfer limits, with the full knowledge of the new information center. The report had no *explicit* ban on the project. So, that simply meant OGR would have to absorb the operating costs of the new information center in its current appropriation.

The February hearing and committee report did not generate any attention by the press or by other members of Congress to the proposed information center. Things were quiet for nearly a month. On Friday, March 6, work began on the temporary building, with an estimated completion time of sixty-five days.[28] It was the calm before the storm. Mellett's week from hell was about to begin.

Attacks by the *Washington Post* and Congress

On Saturday, March 7, the *Washington Post* ran an article with a scarcely concealed slant:

> **Information Center Here to Top All: World's Biggest Under Construction on the Avenue, Between 14th, 15th**
>
> What's that big temporary building the Government is putting up on Pennsylvania Avenue between Fourteenth and Fifteenth Streets Northwest?
>
> Well, it's going to house the world's largest, most expensive and most complicated "information" center.
>
> "U.S. Information" will be the most conspicuous sign on the new building, and it will show the way to one of the world's largest information desks. It will be on the central portion of the building, and this portion will go up three stories while the other part is two.

The article went on to describe the building's layout, how the information center would operate and be staffed and general information about OGR. The next day, in the Sunday paper, the *Post* continued reporting about the information center in the same vein. Its daily column for federal employees said that many government agencies doubted the value of the center, felt it duplicated their work and were resistant to sending their own employees to help staff the center. The column quoted Hamblet's testimony about taxi drivers and bellboys and then sympathetically reported that Senator McKellar "exploded at the suggestion." It insinuated something illegal about the construction of the building: "Despite failure to receive Congressional approval, the building is being constructed by funds of the Public Building [*sic*] Administration." Finally, it noted that across the street of the new building there already was an information center helping people find housing and helping servicemen.[29] That same day, the *Post* ran an editorial opposing the Center. The headline said it all: "The Great Boondoggle." It described the "resplendent" building as "the brain-wave of Lowell Mellett" and nicknamed it "Mellett's Mad-House." It editorial concluded:

> The tragedy of it is that hundreds of little people will step up to the income tax window next week and proudly pay up, thinking their money is going for planes, trucks, ships and the protection of their beloved land. We would hate to have the job of telling them that their money is going for Mr. Lowell Mellett's boondoggle.
>
> If by some miracle Gen. Douglas MacArthur could march his weary, bewhiskered, ragged, blood-stained troops up Pennsylvania Avenue tomorrow, with all Washington on the curb, we feel certain that a number of the self-glorification gentry in this town would dash for the nearest manhole and pull it in after them.

This weekend coverage was all that was needed for Washington's echo chamber and Roosevelt's opponents to move into high gear. For conservative Democrats, here was a chance to attack the New Deal without taking on highly popular programs. For Republicans, this was an opening to criticize Roosevelt while still supporting the war, with the goal of doing well in the November 1942 congressional elections. For both of these groups that comprised the conservative coalition in Congress, this was a perfect issue to use against FDR as part of the larger "ferocious antagonism between Roosevelt and Congress."[30] Catton sarcastically observed, "The East Indies had fallen, Bataan was gone and Corregidor was going, but for a time it seemed as if the crucial issue of the whole war was the projected opening of Mellett's Madhouse."[31]

The next day, Monday, March 9, two of Washington's other five daily newspapers[32] also covered the story. According to the *Washington Daily News*, "Lovely lassies will be tricked out in fancy uniforms the better to inform the business men."[33] The *Washington Evening Star* reported that the information center was causing "considerable controversy on Capitol Hill" and that chairs of two Senate committees said they were going to investigate the issue.[34] Meanwhile, the *Post* kept up its drumbeat by depicting Mellett on the defensive and needing to justify the unjustifiable. The headline, again, said it all: "The Great Boondoggle: Mellett Defends 'Madhouse' Idea Rejected by the Senate."[35] The *New York Herald Tribune* also joined the fray, indicating this was becoming a national, rather than local Washington, story.[36]

On Monday, Senator Harry F. Byrd (D-VA), chair of the Congressional Joint Committee on Reduction of Nonessential Federal

Expenditures, sent a letter to Mellett demanding answers to seven questions about the information center. The last question indicated he had already made up his mind. It requested "A complete statement as to the need for the services you propose to render, in view of the fact that practically every department and agency of the government now has a more or less costly and well-manned information bureau."[37] That day, too, Congressman Daniel Reed (R-NY) inserted the *Post*'s Sunday editorial into the *Congressional Record* and prefaced it with the observation that "An all-out war cannot be fought successfully by political boondoggling, of which the 'great boondoggle,' referred to in the *Washington Post* of March 8, 1942, is only one of thousands which have no relation to an effective national defense or offense."[38]

On Tuesday, Congressman Dave Satterfield Jr. (D-VA) introduced a bill to prohibit use of federal funds for the information center[39] and it was referred to the House Committee on Public Buildings and Grounds. He said the center was "in no way related to the war effort . . . there is a definite choice here as between information for visitors who come to Washington and the procurement of instruments of war."[40] Congressman Everett Dirksen (R-IL) said, "I suppose they think a press release from down there will be more effective than a 1000-pound bomb."[41] That day, the *Washington Post, Times-Herald, News,* and *Evening Star* all had stories about this new controversy. The *Post*'s headline read, "The Great Boondoggle: Mellett's Monster Won't Lack for Funds Despite Congress."[42] The next day's *Post* included a photo of the construction site with the caption, "Prep School for Mellett's Madhouse." A separate, less hysterical, article profiled Harriet Root, the director of USIS. Although it referred to OGR's "huge new building," it also quoted a member of the Capitol Hill Secretaries' Club about how helpful she was to congressional staff seeking information, to the point that they made her an honorary member of their organization.[43]

Acting quickly, on Thursday, March 12, Senator Byrd's Joint Committee held a hearing on the information center.[44] In that morning's edition, the *Washington Post* set the spin for the hearing: "OGR Head Will Be Asked Why He By-Passed Congress on New Building." The article described workmen, meanwhile, "racing" to build the "palatial" structure.[45] At the hearing, Mellett was grilled intensely and aggressively about all aspects of the center. The atmosphere was hostile, with all the members of the committee who spoke, except one, criticizing OGR, Mellett and the information center. He was treated as a guilty criminal, caught in the act. As Senator McKellar usually did with people testifying he was unhappy with, he continuously interrupted him and peppered him with questions intermingled with statements of outrage.[46] At one point Mellett said, after having been interrupted repeatedly, "Now, may I proceed?"[47] Things got so bad that Congressman Woodrum suggested to Senator Byrd, "Mr. Chairman, I think if we let Mr. Mellett finish without any of us interrupting, let him finish answering your questions, we will all get what are looking for."[48]

Senator McKellar thundered at Mellett, "you are disregarding the expressed will of Congress in going ahead with this matter."[49] Mellett's response was that OGR was not exceeding the statutory ceiling on transfers from presidential discretionary funds that McKellar's committee had decided not to change. Further, the costs of construction of the structure were from a discretionary PBA construction account. He asserted he was fully compliant with any explicit and statutory directives of Congress. Congressman Allen Treadway (R-MA) said he had driven by the site of the information center that morning and "it is perfectly astonishing the amount of lumber that is being wasted there to build the building."[50] Senator Glass, up from his sick bed, sarcastically played to the audience: "Do you think there is anybody in the world that can tell you what it is for? [laughter]."[51] Longtime OGR critic Congressman Taber wondered if OGR could handle its work "without this gorgeous set-up that you are talking about having."[52] The only member of the committee who didn't explicitly attack OGR was Congressman Woodrum who was also Chair of the House Appropriations Committee's subcommittee on Independent Offices and second most senior Democrat on the full committee. Because of his personal dealings with OGR's appropriations, he was much more familiar with OGR's activities than most members of the joint committee.[53] However, even Woodrum's support was tepid at best. At most, he was willing to say that the general issues about OGR had been already explored in depth by his subcommittee, "It certainly has been gone into thoroughly many times. It was gone into in the independent offices [bill] hearings this year."[54]

Little new information came out at the hearing. Most was already in the public domain. Rather, this was political theatre, a chance for Republicans and conservative Democrats to assail the administration. The information center was merely the issue-du-jour for a larger campaign by the congressional conservative coalition against FDR, the New Deal, the expansion of the role of the federal government, and the increase in federal agencies and programs. Robert Caro described the mood on Capitol Hill as particularly ugly as 1942 unfolded. After giving Roosevelt just about anything he had asked for at the beginning of the war,

> Then bitterness began to mount on Capitol Hill—against the President, whom not a few conservative congressmen

> viewed as a would-be dictator; against his "ass-kissing New Dealers"; against the administrative agencies which conservatives felt were misusing the powers granted by Congress to extend the New Deal under the cloak of wartime necessity . . . Congress began attempting to reassert its status as a coequal branch of government.[55]

As in the routine course of Washington politics and the roving spotlight of the media, the information center was just one of an ongoing series of controversies that briefly explode on the scene, cause much political machinations, and then disappear as quickly at they came.

The hearing was a major news event. The Thursday afternoon and Friday morning papers covered it extensively, some with pictures from the hearing as well as articles.[56] By definition, such coverage put OGR in a bad light, since Mellett was depicted as defending his agency's controversial project, whereas senators and congressmen were seen as probing for the truth and seeking to save taxpayer funds from being wasted. Searching for a new angle, the *Post* on Friday also had a sidebar story about the construction site. It described the fence around the perimeter of the site of "Mellett's think temple" as a "fancy-topped, dress wood fence thrown as a substantial veil around" the site.[57] However, not all the coverage was negative. Gould Lincoln, veteran reporter (since 1909) and prominent conservative political columnist,[58] dedicated his regular column, "The Political Mill," in the *Washington Evening Star* to a sympathetic view of the project. He wrote, "The new central information office is calculated to serve and to save" and pointed to the hypocrisy of politicians and newspapers previously criticizing the administration for not releasing enough information about the war and who were now criticizing this project to disseminate information.[59] Similarly, Charles T. Lucey, a Washington-based reporter and columnist for the *New York World-Telegram*, commented favorably on the center's purpose of helping "the bewildered individual who comes to this hectic wartime capital to do business, [but] is shunted for days from one agency to another and finally, in frustration, goes home to denounce the confusion on the Potomac."[60]

A friendly Senator, Joseph Guffey (D-PA), inserted Lincoln's column in the *Congressional Record* the next day.[61] But, he did not offer any opinion about OGR or the information center. The day after, Friday, Guffey also arranged for a colleague to insert on his behalf another pro-OGR report, this time a radio commentary by Fulton Lewis Jr. from Thursday evening. Again, there were no expressions of opinion preceding the radio transcript.[62] That same day, Congressman Herman Eberharter (D-PA) inserted the *Washington Post*'s somewhat friendly profile of Harriet Root from its Wednesday edition.[63] Like

Guffey, he made no substantive introductory remarks prior to the reproduction of the text of the article in the *Congressional Record*. Guffey and Eberharter's personal silence is in sharp contrast to the fiery anti-OGR comments members of the conservative coalition. This juxtaposition indicates the asymmetry of the politics of OGR and of government information programs in general. MacCann observed this imbalance when discussing OGR's film activities, "There was perhaps a general public interest in improved, modernized, dramatized Government reporting, but no block of votes in any constituency was going to be shifted because of that issue."[64]

Guffey and Eberharter knew that if they made substantive comments in support of OGR or the information center, they would be open to attacks that they were supporting wasteful federal spending and government propaganda programs instead of the war effort. They were in a no-win political situation and knew it. Contrariwise, congressional conservatives were in a win-win situation—and they knew it. As a rule, no one is for "wasteful" government spending and public-relations programs are easily put in that category. And, partisan or ideological attacks on Roosevelt could be masked as merely prompted by protecting the public purse. That's why they were piling on. The attack on the information center was part of a conscious strategy of the conservative coalition. Knowing that it should not try to cut funding for programs serving constituents, they focused on "those functions behind which no congressional bloc would rally, but which in the long run might critically influence the durability and impact of the programs."[65]

The day after the Byrd Committee hearing, Friday the 13th, President Roosevelt held one of his frequent press conferences.[66] Naturally, the subject came up. FDR took personal responsibility for the idea of the information center and gave a detailed explanation for its rationale and need (see quote near the beginning of this chapter). This was an unusual stance for any politician to take. Normally, when something becomes controversial, the elected official ducks for cover. FDR was especially known for letting members of his administration fight on their own publicly to accomplish particular goals. If they won, great. If they lost, then the president had not spent any political capital needlessly. Given Roosevelt's routine behavior of evading controversial issues and responsibility for them whenever possible, it is that much more striking how firmly and publicly he supported implementation of his idea for a central information building, no matter how controversial it had become with Congress and the media. He went out of his way to take the political heat personally.

He was hoping his comments at the press conference would help turn the tide in this week-old controversy. He only succeeded with the second-tier papers. The Friday afternoon papers headlined his comments: "OGR Project Sound, Decent, Says Roosevelt"[67] and "Mellett's 'Information Booth' Is Sound and Decent, Says F. D.: Helpful to Congressmen's Constituents."[68] However, the key two morning papers gave his comments secondary attention in their Friday editions. The *Post*'s headline was "The Great Boondoggle: Congress' Plan to Give Building to War Agency Gains Support, President Assumes All Responsibility for Information Center Idea."[69] The *New York Times* considered comments he made at the press conference on other topics more newsworthy. Only the third and last sub-headline related to OGR: "Roosevelt Defends Information Center." In the article, his comments about the building were the eighth through tenth paragraphs of the sixteen-paragraph story.[70]

In the meantime, Mellett's week wasn't over. On Friday the House Committee on Public Buildings and Grounds held a hearing on Satterfield's bill to block any funding for the information center. Before Dave Satterfield was invited to testify, Carter Manasco (D-AL), the most junior Democratic member of the committee, asked to insert Lincoln's pro-OGR column into the record. Startlingly—given the asymmetry of the politics of information programs and perhaps due to his lack of prolonged experience in Washington—he verbalized the value he saw in OGR:

> I have heard the Office of Government Reports condemned, but in my experience I have found that it can save more time for your office force than any other agency in Washington . . . It does perform a very valuable service, if your secretary will tell you how much he uses it.[71]

But Satterfield's testimony returned the political rhetoric to its more familiar slant. He ominously warned, "The casualty lists will reveal to the country in bolder and clearer outline the utter madness of the wasters of public funds. This is the first layer on the cake, this temporary building."[72] After his testimony, five members of the committee (three Democrats, two Republicans) made their views known—in the form of questions to Satterfield—that were supportive of his bill. However, another member, James Wright (D-PA) gently challenged Satterfield's position and that of most of the committee members present. Wasn't it true that the amount OGR would save over five years from vacating currently rented offices would equal the cost of the temporary building? Wasn't it true that Congress had appropriated a lump sum for temporary construction to PBA and had not earmarked any of it for or against particular projects? In that case, it could be used legally for any temporary building, including the information center.[73]

Mellett then testified. Generally, he repeated what he had said the day before when testifying at the Byrd Committee hearing. Most committee members asked hostile questions, suggesting that the construction of the building was somehow a contravention of the will of Congress. Congressman Wright, again, was the only member of the committee to present a friendly question. He opined "if my office had to act as a clearing house for all the people, business people in the Pittsburgh district, telling them about all the agencies of the Government, I would have to have three or four hundred clerks."[74] The cross examination of Mellett had not been completed by the time the committee had to adjourn, so the hearing was recessed till Monday, March 16.

Over the weekend, the *Post* continued its attack. Under the headline "Two Information Centers—'Side by Each'," it ran pictures of the construction site of the information center and of the nearby Defense Housing Registry building. A separate story talked about the "spreading determination in Congress . . . [with] the strong backing of Democrats and Republicans in both Houses" to prevent OGR from occupying the site. Byrd was described as preparing a resolution to that effect while the Chairman of the House Public Buildings Committee said he expected the committee to act on the Satterfield resolution after the committee hearing on Monday.[75] The *Post* also published a list of 163 field information offices of the War Production Board throughout the country that were also intended to provide information to businessmen, the ostensible purpose of the OGR Information Center. The point was clear, namely that the facility on Pennsylvania Avenue was surely duplicative of other federal information offices for businesses.[76] Arthur Krock's Sunday column in the *New York Times* was critical of the project. The column mocked Roosevelt's pretensions at being an architect like Thomas Jefferson. "Jefferson was a better architect than the President." Nonetheless, the project "animated the President in his idea, design and location of the government information agency under the Office of Government Reports. The need of the project is highly doubtful."[77]

Monday, March 16, Mellett was to return to complete his testimony before the House Committee. The *Post* story that morning said that Senator Byrd "would confer with members of the House Public Building and Grounds Committee to work out a plan to prevent" OGR from occupying the building under construction.[78] During the hearing, most members of the Committee continued asking Mellett critical questions, but a few were more supportive. United Press wire service reported that "Questioning by committee members today, however, appeared, on the whole, to be more sympathetic toward Mr. Mellett."[79] Congressman Wright pointed out that Satterfield's resolution and the Committee's consideration of it "takes it for granted that this is a nonessential expenditure. From the testimony I have heard it seems to be the opinion of the President . . . that some expenditure along this line is essential." The last witness at the hearing was the commissioner of the Public Buildings Administration, W. E. Reynolds. He blandly told the committee that the information center was just one of many temporary building PBA was constructing or had constructed and that its cost and design were routine and average. Currently OGR was "Quite inadequately housed. The space is very poor." Should Congress so decide, he said, the building could easily be occupied by other agencies. Also, should OGR not need all 60,000 square feet of the building, he had many requests pending from small units of the federal government for space that could take up the rest of the building. He emphasized that his duty was to provide the wartime space needed by federal agencies, not to judge independently the merits of agency programs and mission:

> Congressman Hebert: And supposing that the Congress should decide that they [OGR] should not go into this building, and you would have to provide space for them some place else?
>
> Reynolds: Yes, sir.
>
> Hebert: In other words, by Congress saying that they should not go into this particular business [i.e. building], that would not eliminate entirely future construction in regard to that particular bureau?
>
> Reynolds: No; I think not.[80]

This was a polite way of saying that unless Congress passed an explicit law detailing the permissible space needs of OGR, the information center building was lawful and its development routine. That put the responsibility squarely on the opponents of the building to obtain a majority vote in both houses on the issue. For all the sound and fury, it could not be automatically assumed that these vocal individuals indeed had the support of the *majority* of Congress. Short of such a law, they could not claim to be voicing the views of the entire Congress. Instead, they were merely an informal group of senators and congressmen expressing their individual views.

With Reynolds' testimony completed, the hearing was adjourned. The committee immediately reconvened in a closed executive session to discuss what to do with Satterfield's resolution. It took no action on the resolution that day, an indication that this vocal group didn't have the votes. FDR had tactically outfoxed Congress. Nonetheless, all the headlines and bad press had had an impact. The information center was now a controversial project. The damage was done.

Compromises

Committee Chairman Lanham kept being quoted in the *Post* for several days running, to the effect that the committee would be acting soon on the Satterfield resolution. But the committee never did. Instead, during the executive session after the hearing on Monday, there was a consensus to send a delegation from the committee to meet with the president to discuss the project. This idea was a political facing saving device that gave the appearance of action, yet really confirmed the lack of support for taking formal action on the Satterfield resolution. Also, the purpose of a meeting with the president was so bland that even members of the committee sympathetic to OGR—such as Wright and Manasco—couldn't object. A three-person delegation from the committee consisted of Chairman Lanham, C. Jasper Bell (D-MO), the most senior Democratic member of the committee after Lanham, and Pehr Holmes (R-MA), the ranking Republican member of the committee. Of the three, both Democrats had made statements during the hearings against the information center and sympathetic to the Satterfield resolution, while Holmes had asked several neutral questions and did not indicate a position. (Nonetheless, as the sole Republican on the delegation, he would be under pressure from his Republican colleagues to oppose the project, if only because that was the role of the opposition party.) The delegation met with the president on Thursday, March 19.

At the meeting, FDR reiterated his belief in the need for the center, especially to help businessmen, but slyly said that if the Congress took overt action that prohibited any appropriation for use of the building as an information center, he would of course defer to that. Other agencies could occupy the building. This implicitly challenged them to pass the Satterfield resolution in statutory form and in both houses—a difficult task that he knew and they knew was unlikely to happen. In an effort to appear conciliatory and bring the controversy to a conclusion, Roosevelt blithely promised them "the building would be staffed without any substantial additional costs from the staffs" of OGR and other departmental information offices. As soon as the meeting was over, the president summoned BOB Director Smith. He told him of his no-new-staff promise to the delegation and rather sheepishly asked Smith if reducing information staff in other departments and transferring them to OGR could simultaneously accomplish his promise as well as his desire for the information center to function successfully? Smith said that BOB had just finished a survey of federal information personnel and felt transferring staff from other agencies to OGR could be accomplished without significant impact on those departments' information programs.[81]

Yet even with the House Committee co-opted and no action forthcoming from Congress, the *Post* kept up its barrage against the Information Center:

> March 20: "World's Costliest Information Booth Rises Rapidly"
> March 26: "Work on 'Mellett's Madhouse' Races for Finish"
> March 29: "While the Colossus Grows: Eight U.S. Information Centers Already Are Functioning Here"
> March 31: "Many Private Agencies Here Guide Steps of Businessmen"
> April 2: "Early M-G-M Period, Maybe, or Late Coney Island: Of What Strange Architecture is Mellett's Madhouse Built?"
> April 3: "Found: A Man Who Could Use Mellett's Madhouse"

The *Post*'s campaign still had a sympathetic partner in Senator McKellar. Although the House Committee had been placated, he hadn't been. An ally of FDR, former senator and then-Supreme Court Justice James Byrnes tried to resolve the matter. This was a typical political role he played while on the court.[82] On Saturday, March 22, two days after FDR had met with the House delegation, Byrnes talked with FDR and received the go-ahead to try to work out a compromise with McKellar.[83] He quickly met with McKellar. McKellar agreed that if FDR would promise not to undercut Congress with transfers of discretionary dollars, he would work with Mellett and Woodrum on a compromise. Byrnes and McKellar drafted a letter to the president from McKellar. In it he said, "I am satisfied that the Information Service could be enlarged to be of service to those who have business with the Government, but I do not believe that it should be enlarged to the extent proposed." Specifically, he wanted to FDR to commit to the maximum amount he would transfer to OGR from discretionary presidential accounts.[84]

In response, FDR agreed to sign a letter also drafted by Byrnes. The tone was conciliatory. He reaffirmed his support for the information center building and expanding OGR but noted, "I am satisfied that the matter is not of sufficient importance to justify the time that has been devoted to a discussion of the subject." He recognized that Congress had the power to act in a binding way. He even agreed to limit his use of discretionary funds for OGR if Congress would act "definitely" to specify the funding level it desired for OGR. In other words, he would not defy Congress if it enacted an unambiguous statute. However, he was saying implicitly, resolutions introduced, hearings, letters, petitions and speeches didn't count.[85] After receiving the letter, McKellar then told the press that he was satisfied with the President's response and was now ready to "reach a fair and just conclusion about the matter." Blithely saying, "There never was a question about the President's right to construct the building," he contradicted completely what he had said to Mellett at the Byrd Committee hearing. He said he continued to feel that OGR could equip and operate the building with less funding than it had requested.[86]

Still, it remained to be seen what concrete actions McKellar would take to reflect his part of the compromise. Later in the spring, when the Senate Appropriations Subcommittee for the Independent Offices Bill held a hearing on PBA's budget, both Subcommittee (and Committee) Chairman Glass as well as McKellar were alert, on guard and ready to keep picking at the issue. When the PBA representatives submitted a list of sixty-five buildings they were dealing with, the first item that Glass and McKellar asked about was the information center. They wanted to know what was the $47,000 item for the "madhouse," as Glass referred to it, for? Heating, lighting and cleaning, responded the PBA witnesses. McKellar, remembering down to the minutest details of the controversy, wanted to be sure: "It does not include furniture for the building?" No, Mellett had kept his word about the cost of the furniture having to be absorbed by OGR. Glass and McKellar still wouldn't let go of the subject. Glass asked: "Why do you have to rent additional space [for all federal agencies in Washington], at a cost of some $4,000,000, when they are building a great 'madhouse,' as it is called, at the corner of Fifteenth and Pennsylvania Avenue?" When McKellar noticed that PBA's $4.5 million budget proposal included renting additional space for OGR at another location at a cost of $391, he demanded to know what the additional space was justified for.[87]

The subject generally dropped off the ever-changing list of "hot" news stories from Washington. Then, on April 23, the Senate Appropriations Committee dropped its bomb. It recommended that OGR's fiscal year 1943 budget cut by $406,270, a twenty-seven percent cut to $1,075,000 from $1,500,000 recommended by the House. It also recommended extending for another year the $800,000 cap on transfers to OGR from discretionary presidential funds, instead of the $900,000 recommended by the House.[88] Many other agencies were cut in the bill, reflecting the politics of the McKellar-Byrd-Tydings[89] "economy bloc," especially McKellar's claim that expenditures for information, travel, purchase of cars and employment of lawyers were a waste of public funds.[90] OGR had "one of the severest cuts."[91] McKellar described what he intended to accomplish with this cut. OGR could still move into the new information center building,

> but they haven't enough funds to occupy but a part of the building. They will have to economize sharply, and they can't use the very large staff they had planned, but we have allowed them enough money to do a real job of information if it is properly spent. We haven't allowed enough for any frills.[92]

The size of the cut startled the White House, which was expecting a much more status quo figure. This did not seem like a compromise. Certainly, McKellar had not negotiated that figure with Woodrum and Mellett before the Committee action as he had told Byrnes he would. He did this unilaterally. From the White House's perspective, McKellar wasn't keeping his part of the deal. This confirmed the general feeling by many in the administration that McKellar was not to be trusted.[93] Senior administration officials viewed the cut as "severe" and decided to work to undo it. As a political strategy, Roosevelt approved a recommendation from aide Marvin McIntyre and Budget Director Smith not to challenge McKellar when the committee report reached the floor of the Senate. Instead, the administration would work with the friendlier Woodrum to restore the funding during the conference committee negotiations.[94]

Open for Business

In the meantime, the building was finished. It had been built in about forty-five days at a final cost of $530,000, less than the original estimate of about $600,000. The two-story building fronted on Pennsylvania Avenue and had 70,000 square feet of occupiable space. Over the front entrance were the words "US Information." That doorway led to a long rectangular two-story main hall. This central information hall was finished in a combination of birch and gumwood, a type of plywood. Earlier plans for decorative treatment of the walls of the central hall with painted and lettered panels depicting photomontages were cancelled once the controversy over the "fancy" building had erupted.[95] Running down the middle of the hall was an oval information counter, staffed by eighteen information "generalists" (usually women). Along the two long sides of the hall were private offices, staffed by twelve information "specialists" (usually men) who would handle the most specialized and unique inquiries the counter staff couldn't. In one of the wings of the building were offices of staff specialists from the major agencies. Small exhibits and displays were also part of the main

Figure 8.1. Main Hall, US Information Center, 1942. View from Pennsylvania Avenue entrance/side of building. Mellett presented this picture to Roosevelt with the inscription: "With compliments to the author" (underlining in original). Credit: Franklin Roosevelt Presidential Library, National Archives.

hall.[96] Besides the staff of OGR's USIS, the services provided to the public on the ground floor included:

- Staff from the War Production Board, Department of Commerce, Office of Price Administration, Treasury Department Procurement Division, Federal Works Agency and Civil Service Commission to handle highly specialized public inquiries
- Direct telephone lines to the inquiries offices of the War Department and Navy Department
- The Defense Home Registry (to help people find lodgings in Washington)
- The District of Columbia Council on Defense (to provide information to members of the armed forces—previously located in a small building nearby)
- Outlet for buying US Savings Bonds from the Treasury Department

Figure 8.2. Main Hall, US Information Center, 1942. Looking toward Pennsylvania Avenue entrance. Credit: National Archives, Record Group 44, Box 996.

Figure 8.3. Main Hall, US Information Center, 1942. View from Pennsylvania Avenue entrance/side of building. Credit: National Archives, Record Group 44, Box 1000.

- Recruiting office of the US Marines
- Recruiting office of the Coast Guard
- Free publications from various federal departments and agencies
- Outlet for buying publications of the Government Printing Office
- A library with government documents and reference materials

The second floor of the building included the telephone-service room, with information specialists/operators seated at desks parallel to a wall of filing drawers containing 7,000 cards with information to commonly asked questions. The remaining parts of the second floor were occupied by the rest of OGR's operations such as the staff for the *US Government Manual*.[97] The only Washington-based OGR activity that didn't move into the new building was its press clipping service that remained at its previous location. (Picture of building on cover.)

Figure 8.4. Telephone inquiries room, second floor, US Information Center, 1942. Credit: National Archives, Record Group 44, Box 1000.

In late April, Mellett and his staff began moving in. Special training sessions for the staff were held during the last two weeks before the center was to open.[98] On Saturday, May 2, Mellett hosted a press conference at the new building, giving reporters a chance to see it. In his press statement, he outlined the services and agencies to be available at the center. Impoliticly, he used the occasion of the press conference to respond to another attack on OGR by Senator Byrd. The day before Byrd had claimed in a speech on the Senate floor that the federal government spent $19.5 million on "publicity" and included OGR in that category. Mellett said OGR did not engage in publicity, it merely provided information. He accused Byrd of "wilful [sic] disregard of the truth . . . the Senator, in effect, is saying I lied to his Committee. If one of us is a liar it is not I," he said.[99] Coverage of the press conference in the *Chicago Tribune* described the central counter in the main hall as " a glorified hamburger stand."[100] The *Washington Times Herald* said the purpose of the center was "not that of a feed-box but of an agency to tell you where the feed-box was."[101] On Sunday afternoon, May 3, there was an open house at the center. Although it was open to the public-at-large, specific invitations went to all senators, members of Congress, members of the Congressional Secretaries Club, and heads of all federal cabinet departments and other agencies. Two-thousand people came during the three-hour open house.

That weekend, Mellett sent a picture (see p. 135) of the main hall to FDR and wrote across the bottom, "With compliments to the author."[102] The president responded on Tuesday with a dictated note:

> That is a grand photograph of a glorious room in a magnificent and historic building which, in the generations to come, will preserve democracy for the people of the United States against the sordid attacks of a subversive press.
>
> I have but one final suggestion to complete the perfection of this Temple of that ancient god MEL-ET, and that is that we acquire from Messrs. Ringling Brothers an historic supreme Calliope to be put on top of the Information sign in order that it may discourse sweet harmony capable of being heard in the Halls of the Congress. I suggest also that special loud speaker from said Calliope be inserted into the offices of the Washington Post.[103]

FDR's light-hearted comments also indicate the seriousness and significance of his commitment to disseminating information in a democracy. This was not a minor idea he had, but one that he felt helped implement his vision of a fairer, more just country. It was important and worth fighting for. His note also reflects his anger at the *Washington Post*'s campaign against the information center and the negative impact that it had on accomplishing his goal.

The United States Information Center opened for business at 8:30 A.M. on Monday morning, May 4. In its first two hours, it had 471 walk-in inquiries and 226 phone inquiries. By the time it closed at 10:00 P.M., the Center had had 1,500 walk-ins and another 1,500 phone calls.[104] This was much more business than the USIS had had on a daily basis at its previous location. To test the service, a reporter from the *New York Herald Tribune* called six times with different questions. Each was answered correctly. Yet the reporter couldn't resist taking another potshot at the project, describing Mellett's office on the second

Figure 8.5. Publications display, Main Hall, US Information Center, 1942. Credit: National Archives, Record Group 44, Box 996.

floor office as excessively large, excessively air cooled, and excessively decorated.[105] By the end of its first week of operations, the center had received 20,000 requests for information, combining in-person and phone inquiries. In addition, the District Defense Council had 599 inquiries and the Defense Home Registry found lodging for 264 people.[106] In its last week of operation before moving to the information center, USIS had handled a total 3,600 walk-in, phone and mail inquiries. During its first week at the information center, it received 13,700 inquiries (including mail). There was not an immediate drop off after the novelty wore off. A month later, it received 14,100 inquiries during a week, indicating a relatively stable amount of initial business.[107] The operations of the center quickly became routinized. It was open Monday to Saturday from 8 A.M. to 9 P.M. A daily form kept track of the number of people entering the building from the two entrances in the morning, afternoon and evening. Afternoons were busiest. Inquiries to the counter and phone staff were broken down by federal-government inquiries (functions, personnel or rules and regulations), publications (USIS or others) and District of Columbia (DC government or recreational). It also counted the number of people using the reference library, referred to staff specialists and referred to the editorial section.[108] At the end of May, President Roosevelt brought the subject up when he began one of his regular press conferences:

> President: Lowell says that his sales are increasing every day.
>
> Q: That's that good location you gave him.
>
> President: Good location, Yes, yes. He has got to the point now where he will probably take a full page soon. It's good advertising for the papers. Even the Congressmen are patronizing.[109]

The US Information Center continued in operation after OGR and many other information agencies were merged in mid-June to create the Office of War Information. However, the volume of business gradually decreased. As early as September 1942, hostile press coverage declared that volume "had fallen off almost to the vanishing point."[110] That was an exaggeration. By spring 1943, the average number of inquiries at the counter was down to 730 a day and the average number of calls was about 860. However, including mail, that was still 17,000 inquiries a week. In response to the diminishing workload and congressional budget cuts, staffing was reduced from 148 to 116.[111] In late 1943, Mellett[112] notified FDR of the reduced volumes since it had opened eighteen months earlier. He said the information work could now be accomplished by using only half the building. Knowing how strongly the president felt about the facility, Mellett thought it important that the president personally be involved in any decision to reconfigure the use of the building. Perhaps, he wrote, considering how much criticism had come from the press and Congress about the center before it had opened, some changes should be made now to "forestall unfair criticism"?[113] Roosevelt answered the next day in a dictated note:

> It is understandable that with the passing of the great crush and confusion of the earlier months of the war effort, less space may be required for the Information Center. *There will always be, in my opinion, need for an adequate Information Service in Washington* and it may be that the demobilization period will again require temporary expansion. I suggest therefore that you examine the possibility of contracting the present space in such manner that it can readily be expanded if the need occurs.[114]

FDR had again demonstrated both his personal commitment to the information center concept as well as the strong rationale for its need in modern government and democracy.

Fate of the Building

Throughout World War II, OWI continued operating the US Information Center building, although renaming it the Bureau of Public Inquiries.[115] In May 1944, the center had been in operation for two years. The volume of inquires continued to decline from its peak in 1942. Walk-ins were down from an average of 3,000 a day to 250; telephone calls had dropped from an average of 1,000 a day to 400 and mail went from about 750 a day to 450. Nonetheless, this daily volume of 1,100 inquires, totaling walk-ins, phone calls and mail, reflected the continuation of a need that the information center filled. In response to these declines, the staffing of the center was gradually reduced to forty-six.[116] As a result of the staffing cuts, space opened up in the building. In 1944, OWI moved into the building its Press Intelligence office (formerly of OGR) and the Research Division. This had the effect of consolidating into the information building all of the remaining premerger OGR activities within OWI.[117]

President Truman abolished OWI in August 1945 and transferred its informational activities to BOB, renamed the Government Information Service (GIS) (see chapter 10). The service continued operating the information building on Pennsylvania Avenue.[118] After December 1946, when Truman re-established the Office of Government Reports with GIS as one of its components, OGR was again the operator of the information center.[119] When OGR was disbanded on June 30, 1948, the building was almost totally occupied by agencies providing services for veterans. Only a few rooms were still being used by OGR for its reference library on the day the building ceased serving the purpose for which Roosevelt had built it.[120] Then, like all the other World War II temp buildings in Washington, the "V" building was scheduled to be torn down. To the satisfaction of the House Appropriations Committee of the Republican-majority Eightieth Congress (the Committee that had insisted on defunding OGR), the information center was the first of the temporary wartime buildings to be torn down.[121] The site was then restored to its status quo antebellum as a park. Roosevelt's temple of information disappeared.

In 1981, the triangle was rededicated as the John J. Pershing Park. Today (2005), it contains a statue of Pershing, some marble memorial markers with information about the US Expeditionary Force in World War I and a reflecting pool. Given its central location—the very reason Roosevelt had selected it for the US Information Center—it continues to be a busy place, with federal employees enjoying their lunch hour there, a food kiosk, tables and benches, tourists and even a lunchtime aerobics class.[122] None of the informational markers at the park note the use of the site during World War II. The US Information Center, like the temporary building it was housed in, had totally faded from memory.

Bruce Catton, writing right after the war, viewed the fight over the information center as just another artificial political controversy cooked up by Roosevelt's political and press enemies. It came and went, but the damage was done:

> Like all the other burning issues, this scandal fizzed out at last—and fizzled rather abruptly. One day it was a front-page scandal and a cause for alarms, and the next day everybody was talking about something else. The Madhouse opened for business on May 4, and the republic did not fall . . . it was obviously serving a useful purpose, and anyway the boys had had their fun.[123]

The fight over the US Information Center demonstrates FDR's mastery of both the levers of government and politics. Despite the onslaught from conservative Democrats, Republicans and the *Washington Post*, he had succeeded in creating, building, staffing and

Figure 8.6. Site of the US Information Center in 2003: Pershing Park, looking south at Commerce Department building. Credit: Rod Ross.

Figure 8.7. Site of the US Information Center in 2003: Pershing Park, looking northwest. Treasury Department building on left. Credit: Rod Ross.

operating the center. He protected and nurtured the project from conception to reality. When its traffic levels diminished, he insisted on the need for the building and continuing the services it provided. He was willing to fight for it publicly, willing to take the heat unapologetically. It was something he cared about and that's why he made it happen, even though there was a political price. So, in one sense, FDR had, like so many other times in his presidency, outfoxed his opponents and critics. He got what he wanted.

Yet Roosevelt's success in creating the US Information Center was also the turning point in the fight with Congress over OGR and what OGR symbolized. The conservative coalition had drawn political blood, and knew it. At last, it had found a topic and a way to turn the tide. By packaging the fight over OGR's building in a politically advantageous way, Congress was finding a lever to reassert its centrality and diminish the growth of the powerful presidency. It understood the implications of which branch controlled the dissemination of government information and wanted to minimize the information apparatus of the president. Direct reporting by executive-branch agencies to the public wasn't very important to Congress, despite what Roosevelt said or what the theoreticians of public administration wrote.

Chapter 9

Roosevelt Reluctantly Surrenders, May–June 1942

Notwithstanding fierce opposition from the congressional conservative coalition and some elements of the press, Roosevelt had been dogged and successful in establishing and institutionalizing the Office of Government Reports (OGR). Chapter 2 described how he created the National Emergency Council (NEC) in 1933 and gradually expanded its informational programs. Chapter 3 detailed his efforts from 1936 to 1939 with the Brownlow Committee and the subsequent reorganization process to create through executive order a presidential reporting agency. Chapters 5, 6, and 7 portrayed how from 1939 to 1942 he had always found a way to fund the agency, driven a bill through Congress authorizing direct appropriations to OGR, sharply increased its budget and staffing, and expanded its mission to include radio, movies, and even posters. Finally, fighting determined opposition, Roosevelt had won the fierce battle to open the US Information Center (chapter 8) with few friends in Congress helping him. But, the political costs of all these battles, especially over the US Information Center, were beginning to show. There was no public constituency advocating for information dissemination or lobbying for OGR. It was gradually becoming clear that OGR was just costing him too much political capital. The pragmatic politician could realistically assess the political landscape despite winning the battle to open the US Information Center. Roosevelt had tenaciously nurtured his concept of public reporting from 1933 to mid-1942. Chapter 9 describes the process by which

Roosevelt reluctantly concluded that OGR could not survive politically in the short run. He decided to make it invisible for the duration of the war, with the expectation of re-establishing it after the war when, presumably, it would no longer be quite as controversial as it was at the height of the fight for the US Information Center.

Fiscal Year 1943 Appropriations: A Hint of Weakness

As will be recalled, in January 1942, before the controversy over the US Information Center had erupted, the House passed the Independent Offices Appropriation Bill for fiscal year 1943 giving OGR the full funding that the president had requested: $1.5 in direct appropriation and a raised cap on transfers from other presidential funds to permit OGR's budget to be $2.4 million for the coming fiscal year. Then, in part due to the controversy over the US Information Center, the pace of the bill slowed down. The Senate Appropriations Committee didn't release its report on the bill until April 23, 1942. As punishment for the US Information Center and also due to his general opposition to nondefense expenditures such as information, Senator McKellar had convinced the committee to recommend cutting OGR by $406,270, or about twenty-eight percent and to reduce the limit on presidential fund transfers from $900,000 to $600,000 (see table 9.1).[1]

Table 9.1
Pre-Conference Committee Congressional Decisions about OGR's Fiscal Year 1943 Budget

	Fiscal Year 1942 Base (including changes after Pearl Harbor)	*President's Request (after Pearl Harbor)*	*Approved by House Approp. Com. & House*	*Approved by Senate Approp. Com. & Senate*
General Operations	$1,075,000	$1,475,000	$1,475,000	$1,075,000
Printing and binding	$25,000	$25,000	$25,000	$18,730
Maximum Presidential Transfers	$800,000	No limit, but planned for $902,871	$900,000	$600,000
Total	$2,400,000 (annualized rate. Actual expenditures: $1,821,872)	$2,402,871	$2,400,000	$1,693,730

It was a major blow. Budget Director Smith said it was "rather drastic."[2] Even though the administration was trying to avoid a fight with Kenneth McKellar (see chapter 8), this cut was not acceptable. However, rather than trying to overturn the committee's recommendation as an amendment during the floor debate in the Senate, the White House decided to wait until the inevitable conference committee.[3] It would try to work quietly through Congressman Clifton Woodrum to restore OGR funding levels during the conference committee negotiations. The president was personally involved in pursuing that strategy. As he had demonstrated again and again, he felt strongly about OGR and was willing to intervene personally to help it. On April 27, the president was reminded by his staff to speak to Woodrum that morning about the cuts in OGR and NRPB and the upcoming deliberations in the conference committee.[4]

However, notwithstanding the administration's preferences, in conference committee the House conferees yielded to the Senate's position on direct appropriations to OGR, thus cutting OGR's funding by about twenty-eight percent from the president and the House's recommendations.[5] McKellar's reputation was that he "generally got the amendments he favored" in committee meetings, especially when he cared greatly about the topic.[6] However, the conferees could not come to agreement about the maximum amount the president could transfer to OGR from his discretionary funds. The House position had been $900,000 and the Senate's $600,000.[7] Although McKellar was pushing for the House conferees to accept all aspects of the Senate's OGR position, the House conferees were only willing to accept the Senate's position on direct appropriations to OGR. They knew that the higher the cap on presidential-fund transfers, the greater the ability of the president to negate cuts in direct appropriations.

Sometimes, especially regarding large and complex bills, conferees were not able to resolve all issues. This happened occasionally and was not out of the ordinary. For this bill, for example, there were 123 differences between the versions of the bill passed by both houses. They were able to resolve all but thirteen, one of which was the OGR transfer cap. When these situations happened, usually the conference committee would reconvene after the two houses had approved the slew of differences they had agreed on, and a second round of negotiations would occur.

On June 9, 1942, the conference committee report came up for consideration on the House floor.[8] Woodrum, as chair of the House conferees, began his report. Traditionally, such a report would call on the House to accept the conference committee report (i.e., the issues that were resolved) and to refuse to recede from the House position on the items that the conferees had not agreed on. When he began his summary of those items remaining in contention, something out of the ordinary happened. Woodrum suddenly yielded the floor to Everett Dirksen (R-IL), a minority party member of the conference committee. There had been eight House managers on this conference committee, five Democrats and three Republicans. Dirksen was a longtime critic of OGR. Once he had said, "if I had breath in this body of mine I intended to offer an amendment to strike out the provision for the National Emergency Council" to become OGR in the reorganization plan.[9] Having been yielded the floor by Woodrum, Dirksen delivered a three-minute attack against government public-relations spending in general and criticized OGR specifically only incidentally. When he had concluded, Woodrum then suddenly moved that the House recede from its position on the transfer cap ($900,000) and accept the Senate's ($600,000). His unexpected motion was immediately accepted by voice vote.[10] It happened so fast that even if a supporter of OGR and the president's had wanted to fight the motion, it would have been too late to obtain recognition to debate the motion or to insist on a counted vote (which would bring more members to the floor).[11]

Logically, it was inexplicable. Woodrum had managed the bill and advocated successfully the $900,000 cap at the House Subcommittee, the House Committee, the House floor, and the conference committee. The majority of Democrats on the House delegation to the conference committee had refused to give up on the House's position. Suddenly, in collusion with a minority party member and without any notice to the majority caucus, he folded. Given his tepid defenses of OGR and NEC through all the years, one can only conclude that he had tired of the issue and no longer wanted to fight. Certainly, Roosevelt's personally lobbying him in April hadn't made a difference. Perhaps the Democratic majority was no longer willing to push for FDR's desired position, especially after the controversy over the information center. However, that would not explain why the House conferees had refused to accept the Senate position on the transfer cap in conference. For that brief moment, not only was the conservative coalition in control of the House, the Minority Party itself was calling the shots. A few weeks later, in a letter to Mellett, Congressman Louis Ludlow (D-IN), a member of the House Appropriations Committee, claimed ignorance as to what had happened. "I am at a loss to know why some member of the committee did not answer Mr. Dirksen"—ignoring, of course, that Woodrum was a member of the committee, a Democrat and chair of the House conferees. Nor did Ludlow offer to seek an ex post facto explanation.[12] It was an omen about the political weakness of OGR after the fight over the US Information Center.

Reorganizing Information Agencies

During the defense build-up prior to the US's entry to World War II, Roosevelt had created a multiplicity of agencies involved in information activities. Similar to the profusion of New Deal relief agencies in the 1930s, a disorganized and confusing "alphabet soup" of information agencies had incrementally emerged. This was acceptable to Roosevelt, who didn't mind confusing and overlapping agency missions, since that had the effect of assuring that all important decisions would have to come to him for resolution. Also, it reflected his ad-hoc and pragmatic approach to governance, responding to a particular political situation and defusing it by, among other techniques, creating a new agency. An official history of the war, written by the Bureau of the Budget (BOB), characterized these actions as reflecting President Roosevelt's "familiar pattern of establishing a series of parallel agencies whose powers or fields of authority were not sharply limited."[13] This gradually created a collection of seemingly overlapping information organizations, often in competition with each other.

When he had created OGR in 1939, Roosevelt had thought of it as the central information agency that had the capacity to handle foreseeable needs. For example, during a September 1941 press conference he was asked about seemingly contradictory statistics issued by various federal agencies regarding defense production. He answered that the press and the public "will get something absolutely authoritative from a bureau of the Government and—probably would be Lowell Mellett's Bureau—which would get the figures that everybody could agree on."[14] His strong support for OGR and its central and coordinating mission was, in part, why he resisted the repeated efforts by the military—in October 1939, November 1939 and June 1940—to persuade him to create a Public Relations Administration as part of the implementation of the Industrial Mobilization Plan (IMP) (see chapter 4). He felt OGR could do the job.

However, notwithstanding his support for OGR's central role, as developments warranted, he was willing to create other information agencies, as long as they weren't the monolith desired by the War and Navy Departments and were under his exclusive control (i.e. created through executive orders rather than statutes). In mid-1940, when he had activated the Office for Emergency Management (OEM) as the sixth component of the Executive Office of the President (EOP), it included a Division of Information.[15] The division emerged to become a major source of defense-production information and operated largely as an independent agency accountable directly to the White House.[16] In May 1941 he created the Office of Civilian Defense with responsibility for, amongst other missions, national morale.[17] In July, he appointed a Coordinator of Information,[18] and the Foreign Information Service came into existence a month later.[19] In October, Roosevelt created the Office of Facts and Figures (OFF).[20] Finally, less than two weeks after Pearl Harbor and the entry of the US into World War II, he created the Office of Censorship.[21]

The situation was becoming ripe to be exploited as an artificial political controversy, in the same pattern as happened with the US Information Center. After all, the same political coalition that opposed the US Information Center generally opposed federal spending on any aspect of public relations, publicity, and information. Also, they could suggest that the proposed information spending was not directly tied to the war effort, notwithstanding administration claims to the contrary. For example, Senator Harry F. Byrd (D-VA), referring to the several different information agencies and divisions in the executive branch, said, "the multiplicity of publicity bureaus very nearly approaches a national scandal in the waste of public funds."[22] Congressman Richard Wigglesworth (R-MA) asserted that in fiscal year 1941 the federal government had wasted over $27 million in funding for publicity staff and expenditures. He conceded that perhaps some of that was spent answering requests for information from citizens, but nonetheless "in my judgment [it] is a preposterous figure and entirely unjustified for the work in question. . . . I believe it is an expenditure which could be largely eliminated without impeding the proper functions of the Government to the advantage of the taxpayers of the country."[23]

Roosevelt, sensitive to a political issue that could gain traction, had directed BOB to curtail information spending that was not directly related to the war effort.[24] But that didn't seem to be enough. Roosevelt's political advisers continued calling this potential political problem to his attention and suggesting that some action was necessary to preempt the looming political issue. For example, on February 20, 1942, when he submitted a report on information agencies that had been requested by the president, Milton Eisenhower wrote, "Newspapermen are getting critical. There is considerable duplication. Conflicting statements to the public are causing trouble."[25] Similarly, after meeting with the president on March 7, 1942, advisor Sam Rosenman feared "that the President probably would not take any action to clean up the mess until there was another Congressional investigation, such as was threatened in connection with housing reorganization."[26] A month later, the president still had not acted. BOB Director Harold Smith and Rosenman were getting increasingly concerned, sensing that "this whole area is becoming more and more confused and will end up with a Congressional investigation unless something is done in the very near future."[27] By early June, Harold Smith was certain that the issue would explode politically. He explicitly warned the President "the Byrd Committee and the Tydings Committee are prepared to attack these expenditures as being wasteful."[28]

Also, from a management point of view, reorganization was definitely needed. Pearl Harbor and the declaration of war had transformed the situation. Now that the United States was an active combatant in the war, the informational needs of the government would understandably be different. According to Smith:

> The existing war information machinery of the Government was established on a piecemeal basis before Pearl Harbor. The advent of war requires a realignment of both responsibility and organization in order that consistent and accurate war information may be carried to the people of this Nation and of the world.[29]

This political landscape contributed to Roosevelt summoning Eisenhower to see him just a few weeks after Pearl Harbor. Eisenhower, head of the Information Office of the Department of Agriculture, was a respected and competent public administrator.[30] From time to time since becoming president, Roosevelt had given Eisenhower short-term assignments, which Eisenhower had always completed to the president's satisfaction. By now, he had the confidence of the president. Roosevelt told Eisenhower he "wanted these [information agencies] brought together and co-ordinated."[31] He asked Eisenhower to prepare a plan to do that. Eisenhower quickly went to work.

Roosevelt let it be known (whether directly to Eisenhower or perhaps through BOB) that Eisenhower's report should not include OGR. OGR was generally to be left alone and not affected by any reorganization creating a *temporary wartime* information agency—even though that new agency would have domestic as well as overseas responsibilities. After all, OGR was not a war-related information agency. It had existed (as NEC) long before World War II and would continue to have a mission in peacetime, after the war was over. The only aspect of OGR that Eisenhower could include in his reorganization plan was its Office of the Coordinator of Government Films, just recently created and certainly war-related. Yet, the omission of OGR from Eisenhower's review is glaring. Ignoring it would be illogical and perplexing. It was a major information agency, employing over 500 people and involved extensively in information dissemination related to the war. In fact, when Roosevelt gave the assignment to Eisenhower in late 1941, OGR was undergoing a major expansion *because* of the war. To ignore it would be like ignoring the proverbial elephant in the room.

Although OGR was a civilian agency that existed prior to the defense build-up in 1940 and 1941, its operations were intimately tied into defense activities. For example, every Friday it published a weekly digest called *A Week in the War* (before Pearl Harbor it was entitled *This Week in Defense*) that summarized major developments in the previous week. It had a circulation of about 8,500. An abridged version of *A Week in the War* was mailed to about 9,000 weekly and rural newspapers. OGR also compiled semimonthly state-by-state tabulation of *National Defense Contracts and Expenditures* that was distributed by its state directors to about 30,000 addressees.[32] USIS sent out a monthly packet of government publications dealing with war-related topics to 5,000 libraries.[33] One of OGR's few publications of its own included *Defense Employment and Training for Employment*, published in 1941 to handle the "great number of requests" from citizens seeking jobs or training for defense work.[34] To ignore OGR from a survey and reorganization of war-related information agencies is a baffling decision that can only be explained by an external factor such as a directive from FDR.[35]

Although his assignment had come personally from the president, Eisenhower defined his role as a consultant to BOB.[36] He needed to rely on its staff to prepare the background information and its central clearing role for any executive orders that would have to be prepared to implement the reorganization. Eisenhower's first request was that BOB conduct a thorough survey of all the war-related information agencies, divisions and offices.[37] BOB staff compiled data regarding the facilities, personnel, organization charts, and functions of all the agencies likely to be affected.[38] They excluded OGR from the survey, except its Office of Coordinator of Films. Eisenhower submitted his final report on February 20.[39] He called for creation of a War Information Board that would oversee and set policy for the War Information Coordinator. The Coordinator, in turn, would have two deputy coordinators, for domestic and overseas activities. Eisenhower recommended that the new agency be created by combining the Office of Facts and Figures, Foreign Information Service of the Coordinator of Information, press, radio, and motion picture divisions of the coordinator of Inter-American Affairs and—from OGR—the recently created Office of the Coordinator of Government Films.[40] The report "did not even include a description of the functions of OGR" besides the film coordinator.[41] Interestingly, even though his report only affected a minor aspect of OGR, Eisenhower's reorganization plan was based on his assumption (and recommendation) that Lowell Mellett should head the new agency.[42]

BOB now took Eisenhower's report and converted it into the preliminary draft of an executive order. The draft maintained the hands-off policy regarding OGR, accepting the rationale that OGR was not a wartime agency and did not have, specifically, a war-related mission.[43] This, of course, contradicted OGR's representations to Congress, justifying its budget increases based on war-related information needs. The only substantive change BOB made in Eisenhower's recommendations was to rename the proposed agency the Office of War Information (OWI). This meant a policymaking board would not formally oversee it and set policy in a binding manner. Rather, the director (title changed from coordinator) would be directly accountable to the president.[44] By March 7, the Justice Department had helped revise the draft to assure clarity and legality.[45]

Rosenman and Smith met that same day with FDR to brief him on the status of Eisenhower's recommendations and get his feedback on the draft executive order. The president wasn't ready to commit to signing the executive order. He wondered about whom to appoint to head the agency. He also wondered about the reactions that Nelson Rockefeller and William Donovan would have to stripping "their" agencies of the information programs they operated. Indeed, right after this meeting a major bureaucratic turf war exploded behind the scenes. It eventually culminated in the secretary of state personally lobbying the president to leave Rockefeller's operation alone.[46] Yet during all the in-fighting over which agencies would and would not be merged into OWI—which was occurring at the height of the controversy over the US Information Center—the evolving draft of the executive order never changed in regards to OGR.[47]

Moment of Truth

In some respects, the winter and spring of 1941–2 had been a period of OGR's greatest successes: an increase in the ceiling on presidential funding transfers, a sharp increase in spending and staffing, addition of film coordination responsibilities, and, especially, the opening of the US Information Center. But these successes had been accompanied with major blows, including Congress's refusal to repeal totally the cap on presidential fund transfers, the substantial cut in OGR's budget and transfer cap in the Independent Offices Appropriation bill for fiscal year 1943 and, especially, the fight over the US Information Center. Roosevelt had, again and again, personally gone to bat for OGR. He demonstrated through his actions how much he cared about the existence of an agency dedicated to public reporting. Yet, the fight over the US Information Center and the cuts Congress adopted in OGR's fiscal year 1943 budget reflected the difficulty of sustaining an executive-branch agency dedicated to domestic dissemination of information. These hits—notwithstanding Roosevelt's personal involvement—reflected the limits of power of a president, even one as effective politically as Roosevelt. There was just so much he could do. And, as the horrible spring of 1942 ground on, that became increasingly apparent. The ferociousness of the rhetoric from the conservative coalition on Capitol Hill reflected in part the Republican strategy of supporting the war while exposing the "mistakes" of the administration. With congressional elections coming up in the fall (the first since Pearl Harbor), much was riding politically on the results of these pre-election tussles.[48] Writing from the perspective of only a few years later, Bruce Catton described the political dynamic that OGR and its information center were caught in:

> the we-hate-Roosevelt people were successful beyond their dreams during the war, and 1942 was the year of their first big triumph . . . It began with the excellent assumption that any action which the administration might take (other than those actions directly concerned with military matters) was sure to be unsound and ill-advised and was more than likely to be revolutionary; thus they always had something to criticize, and the criticism never had to be documented since it was based on an axiom rather than on facts and reasoning. Better yet, this created a game in which both ends could be played against the middle; for the very fact that this criticism was being made could then be used as a basis for further criticism, the idea being that there must be something terribly wrong or the administration wouldn't be under so much attack . . . The tragedy was that the administration wasn't able to stand up against it.[49]

In politics, there's a saying—derived from poker—that "there's a time to hold 'em and a time to fold 'em." Such a moment of truth had now arrived for OGR. During Mellett's awful month of March, when the US Information Center was the controversy du jour, he began wondering if OGR was becoming too much of a political liability to FDR. Mellett was fanatically loyal to Roosevelt and wanted to protect the president from political harm—irrespective of Mellett's own personal preferences or the merits of the issue. On April 2, 1942, right after the Information Center controversy finally dropped out of the headlines and a month before it opened, Mellett talked to Roosevelt.[50] Although no record exists of the conversation, it's likely that at that meeting, or during some other contact around that time, he broached the possibility of folding all of OGR—not just the film coordinator's office—into the soon-to-be-created Office of War Information. Later, Mellett said he had realized it was "necessary to destroy what we considered a good operation in order to dispose of a bad myth."[51] The president responded to Mellett that he shared Mellett's political assessment about the probable future of OGR, but wasn't ready to make a final decision.

By April 27, Smith was trying to pull the pieces together regarding both the OWI reorganization, OGR's future and OGR's appropriation for the next year. He wrote the president, ostensibly about the big cut the Senate Appropriations Committee had recommended for OGR's fiscal year 1943 budget:

> I have talked to Mellett since he talked to you. Considering the present situation in the light of the history of difficulties, I suggest that in connection with the Information Order the entire Office of Government Reports be transferred for the duration of the war. Thereafter, its proper location and functions can be more clearly defined. I believe that Mellett will agree with this solution.[52]

Although Mellett and the president had already talked about OGR's political difficulties, it is clear from Smith's memo that they hadn't definitively come to any conclusion. They may have been leaning towards merging OGR into OWI, but Roosevelt hadn't not yet made a final decision. Smith needed such a firm decision, since it would affect the planning for the OWI executive order. Roosevelt didn't give Smith any response to his April 27 memo, even though they saw each other almost every day. Nearly a week passed. Smith felt obligated to keep raising the issue. He needed a decision.

It was Friday, May 1, 1942. The US Information Center was due to open on the next business day, Monday, May 4. That day, Smith had another one of his routine meetings with the president. As usual, he brought with him a long list of issues he needed Roosevelt to decide. The last item was OGR. When they got to that, Smith summarized the situation: Mellett and the president had had some conversations about whether, given the fallout over the information center, to include OGR into OWI after all. Smith, however, felt he must have a specific directive from the president. Before adding OGR to a revised draft of the OWI executive order, he needed to confirm explicitly that this truly was the president's final and firm decision. Is this how the president indeed wanted Smith to proceed? FDR just couldn't say the words. For a change, Roosevelt—usually so ebullient and conversational—was at loss for words, reluctant to verbalize the order to kill

OGR. Smith's dictated summary right after the meeting noted that the president never spoke while Smith was reviewing for him OGR's situation. When Smith was done talking and it was time for the president to respond, he still didn't speak. According to Smith's dictated description, Roosevelt "gave the suggestion the nod." With that description, FDR's sadness and reluctance to lose OGR jump off the page of Smith's dictation. All Roosevelt could do was nod silently.[53] OGR's fate was sealed with a wordless nod. It would go out of existence, at least for the foreseeable future.

Roosevelt's decision was kept secret. No one, besides Mellett, BOB, and the drafters of the executive order at the Justice Department, knew what was going to happen. The grand opening of the US Information Center and its first month of operation occurred without the shadow of the president's decision falling on it. But the smooth administrative machinery that Smith presided over quickly assimilated the president's decision. By May 11, the next draft of the executive order included the complete transfer of OGR to OWI, instead of just its film coordination office.[54] The president still delayed signing the OWI executive order. Some wondered if he didn't want to sign the order until he had decided who would head the new agency. One BOB staffer speculated that Roosevelt was waiting for OGR's fiscal year 1943 appropriation (albeit at a level lower than he had wanted) would be finalized by Congress.[55] Otherwise, if Congress knew OGR was about to be killed, it might delete the entire appropriation from the Independent Offices Appropriation Bill at the last minute, thus cutting the beginning base budget of OWI. FDR couldn't delay indefinitely. Smith was pressing him for action before sending to Capitol Hill any additional budget estimates on informational activities.[56] Finally, on Saturday, June 13, Roosevelt signed the executive order creating OWI and merging OGR into it. Simultaneously, he named Elmer Davis, a radio news commentator for the CBS network, to head the agency.[57]

Even though Congress was still debating the Independent Offices Appropriation Bill when the OWI executive order was signed, by now the bill was so far along in conference committee process that the two houses were focusing solely on the short list of remaining issues dividing them. Another conference committee met to review the last issues in contention. It released its report on June 18.[58] As is normal for the legislative process, no effort was made to reopen a closed issue, such as the OGR provision. Reopening it would have created a precedent of reopening every issue. That would be going in the opposite direction of the legislative process at this stage, namely of narrowing differences and moving towards their final resolution. The OGR section remained intact. (For the details of that appropriation, see discussion earlier in this chapter.) FDR received the bill and signed it into law on June 27, 1942, two weeks after merging OGR into OWI and about two months after opening the US Information Center.[59]

The Office of Government Reports and Office of War Information

One of the important immediate issues, upon the establishment of OWI, was its internal organization. It was a conglomeration of four different independent agencies, three of which engaged in domestic dissemination of information: OGR, OFF, and the OEM Division of Information. How to structure OWI? BOB started thinking about this even before the president signed the executive order. In an internal memo, the staffer leading the project suggested that there should be a merger of all related operations coming from the three agencies, to create one consolidated division for each function. For example, "certain duplications which now exist in the field of intelligence, service to weekly newspapers, and liaison with information agencies could be eliminated."[60] A week before the executive order was signed BOB still had not resolved the question. A status memo on general questions yet unsolved included "The place of the OGR."[61] When Milton Eisenhower was briefed by BOB staff on the last-minute inclusion of OGR into the executive order draft, he suggested "it would probably not be advisable to continue the State representatives of OGR in their present capacities, but that an attempt might be made to work them into the field information work of other agencies."[62]

These few preliminary observations all pointed to a disassembling of OGR once OWI was established. However, that was neither the expectation of the press nor of OGR's leadership. A few days after creating OWI, President Roosevelt was asked at one of his frequent press conferences about Mellett's role in OWI. A reporter specifically asked if Mellett, who was in the room, was "going to be anonymous, or does he remain conspicuous?" Roosevelt ducked the question by quipping, "I can't imagine his being anonymous, can you?" A follow-up questioner tried again: "Can you clarify specifically, sir, the status of Lowell"? Again, the president refused to comment saying, "You had better ask Mr. Davis."[63]

More than two weeks after OWI was created, Mellett was using the title of director of Office of Government Reports *Division*, Office of War Information.[64] That same day, Hamblet sent a message to all state directors calling for reports on current topics.[65] It was as though nothing had changed. The pre-OWI OGR was intact as an entity within OWI and was functioning in a business-as-usual mode. But, the new leadership of OWI did not want this situation to be a permanent one. A week later, Hamblet notified the state directors that

> We have since been told that the OGR must both in Washington and in the field completely lose its identity. . . . Certain of the functions must be maintained almost intact for OWI, others are to be abolished. The field offices as now constituted are among the activities that are to be abolished. . . . There are to be no more State Directors.[66]

OWI was organized into three basic units: Policy Development, Domestic Branch, and the Overseas Branch. OGR's components were dispersed all over OWI. The Division of Press Intelligence was merged with the OFF's Bureau of Intelligence to create the Intelligence Bureau of Policy Development, later called the Bureau of Special Services. Other parts of OGR contributed to three bureaus in the Domestic Branch. Its Office of the Coordinator of Government Films became the core of the Motion Pictures Bureau. USIS was abolished and its functions became part of the Public Inquiries Bureau. OGR's field service was merged with the field information offices of OEM's Division of Information to form the Bureau of Field Operations.[67] OGR's top three officials were named to head OWI bureaus in the Domestic Branch. Hamblet, OGR's executive officer, was named to run to Bureau of Special Operations in the Overseas Branch, built out of OFF's Foreign Language Service. Thus, he was disconnected from his previous OGR responsibilities. OGR Assistant Director Katherine Blackburn was appointed to run the Bureau of Public Inquiries, largely the former USIS. Mellett, incongruously, was appointed head of the Motion Picture Bureau within the Domestic Branch. Given that he was simultaneously serving as one of the six presidential administrative assistants in the White House, that meant he was the advisor to his boss's boss's boss, since the president oversaw the OWI director who oversaw the director of OWI's Domestic Branch who oversaw Mellett in the Motion Picture Bureau!

In the context of the structuring of OWI, Harold Gosnell judged that "in general the functions of the Office [of Government Reports] did not fare well in the new setting."[68] Similarly, executives from OFF dominated the leadership of the new OWI.[69] Of the 856 employees who worked for OGR when it merged into OWI, only seventy-three were still working for OWI a year later.[70] OGR and its staff no longer existed, neither as an intact division within OWI nor as a management team. Its various units were merged, abolished, renamed and reshuffled into OWI's table of organization. Its leadership was dispersed and generally subordinate to former OFF executives and new-from-the-outside OWI managers. OGR, its leadership team and its staff had disappeared not merely from sight, but were totally disbanded. The agency no longer existed, even on a de facto basis within OWI.

At the same press conference when he was asked about Mellett's role in OWI, Roosevelt sent a public hint about his own role vis-à-vis the new agency compared to OGR. Earlier that year, at the height of the controversy over the US Information Center, FDR had said at a press conference that the idea of the center "was mine . . . My shoulders are quite broad." He was voluntarily stepping forward to take the blame and criticism from Congress and the *Washington Post*.[71] Now, two months later, he expressed a very different attitude about OWI. "If only we let Mr. Davis operate, things will be all right, but the whole thing would fall down if he was subjected to Presidential interference."[72] Clearly, he was explicitly distancing himself from the agency, just the opposite of his public comments about Mellett, OGR and the information center. In fact, throughout the war, Roosevelt would not put his own prestige on the line for OWI. According to Sydney Weinberg, Roosevelt "never took much interest in OWI."[73] Similarly, Allan Winkler's history of OWI observed that Roosevelt "had no intention of going out of his way to protect the new agency. Davis was on his own."[74] This was typical of Roosevelt's normal treatment of agencies in his administration. Only few projects close to his heart, like OGR, merited special treatment.

OWI went on to have a tumultuous and controversial existence. Internally, the office never succeeded in merging its predecessor units into a single cohesive agency that successfully worked on an integrated basis. Two historians described it as "a not altogether happy amalgamation."[75] According to Winkler, "Congress had been suspicious of OWI ever since its organization, and the random sniping that began then grew in intensity as the war continued."[76]

This chapter covered the death of OGR, at least for the duration of the war. Roosevelt reluctantly agreed with Mellett's assessment that the fight over the US Information Center had permanently damaged OGR and was starting to hurt Roosevelt. They decided that it would be prudent to merge OGR into the war-time Office of War Information and then resurrect it after the end of the war, when—they hoped—the controversial nature of the agency might have faded somewhat. The next chapter describes President Truman's effort to re-establish OGR after World War II—exactly as Roosevelt had intended—and the resistance by the Eightieth Congress to his plans.

The events described in this chapter summarize one particular example of Congress succeeding in asserting its preeminence over the executive branch, in this case in the area of public information. Increasingly, the issues of institutional power and control of communication were becoming intertwined. Political success, it was becoming clear to all the players, was dependent in part on comprehensive communication campaigns. To defeat a president's efforts to disseminate information was to reassert congressional dominance. Information was, indeed, power.

Chapter 10

Truman's Office of Government Reports, 1946–48

World War II ended on August 15, 1945. Budget Director Harold Smith acted quickly. Three days later he met with President Truman and gave him an overall plan for demobilization of wartime agencies.[1] Writing about the plan to presidential advisor Samuel Rosenman, Smith emphasized the need to act quickly and secretly, "so that the forces would not unite against" it.[2] He and Rosenman remembered all too well the agency turf battles that had occurred when the draft plan to create the Office of War Information (OWI) was circulated in spring 1942 (see chapter 9). Back then, several agencies had mobilized to lobby against the plan and in favor of maintaining their separate and independent existence. Smith and Rosenman didn't want the same thing to happen again. Smith's plan was a comprehensive one, covering almost all the wartime emergency agencies. Regarding OWI, he recommended it be disbanded, with the programs of the overseas branch temporarily shifted to the Department of State until a more permanent decision about the need for an international information agency in the nascent Cold War could be made. He suggested that OWI's domestic branch "should be eliminated" except the *US Government Manual*, which "should be lodged in a suitable permanent agency."[3] Truman accepted Smith's recommendation regarding OWI. On August 31, he signed an executive order liquidating it.[4] Regarding the domestic branch, he announced he was discontinuing the activities of "cooperation with the press, radio, motion pictures, and other informational media in explaining governmental programs" since they were no longer needed. Only "certain prewar information activities, placed in OWI as a wartime measure" would continue to be performed, specifically "the United States Government Manual and answering inquiries from the public."[5] This was a clear reference to the pre-war Office of Government Reports (OGR) and its non-war-related activities. The executive order transferred these programs to the Bureau of the Budget (BOB).

During the war, OWI had undergone innumerable reorganizations. By mid-1945, its Bureau of Special Services contained most of the pre-war OGR functions. The bureau had three divisions, Public Inquiries (essentially the US Information Service, including the staff for the *Government Manual*), Press Intelligence and Research.[6] In essence, what Truman and Smith had just done was implement the original 1937 recommendation of the Brownlow Committee, namely that an information service be created in BOB. In fact, when testifying before Congress about the transfer of OWI's domestic information functions to BOB, Smith specifically reminded the subcommittee members that the original reorganization plan had contemplated an information function within BOB.[7] What he did not tell the committee was that he had been reluctant to accept that original recommendation and was relieved when President Roosevelt instead suggested that the National Emergency Council (NEC) be broken up, with the US Film Service going to the Office of Education and the rest of NEC reconstituted as a separate agency in EOP (see chapters 3 and 5). Smith hadn't changed his mind, either. He continued to be uncomfortable with a BOB information arm that would not be related to the core mission of a budget-control agency.[8] The continuation of these non-war related functions of OWI, derived from OGR, was an implementation of FDR's original intent of merging OGR into OWI only for the duration of the war. That had been his way of putting out of sight, temporarily, what had become a controversial agency. In fact, a later BOB document referred to the functions Truman transferred from OWI to BOB as "in reality the remaining activity of the former Office of Government Reports."[9]

BOB's Government Information Service: OGR by Another Name

The same day that Truman signed the executive order, BOB's personnel officer immediately began making plans for the absorption of the OWI's Bureau of Special Services into BOB. The information he collected included the observation that Katherine Blackburn, the head of the bureau, "is very energetic and very likeable." On the other hand, "there were more personnel headaches in this particular section than anyplace else in OWI."[10] The new unit was quickly renamed the Government Information Service (GIS) of BOB and it continued to be headed by Blackburn. GIS continued to function out of the information building on Pennsylvania Avenue, rather than be consolidated with BOB's offices in the Executive Office Building across from the White House.[11] It had about 145 employees and a budget of about $375,000 for fiscal year 1946.[12] So, besides the name change, little had actually changed. The (former OGR) information program continued uninterrupted and at about the same level as during its last year within OWI.

The Division of Public Inquiries—the pre-war US Information Service—handled about 300,000 inquiries in 1945, about 50,000 by mail (with 45,000 addressed to Uncle Sam or US Government), 185,000 phone calls and the rest were walk-ins to the information center.[13] It also mailed monthly information packets to 3,300 public libraries consisting of key federal publications on important issues of the day as well as catalogs of other publications that could be obtained by request. It continued publishing the *Digest of the Functions of Federal Agencies* and the *Government Manual.*

The Division of Press Intelligence reviewed 225 daily newspapers, ten major weekly magazines, radio news programs, and nine "Negro" weeklies.[14] The review of these publications generated 3.5 million clippings, with about 3.2 million going to departments and agencies, 200,000 to Congress, and about 130,000 to the White House. It also produced daily digests summarizing the content of newspaper and radio-news broadcasts,[15] with thirty copies going to the White House and ten to BOB.[16]

Facing Congress

BOB Director Smith decided that GIS should neither be expanded nor significantly reduced in operation. So, his recommendation to President Truman for BOB's fiscal year 1947 budget contemplated funding GIS at approximately the same level it had functioned during the last half of fiscal year 1946.[17] He also decided to preserve only the two units most closely derived from the core of OGR's pre-war activities: the Divisions of Public Inquiries and Press Intelligence. He decided to liquidate the research division as well as the New York City office.[18] Truman accepted Smith's recommended BOB budget without change.[19] In his formal fiscal year 1947 budget message to Congress in January 1946, Truman requested $411,530 to fund GIS[20] and estimated staffing of about 150.[21]

Smith must have had a sense of déjà vu when he presented his budget to the Independent Offices Subcommittee of the House Appropriations Committee. The pre-war attacks on OGR were renewed, using the same arguments and with the same vehemence. Congressman Richard Wigglesworth reminded the other subcommittee members that Smith was talking about "Mellett's madhouse" and wondered if the function should be funded at all, whether in BOB or elsewhere. Congressman Albert Thomas (D-TX) referred to GIS as "the building up on the Avenue," a reminder to his colleagues of the 1942 controversy over the US Information Center. He suggested that like all other war-related activities, it too should be totally shut down. When Smith responded that GIS consisted of non-war-related and pre-war functions, Thomas shifted to criticizing the need for a clipping service or an office to answer public inquiries. That's what congressmen are for, he argued. Similar to OGR appearances before Congress, no committee member spoke up to defend the information activities. The most Subcommittee Chair Joe Hendricks (D-FL) was willing to do was correct a misstatement made by Congressman Thomas. Smith and his administrative assistant, Frederick Lawton, defended GIS, using similar arguments to those used by OGR before World War II. The centralized clipping service was a cost-efficient approach, since it obviated the natural tendency of every department and agency to create a clipping service for itself. The government should have an office that answered general inquiries that were not directed to a specific agency, such as letters addressed to Uncle Sam or US Government. The *Government Manual* was a widely used and helpful reference source that should be continued. Many members of Congress used GIS's services. Notwithstanding his nuts and bolts orientation to government, Smith briefly shifted to the abstract when he suggested that benefit of GIS's services "in the general interest of democracy."[22]

The House Appropriations Committee recommended substantial cuts in BOB's entire budget request.[23] For GIS, it recommended cutting the budget request in half, from $411,530 to $205,765 with an expected staff cut from about 150 to 75.[24] When the bill reached the floor of the House, the Republicans were ready to pick up where they had left off when OGR had been merged into OWI in 1942. For them, the fifty percent cut was inadequate. Taber quickly hand wrote a proposed amendment to delete all funding for GIS.[25] Besides the usual arguments, a new one was that information activities did not belong in BOB, therefore any funding for BOB's GIS should be eliminated. One congressman said he supported the amendment because clearly government funding was being wasted and misspent. The hospital for veterans in his district in Utica, NY, was being closed for lack of funding—yet there was enough money to fund GIS?

This time, House Democrats were more willing to defend GIS, given that they were defending a fifty percent cut in its budget. After all, one of them said, look at the authorizing legislation for OGR that had permitted spending up to $1.5 million annually on these activities. Now we've got that down to $200,000, so surely we've been tough budget cutters. Some were even willing to defend the substance of GIS's work: the value of having a centralized clipping service, a unit that answered calls and letters that were not directed to a specific agency or member of Congress, and the *Government Manual*. These were all valuable functions, just as long as they were funded at rock-bottom levels. Even Congressman Thomas, who had pressed for liquidating GIS during the hearing, spoke in support of the committee's recommendation and against the floor amendment. With the conclusion of the debate on Taber's amendment, the House voted. It passed.[26] GIS was to be defunded and liquidated. But, that vote had been a voice vote. The Democratic leadership was not willing to let the Republicans (who were the minority party) make budget decisions. That's what the majority party was supposed to do. And the president was a Democrat. The Subcommittee chair then asked for a recorded vote, which would have the effect of bringing more members to the floor, since not all were normally present during preliminary consideration of bills. That vote, as would be expected, reasserted the majority party's control of the House. The results of the voice vote were reversed.[27] The amendment was defeated 152 to 177.[28]

Now the bill went to the Senate. Playing its traditional role as a court of appeals, the Senate Appropriations Committee held a hearing on January 30, 1946, on BOB's budget appeals. Director Smith asked that the Senate reverse the House action regarding BOB's entire budget. The House had cut the president's budget request for BOB for fiscal year 1947 by $882,600. Smith requested a full restoration, which would include funding GIS at about $400,000 for the year. During the public hearing, the senators focused on larger BOB issues and GIS did not attract their attention.[29] The committee eventually decided to split the difference. It recommended adding $450,000 to BOB's budget, restoring about half of the House cut.[30] The Senate adopted the committee's recommendation. During the floor debate there was no attention to GIS, compared to the significant floor fight and floor amendment in the House.

In the conference committee, the Senate managers emphasized that they had not reversed the House's BOB cut; they had simply compromised by restoring half of the cut. This meant that the Senate had already split the difference between full restoration and the House level. If the two houses were to have a fair compromise, with each giving/getting half, then logically, the House conferees should accept the BOB funding level as recommended by the Senate. The House managers accepted the Senate's logic.[31] President Truman signed the bill on March 28, 1946, three months before the beginning of the fiscal year.[32] Even though BOB had gotten about $400,000 less for fiscal year 1947 than requested, most of that would have been dedicated to enlarging the size of the agency. Therefore, based on internal allocations, GIS's budget for the upcoming fiscal year was $417,000, very much a status quo funding level. GIS had survived the fifty percent budget-cutting attack in the House of Representatives with a cost-to-continue budget. It appeared to be attaining a state of normalcy and permanence.

Other Presidential Communication Activities

During World War II, the advertising industry had sought a public service role for itself by creating the War Advertising Council. It coordinated free advertising donated by advertising agencies, newspapers, radio stations, and the motion picture industry. The council worked with OWI to solicit suggestions for advertising campaigns from federal agencies and departments. OWI served as a central body to receive, organize, coordinate, and prioritize the requests from departments. It also worked with the advertising council to select themes for public service campaigns from the requests submitted by federal agencies.[33] With the end of the war and the liquidation of OWI, the question before the council was its future. To continue similar public service campaigns after the war, it would need to change its name back to its pre-war one, the advertising council, and find a new coordinating body in the federal government to replace OWI.[34] The industry's condition for continuing to donate advertising was that a federal coordinating unit would "relieve them of the responsibility of making priority decisions" for public-service campaigns.[35] After some high-level conversations, on October 15, 1945, President Truman directed the Office of War Mobilization and Reconversion (OWMR) to create a "unit which will correlate the information policies of the Federal government on which public campaigns using" the advertising council would be selected and conducted.[36] OWMR was one of the many emergency wartime agencies that existed in Washington. However, unlike most of the temporary wartime agencies, OWMR was a central, coordinating, higher-level body that had the status of a presidential agency,[37] with its director having an office in the White House.[38] Its first director, James Byrnes[39] had been viewed as so powerful and central to the federal war effort that he was sometimes referred to as the assistant president. Also, OWMR's importance was enhanced when, during the war, Congress gave it statutory status and enhanced powers.[40] Therefore, OWMR was viewed as the most appropriate home for post-war liaison with the advertising council.

A small office in OWMR, called the Media Programming Division, was quickly established later that month.[41] On October 30, 1945, OWMR hosted a meeting at the White House for the Information Directors of federal agencies and departments to brief them on the proposed work of the Media Programming Division with the advertising council. By the end of the meeting, there were twenty-eight requests for public service campaigns.[42] Moving quickly, during 1946, the division accepted and the council conducted twenty-five continuing campaigns and twenty-three short-term programs that focused on time-limited events.[43] The total donated value of the advertising during that year was estimated at $100 million.[44]

The division was relatively small. Its chief had first sketched a budget of between $140,000 and $175,000 with about twenty-one staffers.[45] However, he was allotted $62,760 and twelve staff positions.[46] In mid-September 1946—slightly less than a year since Truman's original directive to create the OWMR Media Programming Division—ninety businessmen associated with the advertising council were invited to the White House for a two-day conference to hear briefings from cabinet members and other senior administration officials on key national issues and their hope for help from the council.[47] A message from the president to the conferees noted that "A year's experience has proved that, in peace as in war, there is no substitute for teamwork between business and government in the solution of problems which both agree are in the public interest."[48] At the end of the conference, the participants committed to continuing their cooperative efforts.

For the first six months of its existence, the Media Programming Division handled liaison not only with the advertising council, but also with the motion picture industry. In November 1945, OWMR Director John Snyder met with some leading producers, distributors, and exhibitors to encourage them to continue their wartime policy of presenting short films promoting goals and themes similar to those of the advertising council.[49] During this period, it became apparent that the noncontroversial and nonpolitical messages of the administration were not reaching the movie audience as comprehensively or systematically as the work through the advertising council was reaching radio listeners, newspaper and magazine readers, etc. Generally, exhibitors were willing to cooperate and show government-produced shorts but wanted to be protected "from indiscriminate demands of the many agencies" to have their shorts shown in movie theatres.[50] However, unlike the advertising industry that had kept the War Advertising

Council intact after the end of World War II, the film industry disbanded the War Activities Committee by early 1946. So, there was no longer an industry-wide organization to select, approve, and manage a government film program.[51]

One of the problems was that there were four major exhibitor groups, all competing with each other. None was willing to enter into a formal arrangement with the government if that meant an organization would have to "subordinate itself to any other."[52] Another problem was the desire of the motion picture business to have separate recognition, rather than be associated with the advertising council.[53] Following some negotiations with the American Theaters Association and a meeting in Washington on July 3, 1946,[54] an agreement was reached. A key part of the agreement was that if a central federal office "would screen those things out for them, so that they would not be subjected themselves to deciding which one of the agency films should be rejected, they would carry out the program for us."[55] To implement the agreement, President Truman signed a letter designating OWMR as the "liaison and clearance office" for contacts between all federal agencies and motion-picture exhibitors.[56] In response, a Motion Picture Division was created in OWMR, headed by Arch A. Mercey, who had been involved in OGR's Film Coordinator Office.[57]

Notwithstanding its grandiloquent designation as a division, the Motion Picture Division was tiny, consisting of "only a two-man staff."[58] By October the two had developed a program for fiscal year 1947. It consisted of producing about four short films for about $60,000 on such subjects as economic stabilization and the federal budget. Also, it would approve for presentation short movies produced by federal departments and agencies, such as a fire-prevention film from USDA's Forest Service and one about veterans from the Veterans Administration.[59] However, the lack of a movie counterpart to the advertising council continued hampering the work of the Motion Picture Division. The division arranged for a high-level meeting at the White House of representatives of all elements of the movie business on November 19, 1946. As a result of the meeting, an industry-wide study committee was created "to explore details as to whether or not the industry should cooperate and if so, by what procedure." The committee recommended to its constituent members creation of an overall coordinating committee and a national review group.[60] After a bumpy start due to these industry problems, things seemed to be falling into place for OWMR's Motion Picture Division. As with the Media Programming Division, the Motion Picture Division appeared to be a permanent part of OWMR.

Reestablishing the Office of Government Reports

There was one problem. OWMR was a wartime agency. Certainly, reconversion would properly be an extensive process following VJ Day, lasting for several years and therefore necessitating a continued role for OWMR. But, along with the other wartime agencies, OWMR symbolized such unpopular activities as price controls and rationing. The public was war-weary and wanted the war to be over "officially" and for government controls over everyday economic life to be repealed.[61] In October, new BOB Director James Webb[62] had submitted a memo to Truman suggesting that it was timely to review the structure of the Executive Office of the President (EOP). One of the three specific items he identified for a decision was "Action either to continue or to redefine the OWMR."[63] According to Herman Miles Somers, the consensus within BOB and OWMR was that OWMR should be retained and not liquidated with the rest of the wartime agencies. Its coordinating and planning functions would be needed for a long time, even in a peacetime civilian economy. Therefore, it should be a more permanent freestanding agency in EOP and its name modified.[64] However, politics was part of the bigger picture. Since 1932, the Democrats had controlled the presidency and were the majority party in both houses of Congress. In a major Democratic debacle, as a result of the November 1946 midterm elections, the Republicans became the majority party in the both houses. The election results were interpreted universally as partly reflecting the public's dissatisfaction with Truman's handling of the pace of reconversion. The political message was that Truman needed to end economic controls sooner rather than later and to disband the bureaucratic structure that had administered these wartime controls.[65] Petitioning Congress to change the OWMR statute to make it a permanent EOP agency with a new name was now out of the question. OWMR had to go. And fast.

After the election, BOB quickly prepared a draft executive order that, among other things, would abolish OWMR. The draft was submitted to the Justice Department for review on November 20. The attorney general approved it for form and content the next day and transmitted it to OWMR's director for action. But, these final drafting stages had brought out several problems about a "clean" abolition of the agency that hadn't been considered up to then. One of the problems with that draft was that it made no special arrangements for the Media Programming and Motion Picture Divisions.[66] It was now becoming clear that it was out of the question to disband these two offices. After all, just a year ago, in October 1945, President Truman himself had committed to designating a central coordinating office high up in the administration to serve as the sole contact point in the federal government for the advertising council. Since then several meetings had been held at the White House, each one reinforcing the original directive to create the OWMR Media Programming Division. On November 15, 1946, OWMR Director John Steelman was preparing for a dinner meeting requested by the advertising council. His director of information, Anthony Hyde, prepped him for the meeting by reminding him that the advertising council insisted that its counterpart in the federal government "be placed somewhere near the top, as it is now, with ready access to the White House. . . . It should be separated as far as possible from any other activity of either a controversial or political nature."[67] The movie industry felt the same way. While the development of a working relationship with it was taking longer, again the president had made a written commitment to create a central contact point for film decisions that would have his backing. Just around the same time the draft executive order was being prepared, the special study committee of the movie industry, created after a White House meeting on November 19, quickly issued its recommendations including its desire to work through "one duly designated agency of the Federal Government representing all branches thereof."[68]

After the November 20 executive order draft was rejected, additional consultations took place within BOB and OWMR and between the two agencies to resolve the problems of that draft, including the future of Media Programming and Motion Picture Divisions after OWMR would disappear.[69] The two divisions could not be moved to a cabinet department or one of the independent agencies, because their raison d'être required them to be *above* regular agencies, having the clout to require cooperation and coordination. Both the advertising and movie industries wanted the prestige of working with an office that was close to the president. Also, wherever the two divisions were to be placed, that "home" must be a permanent government agency, not another temporary one. That meant it must have statutory status, not be based solely on an executive order. Finally, it had to be part of the president's official family, not out in the bureaucratic boondocks.

OGR came up during these internal OWMR planning sessions, which were headed by OWMR's director of information, Anthony Hyde. The staff unanimously recommended to BOB that the two divisions be housed in a new unit within EOP "much in the same way as the Office of Government Reports was." It would be called the Office of Government Programming, Office of Advertising Liaison or something like that.[70] BOB staff saw the advantages of the proposal, but did not explicitly give its approval. They had some reservations.

Clearly, Hyde's proposal had many obvious advantages. Like the defunct OGR, the new entity would be part of EOP, thus placing it inside the president's official family. This would meet the demands of the advertising council and the movie industry. But, BOB officials could also readily identify some serious defects in the proposal. The new office could not exist solely based on the authority of an executive order. That would preclude it from getting annual appropriations from Congress. But, to get to *that* point would mean Congress would have to pass a law creating the new agency or at least authorizing appropriations to it. Who knew how long that would take, if ever? If OWMR was about to be disbanded, there was a need for an entity *now*; one that could start receiving appropriations right away. There could be no gap between the disassembling of OWMR and the new entity. The president's word was at stake.

Hyde's idea of an OGR-like agency inevitably brought OGR itself into play for BOB staffers. How about, instead of seeking congressional approval for a new agency like OGR, the president would revive OGR itself? The idea had many obvious advantages. First, OGR had been one of the five original agencies in EOP, the perfect place for the two divisions. This would clearly situate them at a central and high place in the executive branch, as demanded by the advertising council and the movie industry. Second, OGR was a statutory agency. In June 1941, Congress had passed a law authorizing appropriations to it. That law was still on the books. Congress had not repealed it after OGR was folded into OWI in 1942. So, a revived OGR could begin receiving congressional appropriations immediately. Third, the spending authorization for OGR in that law was up to $1.5 million a year, a funding level more than adequate for the two divisions. Fourth, according to the OGR statute, one of its specific purposes was the dissemination of information about the federal government to the public, a good description of the basic purpose of working with the advertising council and the movie industry. Fifth, again based on the OGR statute, another of its enumerated responsibilities was to serve as "a central clearinghouse," a perfect fit for coordinating the needs of federal agencies with the opportunities available through the advertising council and motion-picture business. Finally, BOB continued to be uncomfortable with GIS as one of its divisions.[71] It was part of BOB despite the reluctance of recently departed Director Smith. Smith had not liked the idea of transferring OWI's domestic activities to BOB. From his perspective, those informational programs had no substantial or substantive connection to BOB's mission and operations. Indeed, this poor fit was apparent during the year that GIS was in BOB. It was not well integrated into the agency: it was not located with all the other BOB offices, but at a different site and it operated autonomously and had little to do with BOB's daily work. So, any opportunity for BOB to unload GIS would be considered desirable and appealing. Trying to put the most positive interpretation on the ill fit between GIS and rest of BOB, Blackburn explained that these were two very different missions and functions: "the Bureau of the Budget is a control agency. Ours is a service agency."[72]

So, BOB began planning on using the empty legal shell of OGR and filling it with the two OWMR Divisions. And, if OGR were to be revived, what about the Government Information Service? GIS's two divisions, public inquiries and press intelligence, had been part of the pre-war OGR. Reverting them back to a reestablished OGR from BOB would restore the status quo antebellum. Thus was born the idea of reviving OGR in the post-war Truman presidency. In some respects, this was precisely what President Roosevelt had wanted to do. His merger of OGR into OWI was only a temporary act, to be undone when the war was over and the degree of controversy over OGR had faded. But, the BOB recommendation to revive OGR was not really being prompted by the desire to implement Roosevelt's desires. Rather, the need to find a home for the OWMR Divisions of Media Programming and Motion Pictures was the driving force behind the initiative. Here was a case of the tail wagging the dog: the convenience of OGR's empty legal shell was what drove the decision to reestablish the agency, not the desire to restore the agency to its pre-war status. Employee staffing numbers demonstrate this backwards situation: of the 150 or so employees that the revived OGR would have, only eighteen came from OWMR.[73] BOB Director Webb explicitly acknowledged this situation when he submitted a revised executive order to the attorney general in early December. One of the differences between the two drafts, he wrote, was that "As an incident thereto, the present draft provides for the reestablishment of the Office of Government Reports."[74] In plain English, OGR needed to be recreated because OWMR was being abolished.

The idea quickly took hold, even though some in OWMR didn't like it much. But, in government, decisions follow the path of least resistance. Reviving OGR was logical and feasible compared to the alternatives. However, the idea had at least one very obvious major disadvantage. The November elections had just given control of both houses of Congress to the Republicans. The GOP's conventional wisdom was that its victory in the elections and its status as majority party was a mandate to dismantle New Deal programs and sharply cut government spending. After sixteen years of criticism as the minority party, it seemed the public now agreed with what they had been saying all along and it was their duty to deliver.[75] It had been the Republican members of the two appropriations committees—especially the House—who repeatedly had criticized New Deal public-relations programs in general and OGR in particular. As long as they were in the minority party, their objections could not be decisive—although their views certainly kept the agency under fire. But now, those same committee members were to be the majority on the subcommittees and full committees, even the chairmen. They could make their views stick. They were in control. And, these Republicans hadn't forgotten OGR. They had opposed it in the run-up to World War II. Then, notwithstanding the national mood during the first few weeks after Pearl Harbor, they continued opposing it. They were part of the loud chorus that opposed the US Information Center. And, just earlier in that year of 1946, they had proposed an amendment on the floor of the House to defund BOB's GIS. It was only their minority party status that had prevented them from prevailing. The technocrats of BOB had come up with an excellent organizational and legal solution to the problem of the future of OWMR's Media Programming and Motion Picture Divisions. But, they were ignoring politics. Although some would argue that civil servants should always leave politics to the politicians, this was an example that demonstrated why such an approach is flawed. Politics is part of government. If public servants want to be effective in their work, they must include political considerations in their decision-making.

On December 12, 1946, President Truman held a press conference to announce his signing of an omnibus executive order to dismantle much of the wartime administrative apparatus. He was signaling the public that he had gotten the message of the November election.[76] His action was interpreted exactly as intended. A front-page story in the next day's *New York Times* depicted the purpose of the executive order as "the liquidation of remaining wartime economic restraints and [to] direct the country's return to the free enterprise system."[77] One of the thirteen sections of the executive order re-established the Office of Government Reports as a combination of GIS and the Media Programming and Motion Picture Divisions of OWMR.[78] Truman was clear that he intended to restore OGR to its status quo antebellum by describing the new agency as "an agency in the Executive Office of the President on the same basis and with the same functions as obtained immediately prior to the promulgation of Executive Order No. 9182 of June 13, 1942" that had created OWI.[79] OGR was reborn. Truman was now giving Roosevelt's original idea a second chance. But the political timing couldn't have been worse.

Office of Government Reports Redux

For the second OGR to operate, some administrative actions were needed right away. This entailed the unglamorous and nitty gritty of government management. First, President Truman quickly designated Katherine Blackburn as the agency's acting director.[80] Having been with OGR from the beginning, and serving most recently as GIS director, this decision provided continuity and familiarity for any problems that would need to be resolved as the new agency came into being. She knew how the agency should operate, what it did and had the executive experience to make it happen. Second, since it was the middle of fiscal year 1947, it was important to assure a smooth personnel and financial transition. OGR needed to begin functioning quickly with the staff from GIS and the two OWMR divisions officially transferred to it and the funding already appropriated to its predecessor units.[81] Third, the agency needed to be brought under one roof. Blackburn arranged for the Media Programming and Motion Pictures Divisions to be moved into the US Information Center on Pennsylvania Avenue.[82] Fourth, the annual presidential budget message to Congress for the upcoming fiscal year was traditionally released in early January, only a few weeks after Truman's recreation of OGR. Given the Government Printing Office's advance printing deadlines, the fiscal year 1948 budget for OGR needed to be determined quickly so that it could be placed in the EOP section of the budget message. The previous year, Budget Director Smith had decided to recommend a cost-to-continue budget for GIS compared to its previous funding in OWI. BOB maintained the same approach for the OGR's first budget. Its funding level would be set to cover costs of the same level of activity as the current year—when OGR's components had operated as subunits within BOB and OWMR. For fiscal year 1947, GIS and the two OWMR divisions had had a budget of about $600,000. Therefore, the president's budget recommendation for OGR for fiscal year 1948 would be the same. Similarly, staffing levels would be unchanged at about 150 staffers.[83]

Once all these managerial and administrative details were in place, the reconstituted OGR consisted of four service-delivery units:

- The Division of Public Inquiries was essentially the USIS in the pre-war OGR. Blackburn re-titled it the Government Information Service.[84]
- The Press Intelligence Division was, while smaller in staffing, essentially the same activity it had been in the pre-war OGR.
- The Media Programming Division was renamed as the Advertising Liaison group and was part of the OGR Director's Office.[85]
- The Motion Picture Division was renamed as the Motion-picture Liaison group and was also part of the Director's Office.[86]

OGR's senior leadership demonstrated the continuity between its pre-war and post-war manifestations. Acting Director Katherine Blackburn had been OGR's assistant director before the war. Similarly, Charlotte Hatton was named Chief of the Division of Press Intelligence, the exact position she had held in the pre-war OGR. Malcolm Morrow, Chief of the Government Information Service, had been a Liaison Officer in OGR's pre-war Division of Field Operations, stationed in Washington.[87] Eleanor Herring, OGR's administrative officer and head of the Administrative Division (a post that existed in the pre-war OGR) had been the assistant chief of the state reports and legislative sections of OGR's Division of Field Operations.[88]

The acting head of Advertising Liaison was Charles W. Jackson, who had worked as a program manager in OWMR's Media Programming Division. The head of the Division, Drew Dudley, had resigned in October 1946 and Jackson was immediately named acting chief.[89] He continued in that capacity in OGR. When the Motion Picture Division was transferred from OWMR to OGR, Arch Mercey had headed it. But only a month later he resigned to take an assignment with the United Nations' World Health Organization.[90] Blackburn named the other professional in that small office, Dallas Halverstadt, acting chief.[91] In summary, the (relatively) strong representation of women in the post-war OGR also continued its pre-war pattern. Of the five senior officers (director, four unit heads and administrative officer) three were women, including the agency director. However, some of the functions of the agency, such as library-type work, were considered "women's jobs" in those days and so the significant role of women may have been more a reflection of OGR's mission than anything else.

With the basic managerial and administrative details resolved, the new OGR was able to function on a day-to-day basis. But, externally, the situation was less clear. President Truman's December 13 announcement abolishing OWMR and transferring the Media Programming and Motion Picture Divisions to the reconstituted OGR had not been cleared in advance with the advertising council and the motion picture industry. So, a top priority was to work with the external constituency groups, reassure them of the continuity of business, emphasize the benefits of the reorganization and continue implementing the work of the pre-reorganization divisions. The first reaction came from the advertising council. On December 17, less than a week after the executive order reestablishing OGR, the council's chairman wrote President Truman how "very much gratified" the council was with the president's decision because the "revival" of OGR accomplished the goal of the council that its governmental liaison continued to be in the president's executive office. The letter also recommended that the president name Anthony Hyde, OWMR's director of information, to be OGR director.[92] The day after the president's executive order, the head of the Motion Picture Division sent a form letter to the members of the motion picture Study Committee. He reassured them that

> Our office has been given to understand by the White House that we are to function as we did under OWMR as the Government's coordination and liaison office on motion pictures. We anticipate no change of responsibilities and we hope that our general relationship to the film industry can remain the same.[93]

However, due to the continuing internal conflicts within the movie industry, there was no substantive answer to this letter for nearly three months. Finally, on March 6, Blackburn received official notice that a new industry committee, called the Motion Picture Industry Coordinating Committee, had just been established and was now ready to begin working with OGR's Motion Picture Division.[94]

During its second incarnation (fourth, if counting NEC and BOB's GIS), OGR's work was similar to its previous activities. GIS responded to thousands of phone calls, letters and walk-in requests for information. It received over 200,000 inquiries in a year.[95] The service was also responsible for the *US Government Manual,* which sold almost 29,000 copies in 1946.[96] The Division of Press Intelligence also continued its work uninterrupted from its most recent placement with BOB. As a clipping service for the entire federal government, the Division responded to about 1,500 standing orders to send clippings and summaries of radio transcripts on specific subjects.[97] It also produced daily summaries of editorial opinions from the major daily newspapers and radio programs, and weekly summaries of editorials and opinion columns in 225 other newspapers and nine "Negro" weeklies.[98]At the request of the White House, it created a new product consisting of an integrated digest summarizing all press and radio comment on domestic and international issues prepared for the President and his senior aides by 8:45 A.M. Monday through Saturday.[99]

The two activities transferred from OWMR also continued their work uninterrupted. The Advertising Liaison group worked with twelve government agencies and the Red Cross to create thirty-seven programs and special events that were accepted by the Advertising Council for public service campaigns.[100] The Motion Picture Liaison office was smaller compared to Advertising Liaison. Nonetheless, in 1947, it aided in the showing of seventeen short film subjects in movie theatres throughout the United States and even abroad. However, due to the slow start of the Motion Picture Industry Co-ordinating Committee, only five of those films were directly related to the joint work of the committee and the liaison group. These movie shorts had much more extensive viewership as a percentage of the total US population than in contemporary times. Since these events were taking place just before the broad popularization of television, the frequency of movie going by average Americans was much higher than after the beginning of the age of television. The office estimated that any of the movie shorts that were approved and disseminated by the Committee were exhibited by 21,500 movie houses to an average audience of ninety-five million people a week.[101]

Blackburn had been invited to give a talk to the American Public Relations Association in 1947. This gave her and her senior management team an opportunity to conceptualize OGR as a coherent and integrated agency with a mission common to all its components. A draft of the speech described OGR as "being a good reporter. We bring a concise, factual report of what is going on in the press and radio to the White House and we report to the advertising and motion picture industry the public relations problems that confront the Government."[102]

Facing Congress

Now that the new OGR was fully operating and in good stead with its external stakeholders, it was time to deal with the agency's largest and most foreboding hurdle: the Congress of the United States, specifically the Republican Eightieth Congress. In January 1947, when President Truman had sent his fiscal year 1948 budget to Congress, it included a request for $600,000 for OGR.[103] Since all appropriations bills must begin—as required by the Constitution—in the House, OGR's first contact with Congress would be at the budget hearings of the House Appropriations Committee. The chairman of the full committee was now John Taber (R-NY) who had criticized OGR many times before it was merged into OWI. Chairman Tabor had announced early in the year that one of his goals for all the fiscal year 1948 appropriation bills would be to cut public-relations budgets of all agencies and, especially, OGR.[104] The Chair of the Independent Offices Subcommittee, which had jurisdiction over EOP, was Richard Wigglesworth (R-MA). Like Taber, he had been equally opposed to OGR during its first incarnation and had tried to cut it during the Democratic-majority years.

The White House was aware of the problem. In a memo to John Steelman, assistant to the president (who had served earlier as the last OWMR Director), aide James Cole wrote:

> Unquestionably O.G.R. is considered to be a controversial case by both Appropriations Committees. . . . At this stage of the game there appears to be little that can be done to change the apparent adverse attitude toward O.G.R. on the hill. The advertising and motion picture functions may be sufficiently popular to salvage some amount from the funds requested. I understand that Mr. Repplier, President of the Advertising Council, has done considerable spade work in the House on behalf of O.G.R'S. [sic] continuance.[105]

Indeed, the advertising council was willing to lobby Congress. Both advertisers and the Motion Picture Committee represented private-sector businesses that were donating their efforts for noncontroversial public-service messages. Although a conservative Republican Congress would understandably be critical of a Democratic president and of an executive communications agency, it should—theoretically—be sympathetic and supportive of the work of the private sector. Presumably, lobbying by businessmen to maintain OGR should carry some weight with the majority party. If the tail had wagged the dog in the reestablishment of OGR, then the question now was whether the tail could save the dog. As early as two days after the executive order creating OGR had been signed, the advertising council had conveyed to outgoing OWMR Information Director Hyde that "it will take the initiative in explaining to the Congress why this completely non-political activity should be carried on in the interest of the Nation."[106]

Even though President Truman had sent his budget message to Congress at the usual time in January, the House Appropriations Committee with its new Republican majority was acting much more slowly than usual. It wasn't until mid-April that the Independent Offices Subcommittee held a public hearing on OGR's budget request. Blackburn, accompanied by the acting chiefs of advertising and motion picture liaison and the agency's executive officer, testified.[107] Much of the subcommittee's questioning focused systematically on each of the four functions of the office, their staffing and budgets. The general premise of the questions was whether these specific services were really needed and, if needed, why were they overstaffed and that staff overpaid? Standard skeptical questions also asked about administrative overhead costs, nonsalary costs such as travel and printing and about any publicity and propaganda activities in the agency. Chairman Wigglesworth extensively asked about the free advertising that the government was benefiting from. Wasn't it correct, he said, if the federal government was benefiting from $80 million worth of donated and free advertising, then wasn't it losing the income-tax revenue it would have if that same space/time was filled with paid advertising, since donated space/time is tax deductible? Advertising Liaison Acting Chief Jackson patiently and repeatedly tried to explain that this wasn't the case, but the questioning by Wigglesworth was so persistent that it left the impression that there was some validity to his premise. Representatives of the advertising council were present in the room during the hearing, but they were not given an opportunity to testify.[108]

It wasn't for another two months before the House Appropriations Committee finally reported out the fiscal year 1948 Independent Offices Bill. It was now mid-June, only two weeks before the beginning of the fiscal year. Without comment or explanation in its report, the committee recommended defunding OGR totally, eliminating $600,000 in expenditures.[109] In an effort to call to the attention of all the House members the significance of the recommendation, on June 18 Blackburn wrote the traditional annual letter asking Congress members if they would like to receive a complimentary copy of the latest edition of the *Government Manual* and, if so, how many copies. This time the letter also noted the proposed elimination of OGR and hinted that the effect would be to eliminate future free distributions or even future publication of the *Manual.*[110] Similarly the advertising council sought to communicate the implications of the abolition of the Advertising Liaison Office. However, its support was highly qualified. Its public position was that it supported having a liaison office high in the executive branch, in the president's official family. But, in a letter to the chief of the liaison office, the council flatly stated that "(1) this organization did not favor the placing of your functions in the Office of Government Reports, [and] (2) that it believes these functions belong in the White House."[111]

OGR was a minor component in the omnibus Independent Offices bill and the subject was only glancingly mentioned during the debate on the floor of the House. The ranking minority member on the Subcommittee, Joe Hendricks (D-FL) identified himself as "one of the very few, it seemed, who thought they [OGR] served a good purpose."[112] But, he didn't feel strongly enough about it to oppose the bill in total or have enough support to submit an amendment reversing the cut. A Republican member of the subcommittee, Charles Robertson (R-ND), said he didn't totally support the subcommittee's recommendation because he wanted the work of the Advertising Liaison and Motion Picture Liaison offices to continue. He was hoping those functions could be continued, perhaps as part of the White House staff. As for the other aspects of OGR, it "has not had too constructive a record over the years."[113] The version of the bill approved by the House and sent to the Senate left unchanged the committee recommendation to abolish OGR.

Unless the new Republican majority of the Senate Appropriations Committee could be convinced of the merits of OGR, a unanimous recommendation from both House and Senate committees would be expected to be decisive. The advertising council stepped up its lobbying efforts by contacting all the members of the committee.[114] Blackburn and Herring were called before the subcommittee on June 25, less than a week before the beginning of fiscal year 1948. Chairman Clyde Reed (R-KS) started the hearing with a concise comment, "You are threatened with extinction, are you not?"[115] In her prepared testimony, Blackburn tried to make the case as pointedly as possible. If OGR's GIS were disbanded, the federal government would lose

1. the only office in Washington concerned with handling the traffic of telephone, mail, and personal inquiries of a general nature concerning federal agencies or their personnel;
2. a centralized departmental-reference service built on material unique in its value as background for providing general government information;
3. the only central index of all government functions;
4. the only central index of agencies renamed, consolidated, transferred, or abolished;
5. the *Government Manual* and corollary publications which very nearly paid for themselves.[116]

She made similar points about the unique services and benefits of centralization of clipping services, advertising liaison and movie liaison.

Although the same party controlled the House and Senate, the tone of the hearing was very different from the House hearing. Senator Reed volunteered his favorable view of OGR's library.[117] Reed permitted Senator Joseph C. O'Mahoney (D-WY) to dominate most of the session by asking Blackburn leading questions, apparently because she wasn't doing as good a job as most officials appearing before the subcommittee. He told her bluntly, "What I am trying to develop for your record here is some justification for this Service." Besides his questions, she was permitted to insert in the record of the hearing letters of support from Labor Department, BOB, National Archives, Encyclopedia Americana, and the American Sociological Association. On an unplanned basis, representatives from the Bureau of Labor Statistics and the Federal Trade Commission got up and volunteered statements of the value of OGR's work—a sharp contrast to the House subcommittee not permitting representatives of the advertising council to testify.[118]

Toward the end of the hearing, Reed hinted that the Senate would not accept the House recommendation. He said to Blackburn of the House's action, "They just prepared the corpse for burial. They had not entirely interred you." Further action on the bill didn't occur before the beginning of the fiscal year. Therefore, the two houses quickly passed stop-gap legislation extending current appropriations into the new fiscal year until the appropriate legislation had passed.[119] Indeed, when the committee's report was issued on July 11 it had some good news for the agency. The committee recommended a $400,000 appropriation for OGR for fiscal year 1948 with a specific allocation of those funds to Advertising Liaison and the library. Other agency activities, the report said, had "overexpanded."[120]

This recommendation was certainly not what Blackburn had been hoping for. And the sequence of future legislative steps seemed inevitably to be even worse. From the president's recommendation of an annual budget of $600,000, the Senate had now recommended two-thirds of that. So, the range of options of compromise between the two houses extended from zero—if the Senate conferees receded—to $400,000, if the House conferees yielded. Full funding was now legislatively impossible. The most logical political compromise, assuming neither side receded from its house's position, would be to split the difference and agree on $200,000. OGR did not come up during the Senate floor debate and so the committee's recommendation became the Senate's position in conference committee negotiations with the House. In the meantime, the latest edition of the *Government Manual* had just come off the press. Blackburn rushed a copy to President Truman. In her cover letter, she not so subtly requested his intervention, writing "The Conference Committee that will decide our fiscal fate meets tomorrow morning. I do hope we have convinced them that we should continue and that this will not be the <u>last</u> edition of the Manual, because we are really proud of it."[121] But Truman declined to intervene. Secretary to the President Matthew Connelly responded on Truman's behalf the next day. In his note he wrote, "I am sure you presented a good case, and join with you in hoping that the outcome will be successful."[122] The news from the conference committee was about what could logically have been predicted. The two houses compromised on allocating $230,000 for the fiscal year, about forty percent of the president's original recommendation. That level of funding was intended to permit OGR to continue its advertising industry liaison, motion picture industry liaison, and the library. Essentially, Congress was agreeing to maintain as ongoing concerns the two functions that had been transferred to the post-war OGR from OWMR and which the pre-war OGR had not engaged in, along with OGR's library—due to Senator Reed's personal interest. However, the conference report also stated, "The conferees are of the opinion that full consideration should be given by appropriate authority to the liquidation of this agency at the end of the fiscal year 1948."[123] In other words, the funding of the two liaison offices and the library were not to be interpreted as permanent. The House position to zero out the agency had prevailed in the conference committee over the Senate's, merely with a one-year delay. That aspect of the Conference Committee report was accepted without comment during the floor considerations in the House and Senate. President Truman signed the bill into law on July 30, 1947.[124]

Now, the only remaining decision that could save OGR would be if Truman would reject the non-binding recommendation contained in the Conference Committee report and request continued funding for OGR when he submitted his budget request for fiscal year 1949 in January 1948. But, politically, there was little to decide. In 1948, when Congress would be considering his proposed fiscal year 1949 budget, it would still be the Republican Eightieth Congress. There was no election between now and then that could change the majority party status. Also, Truman was in the midst of a fight for his political life. He was viewed as the underdog in the upcoming 1948 presidential election. His influence on Capitol Hill was very low. As part of his reelection strategy, he was about to begin sending to Congress proposals that he knew it would reject so then he could then campaign on their need, casting the blame on the "do-nothing Eightieth Congress" for not passing them.[125] OGR was small potatoes given that the presidency was at stake. All these years it had lacked any significant support in Congress, even from Democrats willing to defend it from Republican attacks. It had survived largely due to FDR's personal commitment to it and his extraordinary political and executive skills. Truman certainly knew the political trap of defending supposedly wasteful public relations spending. So, President Truman made the only logical decision given the circumstances; he reluctantly decided to accept the recommendation of the conference committee report.[126] He agreed to liquidate OGR and not request any funding for it after the end of fiscal year 1948, on June 30, 1948.[127]

End Game: De Jure Dissolution, de Facto Continuation

There were now only two major decisions left to make. First, how to allocate the funding that Congress had approved for OGR for fiscal year 1948? Second, what—if anything—to try to save when OGR would be liquidated at the end of the fiscal year? When Congress had appropriated $230,000 for OGR for fiscal year 1948, it explicitly earmarked the money for three OGR activities: the Advertising Liaison office, the Motion Picture Liaison office, and the library. The funding needed to maintain the agency in full would have required about three times as much money, since the proposed budget for fiscal year 1948 had been $600,000. And the language of the Conference Committee report was explicit about what the money could be spend on—and what it couldn't. Funding at the one-third level of the request would mean that the Division of Press Intelligence and GIS would need to be liquidated right away. All personnel in those two divisions were to be let go. On July 31, Blackburn submitted a staffing plan for fiscal year 1948 for nineteen full-time staff, compared to the 150 or so OGR had had. Her selections were intended exclusively to maintain the three core activities of the two liaison offices and the library that Congress had specified. She went beyond the congressional mandate in only one respect, retaining two professional staffers for the *US Government Manual* which she thought needed to be preserved.[128] Malcolm Morrow, head of GIS, tried to get the administration to reverse Blackburn's decision and keep GIS open. He talked with Richard Neustadt, Webb's Staff Assistant, who suggested he prepare a plan for Presidential Assistant John Steelman.[129] Morrow wrote a three-page memorandum listing the value of GIS, urging it be kept open and making scurrilous accusations against Blackburn, as though the entire problem was her fault.[130] However, nothing came of his effort.

With that responsibility taken care of, she submitted her resignation to the president.[131] President Truman's letter accepting her resignation was generous in its characterization of her work and OGR's mission:

> From personal observation I can bear witness to the zeal and high efficiency with which you have performed your duties in the Government. The genuine contribution you have made to the public's understanding of the functions of our Government should be a source of great satisfaction to you. Please accept my personal thanks for all that you have done in difficult and responsible posts.[132]

The White House announced her resignation on August 7.[133] With Blackburn gone, the president did not name anyone to replace her, not even an acting one. Instead, the de facto head of the agency became John Steelman, assistant to the president. As OWMR's last director, Steelman was familiar with the work of OGR's two media-liaison offices. Steelman promptly appointed Charles Jackson, who had been chief of OGR's Advertising Liaison office, to be an assistant in his office with responsibilities for coordinating the advertising and motion-picture liaison roles continuing in OGR for the remainder of the fiscal year.[134] Jackson's transfer to the White House payroll not only assured continuation of the work with the Advertising Council, but also opened up one of the few remaining funded slots in OGR. Steelman then appointed John Gibson, who had been a staffer in the OGR Advertising Liaison office to serve as Chief of the office for the remainder of OGR's existence.[135] Similarly, he promoted Dallas Halverstadt from Acting Chief to Chief of OGR's Motion Picture Liaison office.[136]

For fiscal year 1948 the liaison work with the advertising council and movie industry continued uninterrupted, unaffected by the OGR liquidation process. Similarly, the OGR library continued its services with the funding received from Congress. Also, while Congress had made no reference to supporting continuation of the *Government Manual*, staff at BOB agreed with Blackburn that it, too, should be protected and continued. When drafting the official letter for the president to sign regarding the liquidation of OGR, a paragraph about the *Manual* was added:

> Since it may prove desirable to submit a measure to the Congress with respect to the administration of functions relating to the United States Government Manual by an agency other than the Office of Government Reports, activities relating to such manual should be so conducted as to permit its continuation.[137]

Blackburn's decision in July 1947 to include two of the *US Government Manual* staffers on the list of the nineteen OGR employees to be funded with the fiscal year 1948 appropriations had preserved this option.

But, what to do regarding fiscal year 1949 and beyond? Were all the functions of OGR going to be liquidated with the demise of the agency? Although Congress had stated its support for the library and two liaison offices for fiscal year 1948, that support was only for one additional year of funding, with no expectation of continued appropriations. It turned out that OGR's imminent death wasn't as automatic as some thought and was, in some respects, more apparent than real.

First, while the Division of Press Intelligence was officially terminated with the fiscal year 1948 funding cut, the White House staff absorbed one of its major activities, preparing a daily summary of news coverage for the president and his top aides. The daily clipping and reporting continued uninterrupted in the Truman White House and to the present day.[138]

Second, the liaison functions for advertising and motion pictures were transferred into the White House budget for fiscal year 1949. President Truman's budget proposal planned on adding to the White House budget $45,000 and seven full-time staff to continue this function after June 30, 1948. This met with the approval of the House Appropriations Committee when BOB Director Webb and associates made their budget presentation to the subcommittee in January 1948. Although Chairman Wigglesworth jovially referred to "the late lamented Office of Government Reports," he had no objection to the expansion of the White House budget to maintain this activity.[139] In the House Appropriations Committee's report on the Independent Offices Bill, it noted the savings of $230,000 due to the abolition of OGR, but the report also included a recommendation for a $17,000 increase in funding for White House salaries from fiscal year 1948 to fiscal year 1949 as well as a $200,000 increase in the president's Emergency Fund.[140] This suggests that OGR's demise was, in part, merely de jure, with some of its activities being continued de facto by being shifted elsewhere. These former OGR activities continued into fiscal year 1949 without interruption. Seven OGR employees transferred to the White House payroll on July 1, 1948.[141] In August, Jackson was able to report to Steelman on the accomplishments of the office in July 1948, its first post-OGR month as a White House unit.[142] Similarly, in June, Halverstadt was busy making plans and arrangements for future film ventures connecting federal agencies and production studios.[143]

The Advertising Liaison office, as a unit within the White House operating under the supervision of a special assistant to the president, continued its work uninterrupted throughout the Eisenhower, Kennedy and Johnson administrations.[144] The White House liaison role was eventually dissolved, apparently in the late-1960s during the Nixon administration. By the Ford administration, the head of the Office of Communications was automatically designated as the contact person in the White House for the Ad Council, but no longer played a role in selecting which proposals from federal agencies would be recommended for public-service campaigns.[145] At that time, the advertising council shifted to working directly with individual federal departments and agencies, rather than through a White House central coordinating office.[146] To the present, the council continues promoting a variety of causes and topics in support of the missions of federal agencies.

Third, BOB worked to preserve the *Government Manual* and its staff. BOB quietly transferred the responsibility for publishing it to the *Federal Register* division of the National Archives.[147] That office then published the 1948 edition of the *Government Manual* based on the data collected by OGR up to June 30, 1948. It next prepared from scratch and published the 1949 edition. Three OGR staffers who had worked on the manual transferred to the National Archives payroll after OGR closed on June 30, 1948, as part of a modest agency-wide staff increase from fiscal year 1948 to fiscal year 1949.[148] In his January 1949, budget message to Congress for fiscal year 1950, President Truman explicitly identified the expansion of the duties of the National Archives' *Federal Register* office to include publication of the *Government Manual*.[149] This added responsibility of the National Archives came up at the annual budget hearing of the House Independent Offices Appropriations Subcommittee. This was the same subcommittee that over the previous two years—with a Republican majority—had insisted on killing OGR. The discussion was brief, business-like and noncontroversial. The *Government Manual* was plainly referred to as having come from OGR. So different from the previous subcommittee hearings, the shared assumption during that part of the hearing was that, of course, it was a good thing to have saved OGR's *Manual* by transferring it to the *Federal Register* Division of the National Archives. That it was a moneymaker was noted with satisfaction, something that had never impressed the critics of OGR when OGR was fighting for its life.[150]

The final decision about retaining OGR functions related to the OGR library. The Senate Appropriations Committee tried to save it. During the hearings on fiscal year 1949 funding in the Independent Offices Bill, Reed did not raise the issue when BOB testified. However, on its own initiative, the full committee included in its version of the bill a new appropriation of $18,000 "for the continuation for 1 year of the library of the Office of Government Reports."[151] The Senate approved that specific amendment to the House version of the bill without debate.[152] But Congressmen Wigglesworth and Taber would have none of it. They had attacked OGR for years while in the minority. Now that they were in the majority, they wanted to kill OGR, not part of OGR, not most of OGR, but all of OGR. Their double standard of permitting some of OGR's functions, such as the liaison offices and the *Government Manual*, to continue as long as they were no longer called OGR, is striking. In an ironic sense, they insisted on having a public-relations victory in their battle to kill this public-relations agency. In conference committee, the House managers "insisted"[153] on the House version of zero funding for OGR. The Senate negotiators agreed to accept the House position and drop the effort to fund the OGR library.[154]

However, clearly, there was some interest in the Senate to retain the OGR library. On February 17, Senator Harley Kilgore (D-WV) talked to the president about his hope that the library could be saved. In a follow-up letter he wrote:

> On several occasions when I have been unable to obtain information and have appealed to this particular library, I have succeeded in finding just what I was looking for. If at all possible I hope that this reasonably small expenditure can be kept in the budget, because I feel that if the library is abolished, the material available there will be lost due to the fact that there seems not to be any place where it could be housed in tact [*sic*].[155]

Truman summoned BOB Director Webb to discuss the request.[156] They decided to accept the congressional decision not to fund the library. The sole remaining decision was what to do with it. The director of the Senate library and the Senate secretary (whose jurisdiction included the library) formally requested OGR's library collection. Their comments indicated the true value of the library that OGR witnesses had represented to skeptical congressman at so many hearings:

- "It is a working collection, closely integrated so that all of its parts are related effectively to overall operation."[157]
- "The value of the library . . . lies not only in the material it contains but in its order and arrangement."[158]
- "The Senate Library's collections are very short in many categories" of OGR's library.[159]

For a while it indeed appeared that the Senate would get the OGR library.[160] However, ultimately the War Assets Administration decided to assign it to the Library of Congress.[161] So, it too, survived the extinction of OGR.

At the close-of-business on Wednesday, June 30, 1948, OGR ended its existence. On that day, it had sixteen employees.[162] However, in fiscal year 1949 OGR actually expended $23,230, caused by costs involved in liquidating the agency and the June 1948 payroll paid on July 2, already the next fiscal year.[163] OGR even spent $243 in fiscal year 1950![164] OGR's odd ending, defunded but still authorized, was somewhat peculiar and nondefinitive. In August 1949, an academic researcher tried to describe it: "The legal status of this Office is clouded, but the weight of opinion is that it is no longer legally in existence, and that is certainly true in practice."[165] In fact, the public law authorizing congressional appropriations to OGR remained on the books for nearly twenty years. Theoretically, Presidents Eisenhower, Kennedy, or Johnson could have resurrected it. The OGR law was finally repealed in 1966.[166]

But, in July 1948, OGR was no more. Congressional opposition to presidentially controlled public relations had been fierce, consistent, and continuing. A political scientist studying EOP commented bitingly in 1949 that OGR was defunded because it "fell prey to congressional imperception."[167] Thus ended Roosevelt and Truman's efforts to institutionalize a presidential communications agency dedicated to public reporting. It would not be until 1969 that another effort was made to create a permanent and comprehensive White House communications organization.

This chapter has presented the final act in the fight over OGR. Congress won. It wanted to win because denying a president one of his methods of communication with the public meant diminishing his power and his ability to dominate Congress. A weaker public voice meant a weaker president. Killing OGR was one step in restoring congressional government and subordinating the president to Congress. As for public reporting, Congress's attitude seemed to be "who cares?" Reporting was not viewed as an important function of modern public administration and certainly not deserving of expending taxpayer dollars on it.

Chapter 11

Since Then, Till Now

Vestiges and Lessons

Chapter 10 described President Truman's failed effort to re-establish the Office of Government Reports (OGR) after World War II. However, he was doing this during the Eightieth Congress (1947–8), the first Republican-majority Congress since Roosevelt had been elected president in 1932. So, the same Republican Congressmen who had fiercely opposed OGR (and NEC before that), but had been unsuccessful because they were in the minority, were now in charge. With this changed political landscape, it is not surprising that Truman was unsuccessful at keeping OGR in existence. In that respect, Congress won in a showdown with the president. OGR had become a symbol of so much of the New Deal that the conservative coalition in Congress hated, including direct communication with the public instead of through Congress, information dissemination that helped institutionalize New Deal programs, and the alleged pro-Administration propaganda inherent in OGR's work.

This chapter describes subsequent efforts to institutionalize a presidential communications program, culminating in the creation of the Office of Communications in the Nixon White House. The Office of Communications is in many ways the offspring of OGR. The chapter then analyzes the three threads of the OGR story that reflect larger and significant trends in modern American government. The causes of legislative opposition to presidential communication efforts in the first half of the twentieth century help put the story of OGR's rise and fall in that larger context.

OGR III? Hoover Commission, 1947–49

Less than three months after OGR had folded, there was an explicit effort to revive it as part of the recommendations of the Hoover Commission. In 1947, President Truman had appointed a Commission to study the structure of government headed by former President Herbert Hoover. Its assignment was to make recommendations regarding the reorganization of the executive branch.[1] In late September 1948, Edward Stanley and Lawrence Sullivan submitted a report to the commission that they had been directed to prepare on *Information Services in the Executive Branch of the Government*. The report did not mention OGR. However, some of its comments and recommendations bore strong resemblance to that recently defunct agency:

- "the obligation to supply factual, unbiased, non-partisan information—this is a proper, important and highly desirable activity of the Executive Branch, one which few would oppose"
- Federal agencies "need to know the climate of local opinion in which they will operate"
- "there [should] be a central point of contact for government information services and communication groups"
- Designate in the White House an "Assistant for Federal Information, to be responsible directly to the President."[2]

Two days after Stanley and Sullivan submitted their report, senior commission staffer Don Price followed up with a memo to Chairman Hoover. Price, a former BOB official[3] was a member of the task force on the Office of the President.[4] He endorsed parts of Stanley and Sullivan's report and explicitly referred to some of the positive benefits of OGR and its field activities. In particular, he agreed with Stanley and Sullivan about the need for a presidential assistant who would have the coordinating and liaison functions OGR had had until recently. Such a staffer "should issue no publications or information himself. I think that the Office of Government Reports and the O.W.I. made their coordinating and liaison functions less effective by undertaking elaborate publications programs of their own."[5]

Price attached to that cover memo a more detailed review of the recent history of federal field coordination and government information with significant focus on the National Emergency Council (NEC) and OGR.[6] In it he noted the importance of the field coordination and government information functions in the institutionalized presidency. Price suggested that he'd like to develop "ideas regarding the type of agencies which should help the President on either of these two problems."[7] Even prior to his work on the Hoover Commission, Price had been an advocate of public reporting. In a chapter he had authored for a textbook published two years earlier, he wrote, "one of the most curious aspects of the attacks on 'bureaucracy' in recent years has been the opposition to publicity programs or to the spending of money for *reports to the public*, as if it were improper or undesirable."[8] But, a presidential role in government information did not interest Hoover[9] and Price never was permitted to plan a successor agency to OGR. Also, the aides to each of the members of the Commission reviewed the Stanley and Sullivan report, but decided not to push their principals to do anything with the report.[10]

Hoover's general attitude toward the subject of a presidential agency for government information—as well as the attitudes of the other commission members—is made clear by subsequent developments. Nothing came of the Stanley and Sullivan report. The final report of the Hoover Commission did not address government information. The closest recommendation was that the Bureau of the Budget (BOB) needed more authority to control and coordinate federal publications in order to reduce duplication and cut costs[11] and that each department should have a uniform structure of seven management officials, including an "Information and Publications Officer."[12] This latter recommendation originated from the commission's Task Force on Departmental Management. It stated "Public relations activities are important and should be so recognized."[13] A position paper recalled public administration's theory of public reporting:

> the department head has another obligation in a democracy—to keep the public informed about the activities of his agency. How far to go and what media to use in this effort present touchy issues of personal and administrative integrity. But of the basic obligation there can be little doubt.[14]

However, that language did not appear in the final report of the commission.

OGR's Legacy to Contemporary Times

Although OGR closed its doors for good on June 30, 1948, its demise was more de jure than de facto not only in the short run (see chapter 10), but in the long run as well. Many of OGR's functions have continued to this day (2005):

- The *US Government Manual* continues to be published. The Office of the Federal Register of the National Archives and Records Administration published the 2003–04 edition. Since the 1990s, its contents have been available free on the Internet.[15]
- The Ad Council continues to provide public-service campaigns for federal agencies.[16]
- The president continues to get daily news summaries prepared by his communications staff.
- The White House correspondence unit answers a broad variety of questions that are mailed in by citizens not sure to whom—specifically—to address their inquiries.
- The White House Office of Public Liaison provides information directly to the public (especially organized groups) about the programs and activities of the administration.[17]
- A DC Visitor Information Center is located in the federal Ronald Reagan International Trade Center Building at 1300 Pennsylvania Avenue (only one block east of the site of the US Information Center). It is operated by the District of Columbia Chamber of Commerce in partnership with the National Park Service.
- From 1948 to 1999 the title "United States Information Service" was revived and used to describe work of the United States Information Agency (USIA) at US cultural and information centers abroad.[18]

The de facto continuation of so many of OGR's programs affirms the literature regarding the difficulty of terminating government functions and programs even when the agencies housing them go out of existence.[19]

White House Office of Communications

One of the historical contexts for OGR is its role in the history of communications and public relations (see chapter 1). The agency's brief existence represented an early manifestation of the centrality of communications in modern society in general and the public sector in particular. Here was an organization whose primary mission was to communicate. In other words, the means had superseded the ends. Communicating with the public was important. Period. *What* was being communicated became secondary. In that respect, OGR presaged the information age, so dominant at the beginning of the twenty-first century: the Internet, 24/7/365, the Freedom of Information Act, CNN, instant communication, cell phones, wireless laptops and handhelds, wi-fi, webcasting, a homepage for every citizen, e-mail and blogging. Life became synonymous with communication. Information equaled public relations. OGR was the "early warning system" of what was to come both for society at large and for the public sector in particular.

In the public sector, perhaps the closest contemporary manifestation of OGR is the White House Office of Communications. First established by President Nixon, it was intended to "circumvent the press"[20] and disseminate through other channels information for the public about administration activities.[21] Roosevelt's OGR and other media activities (such as radio "fireside chats") were similarly oriented to bypassing the daily newspapers because of the Republican-leanings of most newspaper publishers. For presidents since Nixon, the perceived roadblocks were often the Washington press corps. Whatever the obstacle, the underlying purposes of OGR and the White House Office of Communications were nearly identical. However, in the media-saturated environment of the late twentieth and early twenty-first centuries, the methods used by the Office of Communication have usually focused largely on working with other journalistic outlets, such as local and regional newspapers that didn't have a Washington correspondent, local TV stations, etc., whereas for OGR the focus was on means of information distribution other than through reporters.

At its original conception, NEC/OGR would have been even more similar to the White House Office of Communications. In the preliminary planning for the information functions of NEC in late 1933 and early 1934, another of its activities was to be a centralized public-information bureau for the entire executive branch, severely downgrading the information offices of each cabinet department and independent agency.[22] Eventually, that proposed media-relations function was abandoned because senior presidential advisors feared such activities would inevitably lead to criticism that the agency was simply a propaganda arm of the administration. Such attacks would have the effect of undermining all the other information activities NEC would be carrying out. So, the initial plan for a media-relations function was abandoned.[23] Indeed, Roosevelt's aides were proven right, albeit beginning thirty-five years later. The first Office of Communications, of the Nixon Presidency, was described as "something of a propaganda agency."[24] Notwithstanding the criticism, since 1969, the Office of Communications has become a permanent part of White House operations, irrespective of the person serving as president or his party affiliation. Also, as long as it has existed, the Office of Communications has often been criticized—sometimes accurately—as suppressing information from being released by agencies and of putting a pro-administration spin on all its releases.[25]

The raisons d'être of the Office of Communications and OGR are practically identical. OGR's mission was concisely described by one of its senior officials as "bringing the people in closer touch with the President and the President in closer touch with the people."[26] That definition could be used equally today to describe the underlying purpose of the White House Office of Communications. The latter was portrayed shortly after it was created as "the Administration's public relations agency."[27] Stripped of the negative connotation that "PR" has in American usage, that would be an accurate term to describe the work of both OGR and the White House Office of Communications. Both were dedicated to relating the presidency to the public, of connecting the White House with the citizenry. While the primary means and techniques ended up quite different, the rationale was the same. Besides a common mission, there are some close parallels between some activities of OGR and the White House Office of Communications, notwithstanding the latter's general focus on the news media. As shown in table 11.1, at various times in the presidencies since Nixon, the assignment of tasks to the Office of Communications have largely duplicated that of OGR. Those similarities have included responding to general requests for information, sending out packets of information, summarizing news-media coverage and analyzing public opinion.

Winfield has pointed to OGR as one of the components of the Roosevelt's publicity program, which in her view had laid the "foundation for the modern presidency" and its focus on media relations.[28] She suggested that the ancestry of the communications programs of presidents since Nixon can be directly traced to FDR's information agencies and initiatives.[29]

Explaining Congressional Hostility to the Office of Government Reports

Throughout this narrative, OGR's story has been presented within the context of three analytic perspectives: that of political science regarding the balance of power between Congress and the president, the focus of communications on the emergence of the information age in American government and, thirdly, the theory promulgated by public administration on the need for public reporting in modern government. For the remaining sections of this chapter, these three foci are

Table 11.1
Comparing OGR with the White House Office of Communications

	Office of Government Reports	*Office of Communications*
Handle requests for information	United States Information Service (USIS)	Nixon: Office handled requests for information based on the Freedom of Information Act
Correspondence	USIS	Nixon: In a reorganization of responsibilities, this was assigned to Communications Director Klein
General address for people writing the government	USIS received mail sent to "Uncle Sam," P.O. Box 1, Washington, DC	Clinton: Office kept in touch directly with the people, including Web site and e-mail address
Mailing out packets of information	Field Service's distribution of *This Week in Defense*	Reagan: the Office of Public Liaison was under Communications Director Buchanan
Bypass national press by disseminating information directly to local news outlets	Field Service's mailing of *A Week in the War* to 9,000 weekly and country newspapers	All: Office did mailings to local news media outlets of administration positions, news releases, etc.
Daily summary of newspaper coverage	Division of Press Intelligence	Ford: Handled by Office of Communications
Monitoring and summarizing electronic news media coverage	Division of Press Intelligence	Nixon: Handled by Jeb Magruder, Deputy Director of Office
Special reports about public opinion and news analysis	Division of Press Intelligence's Research Unit prepared special studies and reports on news and editorial comment	Clinton: Office of Media Affairs included two News Analysis Coordinators

Sources: Office of Communications activities from Maltese, *Spin Control;* and Kumar, "Office of Communications."

pulled together to analyze in more detail the legislative dynamic that synthesized to kill OGR. By this one action, Congress was symbolically and substantively trying to:

1. reassert its central constitutional role vis-à-vis the executive branch,

2. eliminate a presidential communications infrastructure at a time when communicating was becoming increasingly central to governance and politics,
3. reject the legitimacy of public reporting as an important function in modern public administration.

Clearly, OGR's fate was determined by congressional hostility. While FDR had usually been able to maneuver around the opposition of the conservative coalition given the majority party status of the Democratic Party, Truman—facing a Republican majority Congress—couldn't. Yet, what precisely was the cause of this intense legislative antipathy? Millett blandly tried to explain congressional opposition as OGR being "too 'subjective' and too 'political' to command much enthusiasm from Congress."[30] Yet, this observation hardly comes to grips with any specific institutional imperatives that had been triggered to prompt such intense, continuing and effective hostility.

Certainly, congressional opposition to OGR was partly motivated by partisanship of Republicans opposing a Democratic president as well as ideological differences reflected in the bi-partisan coalition of congressional conservatives philosophically opposed to FDR's expansion of federal government activities.[31] However, partisanship and the conservative coalition were not the sole factors driving congressional opposition to OGR. For example, in 1943, when Congress severely restricted the domestic activities of OWI (essentially its OGR components), the Democratic Party was the majority party in both houses. Conversely, in 1947–8, a Republican-majority Senate tried twice to maintain OGR while the Republican-majority House refused.

Generally, Congress has consistently been hostile to public-relations activities of executive-branch agencies.[32] Marshall Dimock and Gladys Dimock described this as a permanent state of "legislative nervousness," prompted by institutional fears of the impact of effective agency public relations.[33] This generic opposition to agency public information activities certainly contributed to congressional hostility to OGR. Criticizing unnecessary government spending tends to be an applause line that both Democrats and Republicans feel free to pursue and that both Democratic and Republican constituencies tend to approve of. That made OGR a big, fat target for members of both parties. Ridiculing self-serving publicity, flacks on the government payroll and the cost of printing reports that nobody reads are effective generic political attacks. When such public-relations programs exist as part of larger "line" departments, they tend to have less visibility and less likely to be targeted for political attacks. OGR was just the opposite.

All it did was public relations. It had no other mission than the dissemination and collection of information. This was its political Achilles heel.

The Struggle for Ascendancy: Congress versus the President

Roosevelt pursued his New Deal revolution in the basic role of government in face of a conservative Congress clinging to a nineteenth-century view of a small and passive executive branch.[34] Calvin Coolidge, who had concluded his presidency only four years before Roosevelt began his, had aptly depicted that perspective when he said approvingly "if the Federal Government should go out of existence, the common run of people would not detect the difference in the affairs of their daily life for a considerable length of time."[35]

Congress was largely unsuccessful at stopping the deluge of the emerging imperial presidency. But the conservative coalition identified public-relations programs as one of the chinks in Roosevelt's armor. Here was one activity that could be used to prevail over the White House. It could then serve as a battering ram to restore the status quo ante, of a dominant Congress and a weaker president. OGR's political weakness due to its public reporting mission helps explain the tepid defenses that pro-FDR Democratic members of Congress articulated to support the agency. They certainly did not want to fall into a political trap of supposedly defending expenditure of tax dollars on public relations. Supporters of OGR knew the political trap they faced. If they defended OGR, then they would be accused of supporting unnecessary government spending and government propaganda programs. No one wanted to hand this effective attack line to his or her opponent in the next election. So, none could feel safe politically articulating a strong defense of the informational mission of OGR. In the abstract, the agency's services might sound reasonable, but when confronted with fierce criticisms of waste and flackery, public opinion would surely be more likely to side with OGR's critics rather than its (semisilent) supporters. For example, each time an OGR representative testified before a congressional committee, he or she would emphasize that the bulk of informational requests it received were from Congress. In that case, one would expect that Members of Congress would therefore want to preserve a service that helped them look good to their constituents. Yet, these hundreds of satisfied "clients" failed to speak up when OGR was criticized and threatened with extinction. Clearly, the political math on Capitol Hill was that the benefit derived from OGR was less than the political risk and cost that would occur from publicly defending the agency. Richard MacCann observed this dynamic when he examined congressional treatment of the US Film Service:

> It had friends in general, but no special friends. It was part of the New Deal, but no particular part. It was simply a publicity outfit. It was possible, then, to strike at the New Deal through the Film Service without actually striking down any substantive program of the New Deal or injuring any noticeably important special interests.[36]

So, from the perspective of Congress, OGR and other public-relations programs were a venue where imbalance between the Roosevelt presidency and Congress could be righted. And once traditional relationships were re-established in this one area, then perhaps other dominos would become vulnerable, too.

The OGR story is not merely an historical curiosity, nor is it an anachronism of bygone days. Rather, it was merely one skirmish in the ongoing struggle between the legislative and executive branches over predominance, a conflict that continues to this day. These conflicts occur even when the same party controls the White House and Capitol Hill. For example, during the Bush II presidency, the Republican-controlled Congress fought with him over the relaxation of media-ownership rules by the Federal Communications Commission and the growth of the federal deficit.

Public Reporting as a Threat to Congressional Ties with Constituents

The significant element of the OGR story is that of a new activity in the executive branch, public reporting. Public reporting, as envisioned by public administration theorists, would have an unintended but major political consequence. It would destroy the traditional monopoly that Congress had on direct contacts with the citizenry. From their institutional perspective, many legislators believed it was their duty to hold administrative agencies accountable and then report back to the people on government activities. In their view, the executive branch should not be communicating directly with the public. That's what US Senators and Congressmen were supposed to do. For example, during a debate about OGR, Congressman Clare Hoffman wondered, "If this is a representative Republic, why should it not be an Office of Government Reports of the Congress or of the Government? Why make it the tail on the kite of the Executive?"[37] Sydney Weinberg concluded that congressional opposition to OWI's domestic branch (essentially a continuation of OGR) was because it "brought the Administration into direct contact with the public without the traditional intermediaries of *themselves* and private media."[38]

The institutional imperative that contributed to legislative opposition to OGR was not particular to this agency, but rather was part of an ongoing legislative hostility to active information programs by federal agencies. Harold Gosnell suggested that the principle of separation of powers was at the heart of congressional opposition to OGR. "Under the presidential form of government with its separation of powers and jealousy between the executive and legislative branches it is difficult for the executive to maintain conspicuous information services."[39] When reviewing the history of the US Film Service, Richard MacCann agreed, noting that congressional opposition to a federal executive agency producing films was based on its constitutional role. Therefore, its hostility to all federal public-information programs is a permanent one, independent of shifting partisan and ideological majorities.[40] As a generalization, J. A. R. Pimlott observed, a member of Congress "in his constituency . . . has traditionally been the chief spokesman of the central government and the chief medium of communication with the capital."[41] Similarly, Leonard White noted that members of Congress see themselves as "the representatives of opinion" and therefore are hostile to publicity programs of administrative agencies.[42] This attitude, called "overhead democracy"[43] reflected a simplistic view of democratic theory. In this elected-official-centric and mechanistic view

> democratic control should run through a single line from the representatives of the people to all those who exercised power in the name of the government. The line ran from the people to their representatives in the Presidency and the Congress, and from there to the President as chief executive, then to departments, then to bureaus, then to lesser units, and so on to the fingertips of administration.[44]

In this model, there is no role for executive agencies to report directly to the public; rather they are expected to report to elected officials who, in turn, report to the citizenry. For legislators intent in promoting the institutional interests of the legislative branch, OGR symbolized just about everything that was wrong with the immense growth of public administration and executive public relations during

Roosevelt's presidency. Pfiffner directly attributed this perspective as the explanation for the persistent congressional attacks on OGR: "Members of Congress believe that they secure political advantage by disseminating information about Washington *through their own offices* and that they do not want this advantage to be transferred from them to the White House."[45] For example, Congressman F. Edward Hebert (D-LA) said at a 1942 hearing on OGR's proposed information center:

> essentially our constituents, coming from our districts . . . usually come to the office of their Congressman, with whom they are acquainted, and expect him to give them that service, and as a matter of fact, I think we agree that is what we are paid for, to serve them and to give them every service we can.[46]

Congressman John Jennings Jr. (R-TN) was quoted as saying that OGR was unneeded because members of Congress were fully capable of informing the citizens of where to go to get government work.[47] From this perspective, OGR was unwanted by Congress since it was seen as threatening to supplant the tradition role of legislators as the channel of communication with the public at large.

Public Reporting Equals Public Support?

One of the reasons for congressional hostility to OGR was based on fears that executive agencies would use external relations efforts to generate public support for the agency in ways that would, in turn, pressure Congress and limit its freedom of action. OGR's director, Lowell Mellett, tried to meet this argument head on by affirming that OGR was an information agency, not a propaganda agency. He emphasized that Congress was "the national policy-making branch of the government."[48] Yet, since the difference between propaganda and information is in the eyes of the beholder, his assurances were not persuasive to many members of Congress (see section on "A Propaganda Agency?" in chapter 6).

The battle between the legislative and executive branches over the fate of OGR was but one of the many instances during the New Deal and World War II that demonstrated the difficulty of separating public-relations activities aimed at public reporting from those that help develop public support for the agency and its programs. Herbert Simon, Donald Smithburg, and Victor Thompson acknowledged that public-relations efforts by administrative agencies "almost inevitably veer over beyond what is necessary to create mere public understanding" and have the effect of creating public support for the agency to survive and withstand legislative attacks.[49] The continuing validity in the twenty-first century of the connection between effective agency public relations and reporting with public support has been noted by Janet Weiss and by William Gormley and Steven Balla.[50] In fact, during the Roosevelt years, public administration theorists suggested that it was acceptable for administrators to use their publicity programs to generate support for their agencies and programs. For example, in 1935 Pendleton Herring asserted that it was now legitimate for public administrators to use public-relations efforts "to secure the active support or a favorable attitude on the part of the general public or of some particular group."[51] Following a survey of publicity experts in the federal government, James McCamy four years later created a theoretical framework of six objectives of administrative publicity, including "getting approval from the large public."[52] He, approvingly, connected public reporting with obtaining public support. Public administrators should "take to the citizen an explanation of why certain public policies are adopted, will show him the benefits to be gained from certain practices, and *will enlist his support for public agencies working in his interest.*"[53] Certainly, FDR was explicit in viewing OGR as a way to bypass Congress and generate support from the public for his New Deal programs. According to A. J. Wann:

> Roosevelt thought it was highly important that people should know what was taking place and should have a reasonably complete picture as to how the New Deal program was progressing. Accurate and comprehensive explanations of the various measures, Roosevelt felt, would build support from the public for what was being done. Consequently, he visualized the National Emergency Council and the subordinate state and county branches to be created under its jurisdiction as an unexcelled channel for the wide dissemination of information to the people.[54]

This institutional motivation for legislative opposition to executive public-information programs is indicated by some of the congressional descriptions of OGR. Congressman Everett Dirksen described it as "a propaganda agency pure and simple."[55] According to Congressman Frank O. Horton (R-WY), with OGR "the danger to Democratic processes is very great if the Congress is to be surreptitiously influenced by sentiment manufactured through the distribution of political propaganda designed to affect the deliberations of this body and the legislation enacted here."[56] Similarly, Congressman Earl Michener (R-MI) zeroed in on the uses of public relations to build support: "if a new agency is set up by act of Congress or by Executive order, that new agency sells itself to the Government, to the people, through this propaganda agency."[57] Longtime critic of public-relations spending in general and OGR in particular, Congressman Richard Wigglesworth (R-MA) said that

> the enormous governmental propaganda set-up is not only a gross waste of the people's money, but, over and beyond that, makes for the destruction of the proper exercise of the legislative functions of the Government. . . . [This] leads inevitably to the domination of Congress and the people by the executive branch of the Government. Government work, efficiently performed, needs no paid propaganda campaigns.[58]

Notwithstanding these indications of congressional opposition to public-relations programs having the effect of generating support for the agency, public administration theory continued after OGR's demise to endorse such activities and was blind to the political and institutional implications. In 1947, an article in *Public Personnel Review* approvingly noted the public relations value of annual reports in "building understanding, good will, and public support."[59] A few years later, George Graham presented a definition of public administration for educational purposes. It included a seemingly noncontroversial assessment that "achieving and maintaining support for sound public policies is as much a part of public administration in a democracy as is the execution of policies."[60] The 1953 edition of John Pfiffner and Vance Presthus' long-running textbook included a chapter entitled "Building Public Support."[61] Marshall Dimock suggested that communication efforts by public administrators to build program support were not only legitimate, but "in many ways the most interesting and productive part of any executive's responsibilities."[62] The perspective of bureaucratic politics led Francis Rourke to observe:

> Because public opinion is ultimately the only legitimate sovereign in a democratic society, an agency which seeks first a high standing with the public can reasonably expect to have all other things added unto it in the way of legislative and executive support. Power gives power, in administration as elsewhere, and once an agency has established a secure base with the public, it cannot easily be trifled with by political officials in either the legislative or executive branch.[63]

However, given how controversial an agency's efforts to obtain public support can be with the legislative branch, the endorsement of such support-seeking activities has largely disappeared from the literature in recent decades.

In summary, congressional zeal to kill OGR encompassed multiple interrelated motivations. OGR symbolized the emergence of the modern presidency overshadowing the traditionally principal role that Congress had played up to that point. Yet, unlike some other elements of the modern presidency that Congress could not roll back, OGR was a politically weak and vulnerable target. Fighting it and eventually killing it was a statement not only about the agency itself but also a message about how Congress reacted to its diminished role as the twentieth century progressed. OGR was an early warning system to Congress of the coming communications revolution. Congress still had some advantages over the president in the balance of power between the two branches at that time. But this was merely a stumble toward the reshaped relationship where presidents have overwhelming lead over Congress.

Public reporting as a new activity in public administration threatened the traditional role of Congress with the citizenry. Congress was attempting to protect its role in communicating to the public-at-large about the operations of the federal government. This approach, called "overhead democracy," viewed elected officials as the primary information channel between citizens and government. Congress understood that a federal agency with high levels of support from the public—obtained through effective public reporting programs—was relatively immune to congressional control and cutbacks. Publicity led to a popular image and that led to freedom from legislative threats. In short, administrative efforts at survival could be choked off through legislative restrictions on direct public reporting. Weinberg summarized congressional hostility with the observation that "this field publicity proved particularly repugnant to Congress, for when an official information service attempts to influence opinion in favor of the Administration, the closer it comes to the people, the greater the threat to individual Congressmen."[64]

Reporting in the Aftermath of the Office of Government Reports

Chapter 1 contained a brief review of the literature on government reporting when OGR was created. These writings were emphatic about the legitimacy and imperative for governments in the era of large administrative apparatuses to report to the public on their record of activity. It appears that as the OGR story percolated through public administration practitioners and academics, what happened to OGR contributed to a gradual shift of attention away for public reporting. The historical "lesson" from these events helped focus a perception that public reporting can be controversial and raise the ire of the legislative branch. Whether directly or indirectly, public administration textbooks referred to the public reporting obligation of the government manager less and less, until the topic had largely disappeared from public administration pedagogy except municipal administration's continued interest in annual reports.

OGR did not disappear immediately from public administration literature. As an effort to implement the public administrator's obligation to engage in public reporting, it was still being mentioned after its demise. Albert Lepawsky's 1949 textbook featured a four-page description of OGR's mission and activities while noting that it "was discontinued."[65] Subsequent printings of the book, as late as 1965, retained the OGR section intact.[66] Some other post-1948 general public administration texts and overviews deemed the rise and fall of OGR important to describe and analyze. John Millett's 1959 volume reviewed OGR's history and congressional opposition to it.[67] As late as 1964, Dimock and Dimock included a two-page summary of the life of the agency in their section on public relations, still citing Mellett's 1941 article in *Public Administration Review*.[68] Similarly, discussion of public administration's support for public reporting did not evaporate immediately from the post-OGR pedagogic literature. Even while Congress was in the midst of killing the agency in 1947, a handbook edited by Simon continued to consider it such an important element of municipal administration that it contained a separate chapter on the subject. The chapter provided an expansive definition of public reporting, including "talks before citizen groups, exhibits and demonstrations, motion pictures, radio programs, and printed reports."[69] In the 1950s and 60s, textbooks, handbooks and research-based literature continued focusing on the public reporting duty of the public administrator.[70]

During the same time, practitioners continued engaging in public reporting and experimenting with new approaches, again mostly on the municipal level. San Diego's decision in 1951 to use a motion picture to present its annual report to the citizens was deemed such an important development that *Public Administration Review* devoted an article to it.[71] In 1962, Rosen noted that local governments were experimenting with newer media to accomplish public reporting, such as slides, movies and tapes.[72] In the early 1960s, the Defense Department experimented with annual film report "because the film, unlike a written annual report, can be made available to schools, religious groups, film libraries, and military installations, and it is seen and understood where perhaps a written report would never be looked at."[73] Congress, predictably, refused to fund additional editions of the annual film report.[74] In the mid-70s, the municipal annual report continued to be a "mainstay" of public reporting, but was criticized as needing "more attractive, more readable" formats.[75] However, there was a clear trend pointing to the demise of public reporting as an important subject for public administration theory and practice. In the final decades of the twentieth century, public reporting had largely disappeared from public administration pedagogy and practitioner literature (except annual municipal reports) along with most other attention to public relations. By the 1980s and 90s, public administration education no longer addressed public reporting as a significant topic for government managers in training.[76] Similarly, two de novo encyclopedic overviews of public administration contained no entries in their original print versions regarding public reporting or related subjects.[77]

It is impossible to prove that this diminished focus on public reporting was largely due to OGR. However, it is reasonable to observe the distinct difference in public reporting literature before and after OGR. Before OGR, public reporting was widely emphasized in public administration theory and practice. After OGR's demise, this topic slowly but consistently disappeared from the literature. In that respect, the history of OGR is in full harmony with the trends in the public administration theory and practice. Therefore, whether the OGR case study is a cause or an illustration of a trend in public reporting becomes a relatively minor distinction.

Only a few writers have recently sought to revive the focus on public reporting. In 1985, Heise suggested a new model of public communication, one that would no longer rely exclusively on the news media to inform the public. Instead "government officials would seek not only to communicate with the general public through the mass media but would be equally as concerned to reach various specialized publics and individual citizens . . . through alternative communication channels."[78] In the 1990s, James Garnett similarly emphasized the increasing importance for public administrators to communicate directly with their constituencies.[79] Hindy Schachter proposed reviving the model of reporting used nearly a century earlier, consisting of three types of public reports: a document reporting to the public on the activities of the municipality as a whole, and then reports by every department as well as by each departmental bureau.[80] Robert Behn suggested that one of the duties of a city manager was to regularly report directly to the citizenry about the municipality's goals and performance. This should be done frequently, he suggested, by "month, quarter, year, and decade."[81]

Some contemporary examples from practitioners indicate a modest renewed interest in public reporting in the United States and internationally. The Government Finance Officers Association promotes the goal of public reporting by presenting an annual award "popular annual financial reporting."[82] A report about trends in First World countries noted the potential of the Internet to facilitate direct public reporting.[83] For the emerging democracies in Eastern Europe, Bart Édes identified informing the public directly as one of the seven basic functions of any administrative agency's external communications activities.[84] From the academic perspective, this author observed in 1999, "there is no change in the public relations obligation of the public administrator to keep the public informed" and noted a reinvigoration of "public administration's early attention to direct public reporting."[85]

By the middle of the first decade of the twenty-first century, some governments were experimenting with e-reporting, i.e., using the Internet to report to the citizenry.[86] A significant development recently occurred with the reestablishment of the connection between reporting and citizen participation in policymaking. A report by the Organisation for Economic Co-operation and Development in 2001 stated:

> governments increasingly realize that they will not be able to conduct and effectively implement policies, as good as they may be, if their citizens do not understand and support them. Thus, governments are looking for new or improved models and approaches to inform, consult and engage citizens in the policy-making process. Such efforts to introduce elements of participatory democracy are not intended to replace, but to complement, representative democracy.[87]

This review of the "best practices" of thirty leading Western democratic countries with market-based economies suggested that twenty-first-century efforts to strengthen democracy required a linked and sequential three-stage process. First, governments should engage in reporting, i.e., one-way information dissemination to contribute to an informed public opinion. Second, governments should engage in a two-way consultation process with citizens in order to obtain feedback from the public. Finally, having contributed to citizen awareness and obtained reaction from the public, the last stage calls for active citizen participation in public policymaking. In this way, a true partnership could be built between the citizenry and their democratic governments.[88] Roosevelt's vision for OGR echoes faintly in these recommendations, with a legacy that continues to be valid more than half a century later.

Notes

Preface

1. Lepawsky, *Administration*, 560–3.
2. Mellett, "Office of Government Reports."
3. Reprinted from *Public Relations Review*, Volume 28, Mordecai Lee, "The Federal Public Relations Administration: History's Near Miss," 87–98, Copyright 2002, with permission from Elsevier.

Chapter 1: Introduction and Overview

1. Clinton, *Public Papers*, 79.
2. 55 Stat. 247–8.
3. McDonald, *Federal Relief Administration and the Arts*; McKinzie, *New Deal for Artists*; and Penkower, *Federal Writers Project*.
4. Knepper, *Greenbelt, Maryland*.
5. MacCann, *The People's Films*; and Snyder, *Pare Lorentz*.
6. Relyea, *Executive Office of the President*; Sander, *Staff for the President*; and Hobbs, *Behind the President*.
7. Clawson, *New Deal Planning*; and Warken, *A History of the National Resources Planning Board*.
8. Venn, *New Deal*; and Badger, *New Deal*.
9. Koppes and Black, *Hollywood Goes to War*; Steele, *Propaganda*; Wann, *President as Chief Administrator*; Winfield, *FDR and the News Media*; and Winkler, *Politics of Propaganda*.
10. Childs, "Public Information and Opinion"; Macmahon, "Future Organizational Pattern of the Executive Branch"; Rossiter, "Constitutional Significance of the Executive Office of the President"; and Shils, "Note on Governmental Research on Attitudes and Morale."
11. Kiely, "The Evolution of Federal Field Coordinating Agencies"; Mackay, "Domestic Operations of OWI"; Pope, "Senatorial Baron"; and Weinberg, "Wartime Propaganda."
12. Shull and Shaw, *Explaining Congressional-Presidential Relations*; and Sinclair, "Hostile Partners."

13. Gould, *Modern American Presidency.*

14. Wilson, *Congressional Government.*

15. Wills, *Necessary Evil.*

16. U.S. General Accounting Office, "Chronology."

17. Stephen Labaton, "F.C.C. Plan to Ease Curbs on Big Media," *New York Times*, Sept. 17, 2003, A1, C15; and Jube Shiver Jr., "Rebuffed but Resolute," *Los Angeles Times*, Aug. 25, 2003, C1.

18. Kurtz, *Spin Cycle*; and Gould, *Modern American Presidency.*

19. Winfield, "New Deal Publicity Operation."

20. Maltese, *Spin Control.*

21. Weiner, *Human Use of Human Beings.*

22. Cutlip, *Unseen Power*; and *Public Relations History.*

23. McLuhan, *Understanding Media*, chapter 1.

24. Fuhrman, *Publicity Stunt!*

25. Hiebert, *Courtier to the Crowd*; Tye, *Father of Spin*; and Marchand, *Creating the Corporate Soul.*

26. Barry, *PR Power*; Ewen, *PR!*; Jackall and Hirota, *Image Makers*; Boorstin, *Image*; Levine, *Branded World*; and Aronson, *Hype.*

27. Delorme and Fedler, "Journalists' Hostility Toward Public Relations"; Mallinson, *Public Lies and Private Truths*; and Stauber and Rampton, *Toxic Sludge Is Good for You.*

28. Lee, "Public Information in Government Organizations," especially 190–5.

29. Daniels, *Creating Sustainable Community Programs*; Simonsen and Robbins, *Citizen Participation in Resource Allocation*; Lindstrom and Nie, "Public Participation and Agency Planning"; and King and Stivers, *Government Is Us.*

30. Moynihan, "Normative and Instrumental Perspectives on Public Participation."

31. Milner, *Civic Literacy*; Bennett and Bennett, *Living with Leviathan*; and Price, Cappella and Nir, "Does Disagreement Contribute to More Deliberative Opinion?"

32. Lee, "Intersectoral Differences in Public Affairs."

33. Wilson, "The Study of Administration," 216–7.

34. Beyle, *Governmental Reporting*, 6–7.

35. Kilpatrick, *Reporting Municipal Government*; and Williams, "Measuring Government in the Early Twentieth Century," 647–8.

36. Cooke, *Our Cities Awake*, 197, 204.

37. Ridley, "Municipal Reports"; Ridley, "Appraising Municipal Reports;" and Ridley, "Municipal Reporting Taken Seriously."

38. Simon, "Inter-City Contests;" Simon, "Municipal Reporting" (1938); "Municipal Reporting" (1939); and Lee, "Is There Anything New Under the Sun?"

39. Simon and Ridley, "Trends in Municipal Reporting," 466, italics in original.

40. Pfiffner, *Public Administration* (1935), 472–87.

41. White, *City Manager*; and *Trends in Public Administration.*

42. Foner, *Reconstruction*, 170.

Chapter 2: Origins

1. Jackall and Hirota, *Image Makers*, 11–35; Vaughn, *Holding Fast the Inner Lines*; Mock and Larson, *Words That Won the War*; Creel, *How We Advertised America*; and Committee on Public Information, *Creel Report*.

2. Weinberg, Wartime Propaganda in a Democracy, Ph.D. dissertation, 1.

3. Winkler, *Politics of Propaganda*, 3.

4. At that time, the position he held was much more significant than it is today (2005). There was only one assistant secretary and there were neither deputy nor associate secretaries. Also, the Navy was then a freestanding cabinet department.

5. Fleming, *New Dealers' War*, 115.

6. *U.S. at War*, 211.

7. Winfield, "The New Deal Publicity Operation," 42.

8. Roosevelt, *Public Papers, 1933*, 487.

9. Seligman, "Introduction," xiii–xxix.

10. Roosevelt, *Public Papers, 1933*, 515.

11. Roosevelt, *Complete Presidential Press Conferences*, Vol. 2, Items 510–2.

12. Roosevelt, *Public Papers, 1933*, 530–1.

13. Seligman and Cornwell, *New Deal Mosaic*, 483–4.

14. High, "You Can't Beat the Government," 7.

15. Letter to Frank J. Walker from Miss Mary W. Dewson, Dec. 9, 1933, Box 1000, RG 44.

16. Dewson, Mary, "Rough Plan for Organization of the Information Service," Box 1000, RG 44.

17. *Message of the President Transmitting the Budget, 1935*, 48.

18. Seligman and Cornwall, *New Deal Mosaic*, 48–55.

19. Glaser claimed that the precedent for the *Manual* had been an informational bulletin briefly published by the U.S. Bureau of Efficiency (*Administrative Procedure*, 140).

20. Roosevelt, *Public Papers, 1934*, 81, 83; and "President Demands Ban on Politics by Heads of Emergency Relief," *New York Times*, Feb. 3, 1934, 1–2.

21. USIS was not the first information service for the public-at-large in the federal government. From 1920 to 1933, the U.S. Bureau of Efficiency maintained an Information Service to respond to general inquiries from citizens (Lee, "First Federal Public Information").

22. NEC, Press release: "U.S. Information Service to Assist Washington Visitors," March 14, 1934, Box 1000, RG 44; and "Information Service on Relief Organized in Capital to Direct Applicants for Loans," *New York Times*, March 15, 1934, 13.

23. "Federal Groups Identified for Visitors; Functions of All Organizations Diagramed," *New York Times*, March 25, 1934, Section II, 4; and *Washington Post*, March 15, 1934, quoted in Joint Committee on Reduction, *Reduction: Hearings*, Part 4, 1127.

24. "Capital Keeps Tab on Press," *New York Times*, April 19, 1936, Section IV, 7.

25. Helton, *Preliminary Inventory of OGR*, 11.

26. Prepared Statement of NEC Executive Director Mellett, May 25, 1939. In House Appropriations Committee, *Work Relief and Relief for FY 1940: Hearings*, 286.

27. Form letter to department and agency heads from the President, July 1, 1938, Mellett Papers.

28. Memo to the president from the executive director, Oct. 24, 1935, OF 788.

29. Memo to the president from the acting executive director, Aug. 24, 1936, OF 788; Telegrams to state directors from Leggett, NEC Executive Assistant, Aug. 28, 1936, OF 788.

30. Memo of Conversation Between Mellett and Sidney Hyman, Aug. 8, 1949, Washington, DC. Mellett File, FDR Memorial Foundation Papers, 9.

31. Roosevelt, *Complete Presidential Press Conferences*, Vol. 11, Items 398–9.

32. N.E.C. Employees June 1, 1936, PCAM Papers.

33. Untitled internal planning documents, Box 889, RG 44.

34. House Appropriations Committee, *Work Relief and Relief for FY 1940: Hearings*, 293.

35. Fesler, *Area and Administration*, 57.

36. Memo to the president from the acting executive director, Dec. 29, 1937, Box 890, RG 44.

37. Leggett, Eugene S., Outline of Organization, Aug. 2, 1937, 4, NEC file, Rosenman Papers.

38. Memo to Eugene S. Leggett from Harriet Root, June 9, 1934, Box 1000, RG 44.

39. Seligman and Cornwell, *New Deal Mosaic*, 453.

40. "Information Post Is Run by Women," *New York Times*, May 27, 1937, Section VI, 6; Associated Press, "Nation's Questions Are Answered by Woman," *New York Times*, Aug. 1, 1937, 19; "Woman Answers Nation's Queries," *New York Times*, Sept. 29, 1937, Section VI, 7; "U.S. Information Service," n.d., Box 1000, RG 44; "Notes upon a survey of NEC," PCAM Papers; Leggett, Eugene S., "Outline of Organization, Activities, and Functions," Aug. 2, 1937, 4, NEC file, Rosenman Papers; and House Appropriations Committee, *Emergency Relief Appropriations Act of 1938: Hearings*, 604.

41. "Woman Answers Nation's Queries," *New York Times*, Sept. 29, 1937, Section VI, 7.

42. "New York Office, U.S. Information Service, May 1936" monthly report, Box 996, RG 44.

43. NEC, *Report of Operations, 1938*, 3, Box 1865, RG 44.

44. Graves, "Public Reporting," 226.

45. "New Deal Agencies Described in Manual," *New York Times*, July 19, 1934, 5.

46. "New Gazette to Tell Public How to Get Aid," *New York Times*, Dec. 24, 1934, 11; Seligman and Cornwell, *New Deal Mosaic*, 53; "Special Notice: U.S. Government Manual," Dec. 14, 1934, OF 788; Untitled memo by acting executive director, Jan. 28, 1936, OF 788.

47. OF 788.

48. NEC, *Report of Operation, 1938*, 17–8.

49. McCamy, *Government Publicity*, 150.

50. Barry, *Rising Tide*, 273, 287–9.

51. Adelaide Handy, "Government Bureau Executive Is Calm on Issue of Censorship," *New York Times*, April 20, 1941, Section II, 4. Blackburn's friends and associates referred to her based on the initials of her first and middle name, "KC." She signed informal documents "Kayse Blackburn."

52. Memo to the president from NEC Executive Assistant, Sept. 1, 1936, 1, Box 890, RG 44.

53. Letter to Civil Service Commission from C. E. MacEachran, chief clerk, Department of State, April 4, 1933, Blackburn Papers. Moley was one of the original members of Roosevelt's famed "brain trust." However, within a year he broke with FDR and became a vigorous critic.

54. Note to Commissioners Campbell and Dell from Wales, April 6, 1933, Blackburn Papers.

55. Letter to Howe from P. F. Allen, acting chief clerk, Department of State, May 22, 1935, OF 1275.

56. Letter to P. F. Allen from M. A. Durand, secretary to Howe, May 25, 1935, OF 1275.

57. Adelaide Handy, "Government Bureau Executive Is Calm on Issue of Censorship," *New York Times*, April 20, 1941, Section II, 4.

58. "Capital Keeps Tab on Press," *New York Times*, April 19, 1936, Section IV, 7; House Appropriations Committee, *Emergency Relief Appropriations Act of 1938: Hearings*, 608; Senate Appropriations Committee, *Work Relief and Public Works Appropriations Act of 1938: Hearings*, 302–4; NEC, *Report of Operations, 1938*, 4–5, 20; House Appropriations Committee, *Work Relief and Relief for FY 1940: Hearings*, 294–5.

59. Letter to Howe from Kayse Blackburn, Oct. 20, 1933, OF 1275.

60. Letter to K. Blackburn from Louis Howe, secretary to the president, Oct. 25, 1933, OF 1275.

61. Letter to M. LeHand, secretary to the president, from K. C. Blackburn, Nov. 8, 1934, OF 1275.

62. Letter to K. C. Blackburn from M. Le Hand, Nov. 13, 1934, OF 1275.

63. Memo for Eugene S. Leggett from FDR, Feb. 19, 1937, OF 1275. Based on the subsequent operating levels of the division, the president indeed conveyed how much he liked the work of the division and that he hoped it would not be seriously harmed by the budget cuts.

64. Memo for Lyle Alverson from Stephen Early, assistant secretary to the president, March 12, 1936, OF 788; House Appropriations Committee, *Work Relief and Relief for FY 1940: Hearings*, 348–9.

65. House Appropriations Committee, *Work Relief and Relief for FY 1940: Hearings*, 348–51; Senate Appropriations Committee, *Work Relief and Public Works Appropriations Act of 1939: Hearings*, 250.

66. Memo to Mellett from Bea Andreen, Aug. 11, 1939, Box 889, RG 44.

67. NEC, *Report of Operations, 1938*, 10–1; and memo from Mellett regarding U.S. Government Reports, Aug. 14, 1939, Box 889, RG 44.

68. Snyder, *Pare Lorentz*, 21–78; MacCann, *People's Films*, 56–86.

69. *Budget of the U.S., 1940*, 68.

70. Letter to Mellett from President Roosevelt, Aug. 13, 1938, OF 788.

71. Box 889, RG 44.

72. Letter to Mellett from the president, Sept. 20, 1938, OF 788.

73. Letter to Mellett from the president, Jan. 12, 1939, Entry 78, Box 889, RG 44; letter Studebaker from Mercey, U.S. Film Service, June 28, 1939, Box 1867, RG 44; Senate Appropriations Committee, *Work Relief and Public Works Appropriations Act of 1939: Hearings*, 250–4; and House Appropriations Committee, *Work Relief and Relief for FY 1940: Hearings*, 314, 351.

74. *Directory of U.S. Government Films*, Dec. 1938, U.S. Film Service, Box 1865, RG 44; NEC, *Report of Operations, 1938*, 6–10; and House Appropriations Committee, *Work Relief and Relief for FY 1940: Hearings*, 295–6.

75. Memo to the president from James W. Rowe Jr., Aug. 1, 1940, OF 788.

76. Snyder, *Pare Lorentz*, 79–144; and MacCann, *People's Films*, 87–103.

77. Roosevelt, *Public Papers, 1935*, 253–4 and *1937*, 356–7, 552–3; and *Federal Register* 3 (June 6, 1938), 1356.

78. Roosevelt, *Complete Presidential Press Conferences*, Vol. 11, Item 398.

79. 52 Stat. 810.

80. *Journal of the Executive Proceedings*, Vol. 80, 258.

81. Ickes, *Secret Diary*, 375. Ickes eventually soured on Mellett, when Mellett opposed the push by Ickes and other internationalists before Pearl Harbor for more overt Administration domestic propaganda in favor of the US intervening on the side of Great Britain.

Chapter 3: Planning a Presidential Communications Agency, 1936–39

1. For a summary of its work, see Arnold, *Making the Managerial Presidency*, 93–117.

2. "Notes upon a Survey of NEC," PCAM Papers.

3. Fesler, "Brownlow Committee." Fesler went on to have a distinguished career as a political scientist, retiring from Yale as Alfred Cowles Professor Emeritus of Government in the 1990s.

4. Letter to Alverson from NEC Georgia State Director, July 28, 1936, Box 1003, RG 44.

5. "Comment," n.d., Box 1003, RG 44; and correspondence with Fesler, June 20, 2002, author's files.

6. Harris, J. P., Confidential Memo on NEC, Aug. 28, 1936, 8, PCAM Papers. Harris subsequently had a very successful career as a political scientist at UC-Berkeley.

7. Ibid., 29.

8. President's Committee on Administrative Management (PCAM), *Report*, 19, 60.

9. Summary of meeting with the president, May 3, 1939, Smith Papers.

10. "Financial Management, Tentative Outline," n.d., 2, PCAM Papers.

11. Note on style: *italics* indicates adding wording, ~~strikethroughs~~ indicate deleted material.

12. Tentative Draft of the Report, Dec. 18, 1936, 60, PCAM Papers.

13. PCAM, *Report*, 20.

14. Ibid., 54; and Tentative Draft of the Report, Dec. 22, 1936, 59, PCAM Papers.

15. PCAM, *Report*, 19.

16. Letter to the author from James W. Fesler, Aug. 1, 2001, author's files.

17. Fesler, "Executive Management."

18. Emmerich, *Federal Organization and Administrative Management*, 208.

19. Roosevelt, *Public Papers, 1938*, 179; and Polenberg, *Reorganizing Roosevelt's Government*.

20. Talese, *Kingdom and the Power*, 226.

21. *Public Opinion Quarterly* later evolved into a purely academic and heavily quantitative journal.

22. Arthur Krock, "President Expands Emergency Council," *New York Times*, Dec. 20, 1933, 4; and "In Washington: Events Suggest Need of a Bureau of Explanation," *New York Times*, Feb. 20, 1934, 20.

23. Krock, "Press vs. Government," 46.

24. Polenberg, *Reorganizing*; and Brownlow, *Passion for Anonymity*, 413–4.

25. This was only the second time Congress approved a "legislative veto." It became increasingly popular with Congress in the 1970s. In 1983, the Supreme Court ruled in *INS v. Chadha* that the legislative veto was unconstitutional because it reversed legislative and executive functions.

26. 53 Stat. 1423–30.

27. When Smith was dictating a summary of that meeting, he uncharacteristically added a personal observation about Roosevelt: "The knowledge of the details of the Federal establishment on the part of the president impressed me during this conference as being nothing short of amazing" (Summary of meeting with the president, April 26, 1939, Smith Papers).

28. The demise of President Carter's zero-based budgeting (ZBB) also demonstrates this.

29. House, *Message from the President on Federal Government's Handling of Work-Relief*, H. Doc. 270, 7.

30. Summary of Daily Activities, April 27, 1939, Smith Papers.

31. Summary of meeting with the president, May 3, 1939, Smith Papers.

32. Roosevelt, *Complete Presidential Press Conferences*, Vol. 16, Item 374.

33. Ibid., Vol. 15, Item 92.

34. 53 Stat. 1435.

35. Roosevelt, *Public Papers, 1939*, 316.

36. Ibid.

37. Ibid.

38. Letter to Samuel Rosenman from Mellett, Dec. 16, 1940, Mellett Papers; and memo from Mellett regarding U.S. Government Reports, Aug. 14, 1939, Box 889, RG 44.

39. House Appropriations Committee, *Independent Offices Appropriations Bill for 1941: Hearings*, 54–5.

40. Roosevelt, *Public Papers, 1939*, 309.

41. House Appropriations Committee, *Work Relief and Relief for FY 1940: Hearings*, 289. Mellett apparently deliberately interpreted Taber's question to be about whether NEC's successor would be *physically* in the Executive Office Building (next to the White House) as opposed to whether it would be *organizationally* part of the Executive Office of the President.

42. *Minute and Docket Book of the House Appropriations Committee*, Seventy-sixth Congress, First Session, microfilm M1625, RG 233, 37.

43. House Appropriations Committee, *Appropriations for Work Relief, Relief, and for Loans*, H. Rep. 833, 33.

44. *Congressional Record* 84:7, 7340.

45. Voorhis was defeated for reelection by political newcomer Richard Nixon in 1946.

46. *Congressional Record* 84:7, 7340–1.

47. Horn, *Unused Power*.

48. Senate Appropriations Committee, *Work Relief and Public Works Appropriation Act of 1939: Hearings*, 249–55.

49. Senate Appropriations Committee, *Work Relief and Public Works Appropriation Act of 1939*, S. Rep. 668.

50. 53 Stat. 931.

51. Although the bill accomplished Roosevelt's goal for NEC, he was extremely unhappy with four other provisions in it, including defunding the Federal Theatre Project. By sending the bill to the president two hours before the beginning of the fiscal year, Congress had made it impossible for him to consider vetoing it (Roosevelt, *Public Papers, 1939*, 375–7).

52. Memo to Mellett from the president, July 1, 1939, OF 788.

53. Memo to all employees of OGR from Mellett, July 1, 1939, Box 889A, RG 44.

54. Summary of daily activities, July 21, 1939, Smith Papers.

55. Roosevelt, *Complete Presidential Press Conferences*, Vol. 14, Item 18.

56. *Congressional Record* 84:9, 9278.

57. Summary of meeting with the president, July 21, 1939, Smith Papers.

58. House Appropriations Committee, *Independent Offices Appropriation Bill for 1941*, 8.

59. "May Restore Part of Maritime Cut," *New York Times*, Jan. 27, 1940, 30.

60. House Committee on Expenditures in the Executive Departments, *Authorizing Expenditures*, H. Rep. 177, 5.

61. Roosevelt, *Complete Presidential Press Conferences*, Vol. 15, Item 89.

62. Cooper, *By Order of the President*, chapters 2–3; and *U.S. at War*, 211.

Chapter 4: A Better Idea from the Military?

1. See beginning section of chapter 2.

2. For background, see Thatcher, *Planning for Industrial Mobilization*, 57–146.

3. Ibid., 81. Eisenhower's experience with IMP no doubt contributed to his famous maxim, "Plans are useless, but planning is indispensable."

4. Holland, *Eisenhower Between the Wars*, 161.

5. Holt, *Eisenhower*, 167, emphasis in original.

6. Ibid., 166–7.

7. House, *War Policies Commission*, 791–4.

8. Koistinen, *Planning War, Pursuing Peace*, 236.

9. House, *War Policies Commission*, 376.

10. Ibid., 417, Chart No. 3; and Kreidberg and Henry, *History of Military Mobilization*, 512.

11. House, *War Policies Commission*, 418–9.

12. Ibid., 449.

13. House, *War Policies Commission*, Chart No. 8, facing p. 420.

14. Koistinen, *Planning War, Pursuing Peace*, 58.

15. Ibid., 65.

16. Kreidberg and Henry, *History of Military Mobilization*, 506.

17. Ibid., 506–7.

18. House, *War Policies Commission*; and House, *Documents by the War Policies Commission*.

19. House, *Documents by the War Policies Commission*.

20. Senate Special Committee, *Industrial Mobilization Plan: Revised—1933*.

21. Ibid., xi.

22. Ibid., chart facing p. 14.

23. Ibid., 15.

24. Archaic, but correct, usage meaning "to inspect, check."

25. Senate Special Committee, *Industrial Mobilization Plan: Revised—1933*, 47.

26. Tobin and Bidwell, *Mobilizing Civilian America*, 83.

27. Mock and Larson claimed the 1933 APR plan was based on CPI (*Words That Won the War*, 343).

28. Tobin and Bidwell, *Mobilizing Civilian America*, 82.

29. *Industrial Mobilization Plan, Revised 1936*.

30. Ibid., chart facing p. 14.

31. Koistinen, *Planning War, Pursuing Peace*, 65, quoting from a military document.

32. Kreidberg and Henry, *History of Military Mobilization*, 527.

33. Mock and Larson, *Words That Won the War*, 342.

34. Koistinen, *Planning War, Pursuing Peace*, 65.

35. Senate, *Industrial Mobilization Plan of 1939*.

36. Ibid., 10.

37. Tobin and Bidwell, *Mobilizing Civilian America*, 84.

38. Harris, "Emergency National Defense," 19.

Chapter 5: Congress Authorizes a Presidential Communications Agency, 1939–41

1. Given the pressures on a president's time, the length of their luncheon is an indication of the importance that Roosevelt assigned to the subject of the meeting.

2. See endnote 4, chapter 2.

3. Brownlow, *Passion for Anonymity*, 425, italics added. Later, Roosevelt made the same point publicly, but without the reference to public relations (Roosevelt, *Public Papers, 1940*, 623).

4. Brownlow, *Passion for Anonymity*, 428. See also Somers, *Presidential Agency*, 7; and Fesler et al., *Industrial Mobilization for War*, 10–1.

5. Blum, "Birth and Death," 82.

6. Roosevelt, *Public Papers, 1939*, 491.

7. Ibid., 494. At one point in the process of drafting the executive order, OGR was assigned only the first four missions, but Roosevelt hand-wrote the fifth mission into the draft. He wanted OGR, since it had a field service and was working with all other executive branch agencies in the field, to have the duty to report to him on ways to save money in government operations. Smith, somewhat unhappy about OGR getting a role that he thought more appropriately belonged to BOB, declined to fight about it (Summary of daily activities, Aug. 28, 1939, Smith Papers).

8. Blum, "Birth and Death," 80.

9. War Resources Board, *Report*, 7.

10. Ibid., 11.

11. Roosevelt, *Public Papers, 1939*, 586–7.

12. Somers, *Presidential Agency*, 7; and Thatcher, *Planning for Industrial*, 299–300.

13. Joint Army-Navy Board, *Basic Plan for Public Relations Administration*, 6, PSF-Roosevelt.

14. Ibid., Annex B, Item IV, pp. 11–2.

15. Edison, son of the famous inventor, was later appointed by FDR to be the permanent secretary.

16. Letter to the president from the Secretaries of war and Navy, June 10, 1940, PSF-Roosevelt.

17. Memo for Louis Brownlow and director of the budget, Dec. 14, 1939, OF 25.

18. Memo for the secretary of war from the president, Jan. 2, 1940, OF 25. If such a follow-up conversation indeed ever occurred, Roosevelt would simply have deflected the inquiry.

19. Meeting with the president, Saturday, Feb. 10, 1940, 4, Smith Papers.

20. Letter to the president from the secretaries of war and Navy, June 10, 1940, PSF-Roosevelt.

21. Steele, "Preparing the Public for War," 1641.

22. Roosevelt, *Public Papers, 1939*, 506.

23. Catton, *War Lords of Washington*, 10–1, 52–5, 62–7. During the war, Catton was the War Production Board's Information Director. Later, he wrote best-selling Civil War histories.

24. Its "national morale" mission led to the fan dancer controversy. See chapter 8.

25. Meeting with the president, Dec. 14, 1939, Smith Papers; and *Budget of the U.S., 1941*, 38.

26. House Appropriations Committee, *Independent Offices Appropriations Bill for 1941: Hearings*, Part 1, 51.

27. Ibid., 8–10.

28. Summary of daily activities, Jan. 18, 1940, Smith Papers.

29. NEC had been funded out of relief appropriations bills as a temporary agency.

30. House Appropriations Committee, *Independent Offices Appropriations Bill for 1941: Hearings*, Part 1, 41–71.

31. Summary of daily meetings, Jan. 6 and 16, 1940, Smith Papers; and memo to the president from Harold Smith, Jan. 19, 1940, OF 788.

32. House Appropriations Committee, *Independent Offices Appropriations Bill, 1941*, H. Rep. 1515, 5.

33. *Cong. Record* 86:1, 387. This criticism from a conservative Republican seems odd, since the list's purpose was to prevent anyone from getting aid from more than one program. However, to Dirksen, it was a device to develop a Democratic mailing list of people receiving assistance.

34. Ibid., 419.

35. Roosevelt, *Complete Presidential Press Conferences*, Vol. 15, Items 82–3, 92–3.

36. Henry N. Dorris, "$94,517,206 Slash Is Voted by House," *New York Times*, Jan. 19, 1940, 3.

37. Memo to the speaker of the house from the president, Jan. 23, 1940, OF 788.

38. Summary of meeting with the president, Jan. 24, 1940, Smith Papers.

39. Senate Appropriations Committee, *Independent Offices Appropriations Bill for 1941: Hearings*, 90.

40. Ibid., 21.

41. "May Restore Part of Maritime Cut," *New York Times*, Jan. 27, 1940, 30.

42. "Bill for Farm Aid Is Cut $154,530,263 in Report to House," *New York Times*, Jan. 31, 1940, 20.

43. Senate Appropriations Committee, *Independent Offices Appropriations Bill, 1941*, S. Rep. 1177.

44. *Congressional Record* 86:1, 1047.

45. House Appropriations Committee, *Work Relief and Relief for FY 1941: Hearings*, 34–62.

46. House Appropriations Committee, *Appropriations for Work Relief and Relief, FY 1941*, H. Rep. 2186, 3, 14–5.

47. "Motions to Amend Delay Relief Bill," *New York Times*, May 23, 1940, 20.

48. *Congressional Record* 86:6, 6662. This was not a one-time slip-of-the-tongue. A year later, Senator James Davis (R-PA) said, "The Office of Government Reports may be developed into one of the greatest OGPUs that any country in the world has ever had" (ibid., 87:4, 4245).

49. Ibid., 86:6, 6659–63.

50. Senate Appropriations Committee, *Emergency Relief Appropriation Act FY 1941: Hearings*, 18–28, 107–8.

51. Senate Appropriations Committee, *Emergency Relief Appropriation Act, FY 1941*, S. Rep. 1754, 6. The Committee explained the $20,000 difference from earlier appropriations as NEC's Radio Division budget, which was transferred to the Office of Education when OGR was created.

52. House Appropriations Committee, *Work Relief and Relief Appropriation, 1941*, H. Rep. 2681, 11.

53. 54 Stat. 618.

54. Memo to the BOB director from Mellett, April 22, 1941, Box 889A, RG 44.

55. Authorization letter, to the treasury secretary from the president, May 13, 1941, Box 101, OF 79.

56. *Budget of the U.S., 1942*, 44.

57. Conference with the president, Dec. 18, 1940, 3, Smith Papers.

58. Henry N. Dorris, "$94,517,206 Slash Is Voted by House," *New York Times*, Jan. 19, 1940, 3.

59. *Congressional Record* 87:1, 1032, 1091. Today (2005) they are called the Senate Governmental Affairs Committee and the House Government Reform Committee.

60. Senate Committee on Expenditures in the Executive Departments, *To Authorize Expenditures: Hearings*, 3. The Executive Order had a fifth mission for OGR (see chapter 5, endnote 7). It was deleted from the bill because it could have been attacked as duplicating BOB's role.

61. Davenport, "You Can't Say That!" Mellett believed the article was a payback for rejecting the magazine's offer of free copies to the military, which he thought it was a scheme to recruit post-war subscribers (Conversation with Sidney Hyman, Aug. 8, 1949, Mellett Papers, 10–2).

62. *Congressional Record* 87:2, 1651.

63. Frederick C. Barkley, "Aid Bill Foes Balk," *New York Times*, March 4, 1941, 1.

64. "Says Permanent OGR Ideal Method for Censorship," *Editor & Publisher* 74:10 (March 8, 1941): 14.

65. "Comment," *America* 34:24 (March 22, 1941): 647.

66. Reprinted in *Congressional Record* 87:4, 4253–4.

67. "Propaganda Aim Seen in the New Bill," *New York Times*, Feb. 23, 1941, 23.

68. House Committee on Expenditures in the Executive Departments, *To Authorize Expenditures: Hearings*, 2.

69. "Censorship Intent Denied by Mellett," *New York Times*, Feb. 27, 1941, 10.

70. Krock, "A Shining Mark for Economizers, if Any," *New York Times*, Feb. 28, 1941, 18.

71. House Committee on Expenditures in the Executive Departments, *Authorizing Expenditures*, H. Rep. 177, 1.

72. Ibid., 4–5.

73. *Congressional Record* 87:3, 2542–67.

74. Senate Committee on Expenditures in the Executive Departments, *To Authorize Expenditures: Hearings*, 3.

75. Krock, "The Consolidation Plan for Official Press Agents," *New York Times*, April 2, 1941, 22.

76. "Senate Group for OGR Fund," *New York Times*, April 17, 1941, 11.

77. Senate Committee on Expenditures in the Executive Departments, *Authorizing Expenditures*, S. Rep. 264, 3.

78. Ibid., 6, italics in original.

79. *Congressional Record* 87:4, 4240–70.

80. Senator Hill, as floor manager of the bill, had accepted one amendment from Robert Taft (R-OH) codifying OGR's exclusion from film and radio activities, since NEC's U.S. Film Service and Radio Division were transferred to the Office of Education when OGR was created out of NEC.

81. *Congressional Record* 87:4, 4270; and "Vote News Agency," *New York Times*, May 21, 1941, 18.

82. *Congressional Record* 87:4, 4303 and 87:5, 4683, 4759; "House Delays OGR Bill," *New York Times*, May 22, 1941, 16; and House, Conference Committee, *Authorizing Expenditures*, H. Rep. 644.

83. 55 Stat. 247–8; and "President Signs Measure," *New York Times*, June 11, 1941, 22.

Chapter 6: In Operation, 1939–41

1. Williams, " 'The President's' OGR," 561–2.

2. House Committee on Expenditures in the Executive Departments, *To Authorize Expenditures: Hearings*, 21.

3. House Appropriations Committee, *Second Deficiency Appropriation Bill for 1941: Hearings*, 30.

4. Ibid., 15.

5. Senate Appropriations Committee, *Emergency Relief Appropriation Act FY 1941: Hearings*, 20.

6. Senate Appropriations Committee, *Second Deficiency Appropriation Bill for 1941: Hearings*, 5.

7. House Appropriations Committee, *Work Relief and Relief for FY 1941: Hearings*, 44.

8. Senate Appropriations Committee, *Second Deficiency Appropriation Bill for 1941: Hearings*, 7.

9. House Appropriations Committee, *Second Deficiency Appropriation Bill for 1941: Hearings*, 48.

10. Mellett, "Government Propaganda."

11. Mellett, "Office of Government Reports."

12. Garnett, "Administrative Communication," 3; and Redfield, "Theory of Communication," 12.

13. Shils, "Note on Governmental Research," 473.

14. Steele, *Propaganda in an Open Society*, 99–100; and "Pulse of the People," 203–5.

15. Millett, *Government and Public Administration*, 280.

16. 54 Stat. 618; 55 Stat. 542; *Budget of the U.S., 1942*, 42–3; and *Budget of the U.S., 1944*, 26.

17. *Budget of the U.S., 1941*, 38.

18. Siebert, "Federal Information Agencies," 28–9.

19. With the establishment of OGR as a permanent EOP agency, Blackburn was appointed by the president as OGR assistant director, ending the charade of being an employee of the State Department (see chapter 2) (letter to Blackburn from the Department of State, Sept. 26, 1939 and letter to Mellett from the president, Sept. 27, 1939, Blackburn Papers).

20. Letter to the president from Mellett, Sept. 30, 1940, PPF 5669. With Roosevelt running for re-election to an unprecedented third term in fall of 1940, Mellett reminded the FDR that the six White House administrative assistants (created as part of the Brownlow Committee report) were excluded from the ban on political activities by federal employees under the new Hatch Act. If the president named him to one of the vacancies, if only until November, he'd be able to be involved in the campaign (memo of conversation between Mellett and Sidney Hyman, Aug. 8, 1949, Washington, DC, Mellett File, FDR Memorial Foundation Papers, 9–10). After the election, Roosevelt kept him on as administrative assistant as well as OGR chief, although with only one salary.

21. Felix Belaire Jr., "Brain Trust Far from Dead," *New York Times*, Sept. 17, 1939, Section IV, 7.

22. Roosevelt, *Complete Presidential Press Conferences*, Vol. 16, Item 241.

23. In 1940, the division was briefly called the Report and Coordinating Division (House Appropriations Committee, *Work Relief and Relief for FY 1941: Hearings*, 50).

24. House Appropriations Committee, *Independent Offices Appropriations Bill for 1941: Hearings*, Part 1, 43; and Senate Appropriations Committee, *Second Deficiency Appropriation Bill for 1941: Hearings*, 1.

25. Mellett, "Office of Government Reports," 127.

26. House Appropriations Committee, *Second Deficiency Appropriation Bill for 1941: Hearings*, 15.

27. OGR, *Report of Operations: 1941*, 3.

28. Kiely, *Evolution*, Ph.D. dissertation, 110–5; and *U.S. Government Manual*, Sept. 1941, 64.

29. Mellett, "Office of Government Reports," 129.

30. *Information Digest*, No. 484, June 11, 1942, OGR, Folder 11, Box 13, Cartwright Papers.

31. "NEC Endorsements, 1938–1941" file, Box 4, OF 788.

32. Letter to Congressman John McCormack from the president, Nov. 24, 1939, Mellett Papers; and letter to James M. Curley from the president, July 9, 1941, OF 788.

33. Letter to the president from Senator Abe Murdock, June 17, 1941, OF 788.

34. Letter to Senator Frederick Van Nuys from Mellett, July 7, 1941, Mellett Papers.

35. Memo from Mellett, Sept. 29, 1939, OF 788.

36. Letter to A. D. Folger from the president, Sept. 29, 1939, OF 788.

37. Senate Committee on Expenditures in the Executive Departments, *Authorize Expenditures: Hearings*, 19.

38. Memo to the president from the director, Oct. 17, 1939, OF 788.

39. Memo to the president from Mellett, Oct. 20, 1941, OF 788.

40. Memo to the president from Mellett, March 17, 1942, OF 788.

41. Letter to F. H. LaGuardia from Mellett, Sept. 24, 1941, Box 890, RG 44.

42. Letter to Mrs. Franklin Roosevelt from Mellett, Jan. 22, 1942, Mellett Papers.

43. OGR, *Report of Operations: 1941*, 4–5.

44. "The U.S. Information Service" brochure, n.d., Box 996, RG 44.

45. House Appropriations Committee, *Second Deficiency Appropriation Bill for 1941: Hearings*, 57.

46. Roosevelt, *Public Papers, 1939*, 316.

47. Letter to Thomas P. Ayer, Librarian, Richmond Public Library from Phillip C. Hamblet, OGR executive officer, Dec. 4, 1941 and letter to Congressman Dave E. Satterfield Jr. from Philip C. Hamblet, OGR executive officer, Dec. 4, 1941, Box 996, RG 44. In 1942 the congressman proposed a ban on construction of the US Information Center (chapter 8).

48. "Requests for Information Handled by USIS," Box 898, RG 44.

49. OGR, *Report of Operations, 1940*, 15–6; and OGR, *Report of Operations, 1941*, 18.

50. Webb, "U.S. Information Please"; and House Appropriations Committee, *Second Deficiency Appropriation Bill for 1941: Hearings*, 59.

51. "Requests for Information Handled by USIS," Box 898, RG 44.

52. House Committee on Expenditures in the Executive Departments, *To Authorize Expenditures: Hearings*, 7.

53. Form Letter from Harriet Root, Chief, USIS, Feb. 9, 1942, Box 998, RG 44. By mid-1942, 5,000 U.S. public libraries had signed up (Danton, "Public Library War Information Centers").

54. Jordan, "Teacher's Section: Keeping Up with the War News," 408.

55. OGR, *Report of Operations, 1941*, 17–8.

56. House Appropriations Committee, *Second Deficiency Appropriation Bill for 1941: Hearings*, 57.

57. *U.S. Government Manual* order form, Box Pr162, RG 287.

58. The next major change occurred in the 1990s, when a free Internet version was created.

59. Senate Appropriations Committee, *Work Relief and Public Works Appropriation Act of 1938: Hearings*, 312–4; and House Appropriations Committee, *Independent Offices Appropriations Bill for 1950: Hearings*, Part 1, 275–6.

60. Preceding section based on: OGR publications in the Library of the Wisconsin Historical Society, Madison; Boxes Pr62, Pr63, Pr162 and Pr168, RG 287; references to OGR publications in *U.S. Government Publications Monthly Catalog*; references to OGR publications in OGR annual reports; and memo to the president from Mellett, Nov. 20, 1939, Mellett Papers.

61. House Appropriations Committee, *Second Deficiency Appropriation Bill for 1941: Hearings*, 30.

62. House Appropriations Committee, *Work Relief and Relief for FY 1941: Hearings*, 41; and OGR, *Report of Operations, 1941*, 13–4.

63. Senate Appropriations Committee, *Emergency Relief Appropriation Act FY 1941: Hearings*, 24–5, 28; and Mellett, "Office of Government Reports," 129–30.

64. House Appropriations Committee, *Second Deficiency Appropriation Bill for 1941: Hearings*, 30; and Senate Appropriations Committee; *Emergency Relief Appropriation Act FY 1941: Hearings*, 25.

65. OGR, *Report of Operations, 1941*, 16; Mellett, "Office of Government Reports," 130; and Williams, " 'The President's' OGR," 552–3.

66. Memo to the president from Mellett, July 18, 1941 and memo from FDR, July 21, 1941, OF 788.

67. Memo to the president regarding weekly analysis of press reaction, Dec. 5, 1941, 1, OF 788.

68. To: William Hassett, From: Division of Press Intelligence, March 19,1942, OF 788.

69. House Appropriations Committee, *Independent Offices Appropriations Bill for 1943: Hearings*, 1150. Rather than editing out archaic terminology, it seemed more appropriate to retain the term used then.

70. House Committee on expenditures in the executive departments, *To Authorize Expenditures: Hearings*, 6; and House Appropriations Committee, *Independent Offices Appropriations Bill for 1943: Hearings*, 1151.

71. Memo on personnel problems resulting from increase in volume of work, Box 909, RG 44.

72. Memo to "Officer in Charge of Information" from Robert Berger, Box 889, RG 44.

73. Memo of agreement, June 25, 1940, Box 889, RG 44.

74. OGR, *Report of Operations, 1941*, 10.

75. Congressional Joint Committee on Reduction, *Reduction: Hearings*, 1154–6.

76. Summary of daily activities, Sept. 29, 1939, Smith Papers.

77. Summary of meeting with the president, Oct. 3, 1939, Smith Papers.

78. Letter to Mellett from the president, Nov. 20, 1939 and memo to the budget director from Mellett, Nov. 21, 1939, Box 889, RG 44.

79. Letter to Mellett from Shannon Allen, Radio Section, Interior Department, Box 889, RG 44.

80. Congressional Joint Committee on Reduction, *Reduction: Hearings*, 1227.

81. Eisenhower, *Study of War Information Work: Supporting Data*, 45, Box 82, RG 51.

82. Letter to Mellett from Studebaker, Aug. 3, 1939, Mellett Papers.

83. Letter to Lorentz from Studebaker, Aug. 24, 1939, Mellett Papers.

84. Memo to Mellett from Steve Early, April 3, 1940, OF 788.

85. Memo for the president from James Rowe Jr., Aug. 7, 1941, Mellett Papers.

86. Memo for Jim Rowe from FDR, Aug. 19, 1941, Mellett Papers.

87. Memo for the president from James Rowe Jr., Aug. 7, 1941, Mellett Papers.

88. MacCann, *People's Films*, 104–14; Snyder, *Pare Lorentz*, chapter 7; and USIS form letter, n.d., Box 1000, RG 44.

89. House Appropriations Committee, *Second Deficiency Appropriation Bill for 1941: Hearings*, 49.

90. Memo to the president from Mellett, March 17, 1941, Mellett Papers.

91. Memo on government poster work to Mellett from Arch Mercey, Jan. 1941, Box 889A, RG 44.

92. Memo to the president from Mellett, March 17, 1941, Mellett Papers.

93. Memo for Mellett from the president, March 18, 1941, Mellett Papers.

94. Memo on poster committee to Mellett from Arch Mercey, March 26, 1941, Box 889A, RG 44.

95. To Paul McNutt, Federal Security Agency from Mellett, April 16, 1941, Box 889A, RG 44.

96. Eisenhower, *Study of War Information Work: Supporting Data*, 45, Box 82, RG 51.

97. Carroll, "Dr. Roosevelt's Propaganda Trust," 21–2.

98. "Says Permanent OGR Ideal Method for Censorship," *Editor & Publisher* 74:10 (March 8, 1941): 14.

99. Thomson, *Easily Led*, 284.

100. Walton, "What Is Propaganda?"

101. Stoke, "Executive Leadership and the Growth of Propaganda," 500.

102. Steele, *Propaganda in an Open Society*, 90–1.

103. Ibid., 92.

104. Mellett, "Government Propaganda."

105. "Praises Honesty of Press Services," *New York Times*, Aug. 21, 1941, 10.

106. Memo for Lyle T. Alverson from Stephen Early, Feb. 24, 1936, OF 788.

107. Memo to the president from the executive director, NEC, Jan. 21, 1939, Mellett Papers.

108. Memo for Mellett from FDR, Jan. 23, 1939, Mellett Papers.

109. "Benefits to Wisconsin from Reciprocal Trade Agreements," Box Pr168, RG 287.

110. House, Conference Committee, *Second Deficiency Appropriation Bill, 1941*, H. Rep. 894, 4.

111. 55 Stat. 542–3.

112. Larson, "Publicity for National Defense," 246.

113. Larson, "Official Information for America at War," 76.

Chapter 7: High Water Mark, Winter–Spring 1941–42

1. House Appropriations Committee, *Second Deficiency Appropriation Bill for 1941: Hearings*, 50.

2. *U.S. at War*, 217.

3. Roosevelt, *Public Papers, 1941*, 381. But, later he created the Office of Facts and Figures.

4. 55 Stat. 542. The appropriation also included an additional $18,730 for printing and binding, a separate appropriation category that Congress used at that time for all agencies.

5. Letter to Harold Smith from Mellett, Dec. 12, 1941, Box 899, RG 44.

6. Letter from John McCormack to Mellett, Dec. 16, 1941, Mellett Papers.

7. House, *Proposed Provision on Existing Appropriation, OGR, 1942*, H. Doc. 467, 1–2.

8. House Appropriations Committee, *Additional Appropriation Incident to the National Defense: Hearings*, 38.

9. Ibid., 37.

10. Ibid., 42–3.

11. House Appropriations Committee, *Additional Appropriation Incident to the National Defense*, H. Rep. 1549, 5.

12. *Congressional Record* 87:9, 10041–5. Hoffman was one of the most anti-Roosevelt of all members of Congress (Fleming, *New Dealers' War*, 112, 157).

13. Senate Appropriations Committee, *Additional Appropriation Incident to the National Defense*, S. Rep. 919, 1–2.

14. 55 Stat. 855.

15. Letter to Harold Smith from Mellett, Dec. 20, 1941, Box 889A, RG 44.

16. Memo to the president from Harold D. Smith, Jan. 19, 1942, OF 79.

17. Letter from the president to the secretary of the treasury, Jan. 19, 1942, OF 79.

18. *Budget of the U.S., 1943*, 48–50.

19. *Congressional Record* 88:1, 573.

20. House Appropriations Committee, *Independent Offices Appropriations Bill for 1943: Hearings*, Part 1, 1164.

21. *Congressional Record* 88:1, 572.

22. George D. Riley, "U.S. and Us," *Washington Times-Herald*, Jan. 29, 1942.

23. House Appropriations Committee, *Independent Offices Appropriations Bill, 1943*, H. Rep. 1643, 4.

24. *Congressional Record* 88:1, 572.

25. Ibid., 550.

26. The statement must be judged in the context of the times. The Holocaust and other beyond-belief acts of Hitler's regime were not known. Nonetheless, much was known about the undemocratic and terror actions of the Nazis, thus making Wigglesworth's statement still inexcusable.

27. *Congressional Record* 88:1, 573.

28. Caro, *Years of Lyndon Johnson*, 68–74.

29. Koppes and Black, *Hollywood Goes to War*, chapter 2.

30. *U.S. at War*, 217.

31. Author's files.

32. OF 788; and "Mellett Is Named Film Coordinator," *New York Times*, Dec. 24, 1941, 14.

33. *Federal Register* 7:2 (Jan. 3, 1942), 55–6.

34. Coordination of Government Films, 3, Box 889A, RG 44.

35. Budget estimate, Office of the Coordinator of Government Films, Feb. 6, 1942, Box 890, RG 44.

36. Congressional Joint Committee on Reduction, *Reduction: Hearings*, Part 4, 1213–5, 1225, 1228–30.

37. Pierce, *Sacred Trust*, 117.

38. After the war, Poynter returned to the family's business, the *St. Petersburg Times*. Upon his death in 1978, his will funded the creation of the Poynter Institute, which promotes high standards in U.S. journalism. Retrieved May 27, 2004: http://www.poynter.org.

39. Letter to Brigadier General Lewis B. Hershey from Mellett, Feb. 2, 1942, Mellett Papers.

40. Letter to Mellett from Lewis B. Hershey, Feb. 4, 1942, Mellett Papers.

41. "Movies Are Put in Essential Class by Draft Ruling," *New York Times*, Feb. 9, 1942, 1, 9. The other front page story was the Japanese bombing of MacArthur's forces on Bataan in the Philippines.

42. Associated Press, "Screen Guild for Draft," *New York Times*, Feb. 10, 1942, 24.

43. Letter to John W. McCormack from Mellett, Feb. 18, 1942, Mellett Papers.

44. Pierce, *Sacred Trust*, 253.

45. Shorts were short movies, some documentaries (such as travelogues and historical vignettes) and some entertaining (such as featuring humorist Robert Benchley). Typically, an admission ticket to a movie covered a double feature, a newsreel, a serial, a cartoon, and several shorts.

46. Memo to Mellett from Leo C. Rosten, May 11, 1942, Blackburn Papers. Rosten, who had a Ph.D. in political science, eventually became a writer of popular fiction and nonfiction.

47. Pierce, *Sacred Trust*, 117.

48. Memo on proposed U.S. government movie-radio center to Mellett from Nelson Poynter, April 21, 1942 and letter to Nelson Poynter from Basil Capella, chief, OGR personnel division, May 7, 1942, Box 890, RG 44; and Pierce, *Sacred Trust*, 117–20.

49. Memo to George Barnes from McGee on Mellett statistics, Nov. 14, 1942, Mellett Papers.

50. Short, "Washington's Information Manual for the Motion Picture Industry," 173–4.

51. *War Films*, Box 902, RG 44.

52. Blackburn Papers. Each filled-out form was assigned to a "researchist."

53. Pierce, *Sacred Trust*, 120.

54. Koppes and Black, *Hollywood Goes to War*, 57–8.

55. Gosnell, *Office of Government Reports*, 36.

56. Eisenhower, *Study of War Information Work: Supporting Data*, 44, Box 82, RG 51.

Chapter 8: Roosevelt Fights to Create the US Information Center, Spring 1942

Note: Most newspaper articles in this chapter were located in a scrapbook of press clippings relating to the U.S. Information Center, Box 1002, RG 44.

1. Transcript of March 12, 1942, radio report by Fulton Lewis, reprinted in *Congressional Record* 88:2, 2412; and Hamblet, "Nerve Center for National Facts," 10.

2. Catton, *War Lords of Washington*, 183.

3. Seligman and Cornwell, *New Deal Mosaic*, 454.

4. Roosevelt, *Complete Presidential Press Conferences*, Vol. 19, Items 199–201.

5. Congressional Joint Committee on Reduction, *Reduction: Hearings*, Part 4, 1306.

6. Roosevelt, *Complete Presidential Press Conferences*, Vol. 19, Item 198.

7. Mellett to Coy, Dec. 22, 1941, Mellett Papers.

8. *Subject: The U.S. Information Service*, Jan. 9, 1942, Box 910, RG 44.

9. Memo to executive officer from T. P. Carroll regarding expanded USIS, Jan. 19, 1942, Box 996, RG 44.

10. House Committee on Public Buildings, *Prohibit Use of Money: Hearings*, 28.

11. Letter from Franklin D. Roosevelt to Mellett, Feb. 2, 1942, Mellett Papers.

12. "Mellett to Expand Services of O.G.R.," *New York Times*, Feb. 3, 1942, 13.

13. House Committee on Public Buildings, *Prohibit Use of Money: Hearings*, 29.

14. "Map of Washington, DC, Central Area," April 17, 1942, Box 910, RG 44.

15. Mellett letter to Smith, Feb. 5, 1942, Box 899, RG 44.

16. Senate, *Communication from the President: Obligations by the Office of Government Reports*, S. Doc. 179.

17. Drury, *Senate Journal*, 116. Drury covered the Senate for the *New York Times.* He later became a full-time writer of political fiction. His first novel, *Advice and Consent* was a bestseller.

18. Conference with the president, Nov. 18, 1945, Smith Papers.

19. Caro, *Years of Lyndon Johnson*, 82–3.

20. Pope, *Senatorial Baron*, Ph.D. dissertation, 351.

21. Senate Appropriations Committee, *First Deficiency Appropriation Bill for 1942: Hearings*, 1–21.

22. Ibid., 13–4. The reference to fan dancers relates to dancer Mayvis Chaney, a friend of the First Lady's, who was hired by the Office of Civilian Defense to work on programs to boost public morale (Pope, *Senatorial Baron*, Ph.D. dissertation, 352–3; and Fleming, *New Dealers' War*, 106–7).

23. E. Pagano, "Cabbies to Earn Quick Tips about City," *Nashville (TN) Banner*, July 4, 1996, D1.

24. *Subject: The U.S. Information Service*, Jan. 9, 1942, Box 910, RG 44.

25. Senate Appropriations Committee, *First Deficiency Appropriation Bill, 1942*, S. Rep. 1086.

26. Rosen, *Holding Government Bureaucracies Accountable*, 83–4; Kirst, *Government without Passing Laws*, 66–73; and Fenno, *The Power of the Purse*, 291–3.

27. Presumably, McKellar had failed behind closed doors at convincing the committee to say that in the report. So he had to make the most of the report's silence. The Center for Legislative Archives (maintained for Congress by the National Archives) has no records of those meetings.

28. "Mellett's Monster Won't Lack for Funds Despite Congress," *Washington Post*, March 10, 1942.

29. Jerry Klutz, "Value of Information Center Is Debated," *Washington Post*, March 8, 1942.

30. Fleming, *New Dealers' War*, 558.

31. Catton, *War Lords of Washington*, 184.

32. Pierce, *Sacred Trust*, 67.

33. "Mellett Says Q & A Center is F. D.'s Own," *Washington Daily News*, March 9, 1942.

34. "Economy Unit Begins Inquiry," *Washington Evening Star*, March 9, 1942.

35. *Washington Post*, March 9, 1942.

36. "Capital Is Astir," *New York Herald Tribune*, March 9, 1942, Archives of Media Industries.

37. Byrd letter to Mellett, March 9, 1942, Mellett Papers.

38. *Congressional Record* 88:8, A909–10.

39. House Joint Resolution 290, Seventy-seventh Congress.

40. *Congressional Record* 88:2, 2182.

41. "House Group to Act on Bill Barring OGR Center Funds," *Washington Post*, March 11, 1942.

42. *Washington Post*, March 10, 1942.

43. "Answers Easy for Miss Root, U.S. Authority," *Washington Post*, March 11, 1942.

44. Congressional Joint Committee on Reduction, *Reduction: Hearings*, Part 4, 1125–312.

45. Charles Mercer, "Senate Unit to Question Mellett Today," *Washington Post*, March 12, 1942.

46. Pope, *Senatorial Baron*, Ph.D. dissertation, 361.

47. Congressional Joint Committee on Reduction, *Reduction: Hearings*, Part 4, 1131.

48. Ibid., 1133.

49. Ibid., 1131.

50. Ibid., 1139.

51. Ibid., 1140.

52. Ibid., 1221. Tabor's nickname was "Meat Ax," for his approach to cutting government spending (Donaldson, *Truman Defeats Dewey*, 40).

53. Since the Constitution requires that all appropriations bills begin in the House, the Senate Appropriations Committee always gets the bill second. This focuses the Senate Committee on the more controversial issues, practically an "appeals and review" approach, rather than examining the entire bill. Hence, House Committee members would have a more detailed knowledge of agency operations than their counterparts in the Senate (Horn, *Unused Power*).

54. Congressional Joint Committee on Reduction, *Reduction: Hearings,* Part 4, 1140.

55. Caro, *Years of Lyndon Johnson,* 74.

56. "Can't Prevent OGR Building, Probers Find," *Washington Times Herald,* March 12, 1942; "Mellett Gets Go Ahead on 'Information Booth,' Spanking Came First," *Washington Daily News,* March 12, 1942; "Information Building Was Idea of President, Mellett Declares," *Washington Evening Star,* March 12, 1942; "OGR Building Plan Laid to Roosevelt," *New York Times,* March 13, 1942; and Thomas J. O'Donnell, "Quiz Starts New Probes," *Baltimore Sun,* March 13, 1942.

57. "DC Goes Easy on Mellett's Madhouse," *Washington Post,* March 13, 1942.

58. Caro, *Years of Lyndon Johnson,* 283, 612; and Nixon, *Public Papers, 1970,* 392–3.

59. Gould Lincoln, "Mellett's Information Center," *Washington Evening Star,* March 12, 1942.

60. Charles T. Lucey, "Washington Will Process Inquires," *New York World-Telegram,* March 5, 1942, Archives of Media Industries.

61. *Congressional Record* 88:8, A971–2. Guffey was a very liberal and pro-New Deal Senator (Fleming, *New Dealers' War,* 243, 359).

62. *Congressional Record* 88:2, 2412.

63. Ibid. 88:8, A1006.

64. MacCann, *People's Films,* 108.

65. Burns, *Roosevelt,* 370.

66. Most of Roosevelt's press conferences were not large and formal events, as they are now. Rather, the handful of White House reporters were taken to the Oval Office for a short meeting.

67. *Washington Times Herald,* March 13, 1942.

68. *Washington Daily News,* March 13, 1942.

69. *Washington Post,* March 14, 1942.

70. "President Plans Housing on Mall, *New York Times,* March 14, 1942.

71. House Committee on Public Buildings, *Prohibit Use of Money: Hearings,* 2.

72. Ibid., 6.

73. Ibid., 11–2.

74. Ibid., 17.

75. Charles Mercer, "Effort Also Continued to Take PBA Funds," *Washington Post,* March 14, 1942.

76. House Committee on Public Buildings, *Prohibit Use of Money: Hearings,* 25, 39.

77. Arthur Krock, "Roosevelt Adventures in the Role of Architect," *New York Times,* March 15, 1942.

78. "Mellett Faces House Inquiry Again Today," *Washington Post*, March 16, 1942.

79. United Press, "OGR Critics 'Aiding Enemy'," *Washington Daily News*, March 16, 1942.

80. House Committee on Public Buildings, *Prohibit Use of Money: Hearings*, 44–5.

81. Conference with the President, March 19, 1942, Smith Papers. The BOB survey was part of the planning to reorganize federal wartime information offices (see chapter 9). Information staff from the War Production Board and the Commerce Department were transferred to USIS to staff the information center (press statement of Mellett, May 2, 1942, Mellett Papers).

82. Robertson, *Sly and Able*, 298–307.

83. Byrnes letter to Roosevelt, March 26, 1942, OF 4850.

84. McKellar letter to Roosevelt, March 24, 1942, OF 4850.

85. Roosevelt letter to McKellar, March 26, 1942, OF 4850.

86. "Roosevelt to Let Congress Choose User of 'Madhouse'," *Washington Post*, March 30, 1942.

87. Senate Appropriations Committee, *Independent Offices Appropriations Bill for 1943: Hearings*, 308–10, 312.

88. Senate Appropriations Committee, *Independent Offices Appropriations Bill, 1943*, S. Rep. 1266, 3.

89. Tydings was one of the Democratic senators FDR had tried to "purge" in the 1938 elections.

90. Pope, *Senatorial Baron*, Ph.D. dissertation, 353–4.

91. Robert C. Albright, "Senators Slash Funds of Nonwar Agencies: Mellett's OGR Is Among Hardest Hit, Taking $406,270 Cut; Few Escape," *Washington Post*, April 25, 1942.

92. Ibid.

93. Pope, *Senatorial Baron*, Ph.D. dissertation, 319–20.

94. Memo for the president from BOB Director Harold Smith, April 27, 1942, OF 788.

95. Public Buildings Administration letter to Hamblet, March 9, 1942, Mellett Papers.

96. "Comrades in Arms," *Washington Star*, May 18, 1942.

97. Hamblet, "Nerve Center for National Facts"; Root, "The U.S. Information Center"; and n. a., "U.S. Information Center" (in *American Foreign Service Journal*).

98. "Training for Duty in 'Mellett's Madhouse'," *Washington Post*, April 19, 1942.

99. Press statement of Mellett, May 2, 1942, Mellett Papers.

100. "Open 'Mellett's Madhouse' Amid Oral Fireworks," *Chicago Tribune*, May 3, 1942.

101. "2,000 Help Mellett Open OGR Offices," *Washington Times Herald*, May 4, 1942.

102. Underlining in original.

103. E. Roosevelt, *FDR, His Personal Letters*, 1316–7.

104. "Queries Flood Mellett Center on First Day," *Washington Times Herald*, May 5, 1942.

105. Leo P. Cullinane, "New U.S. Center of Information," *New York Herald Tribune*, May 5, 1942.

106. "Information Office Gets 20,000 Calls for Service," *Washington Sunday Star*, May 10, 1942.

107. "U.S. Information Service Inquiries," Box 996, RG 44.

108. "Inquiries Report and Tabulation, June 9, 1942," Box 1002, RG 44.

109. Roosevelt, *Complete Presidential Press Conferences*, Vol. 19, Item 357.

110. Leo P. Cullinane, "Capital Center of Information Is Losing Its All," *New York Herald Tribune*, Sept. 10, 1942, Archives of Media Industries.

111. Memo to Miss K. C. Blackburn from Harriet Root, March 12, 1943, Box 1681, RG 44; and House Appropriations Committee, *National War Agencies Appropriation Bill for 1944: Hearings*, 907.

112. Since OWI had absorbed OGR in 1942, Mellett was writing as assistant to the president.

113. Memo to the president from Mellett, Dec. 30, 1943, OF 4850.

114. Memo for Mellett from the president, Dec. 31, 1943, OF 4850, italics added.

115. Leo P. Cullinane, "Capital Center of Information Is Losing Its All," *New York Herald Tribune*, Sept. 10, 1942, Archives of Media Industries.

116. OWI briefing paper for Congressional testimony, n.d., Box 1681, RG 44.

117. "Outline History of the Bureau of Special Services," Oct. 30, 1945, 5, Box 1873, RG 44.

118. *Congressional Directory, Seventy-ninth Congress, Second Session*, first edition, information as of Jan. 1, 1946, 318.

119. *Congressional Directory, Eightieth Congress, Second Session*, second edition, information as of May 19, 1948, 313.

120. Crosby Noyes, "Miss Clara Edmunds Loses Fight to Save Information Library," *Washington Evening Star*, May 27, 1948, OF 569.

121. Ibid.

122. Private communication from Alan Ehrenhalt to the author, July 16, 2002, author's files.

123. Catton, *War Lords of Washington*, 184.

Chapter 9: Roosevelt Reluctantly Surrenders, May–June 1942

1. Senate Appropriations Committee, *Independent Offices Appropriations Bill, 1943*, S. Rep. 1266, 3. Although the report lists $800,000, all subsequent references in Congressional documents are to $600,000 (*Congressional Record* 88:3, 3822; and House, Conference Committee, *Independent Offices Appropriations Bill, 1943*, H. Rep. 2207, 10).

2. Conference with the president, May 1, 1942, 2, Smith Papers.

3. Memo for the president from BOB Director Harold Smith, April 27, 1942, OF 788.

4. "Reminder to the President," attached to memo to the president from BOB Director Smith, April 27, 1942, OF 788.

5. House, Conference Committee, *Independent Offices Appropriations Bill, 1943*, H. Rep. 2207, 6.

6. Pope, *Senatorial Baron*, Ph.D. dissertation, 362.

7. House, Conference Committee, *Independent Offices Appropriations Bill, 1943*, H. Rep. 2207, 10.

8. *Congressional Record* 88:4, 5047.

9. Ibid. 84:7, 7340.

10. Ibid. 88:4, 5048.

11. The more normal scenario, where the majority party leadership would arrange a re-vote to reestablish its control, is what happened regarding the fiscal year 1947 budget. See chapter 10.

12. Letter from Louis Ludlow to Mellett, June 23, 1942, Mellett Papers.

13. *U.S. at War*, 211.

14. Roosevelt, *Complete Press Conferences*, Vol. 18, Item 150, underlining in original.

15. Roosevelt, *Public Papers, 1940*, 698, 701.

16. Catton, *War Lords of Washington*, 10–1, 52–5, 62–7; Gulick, *Administrative Reflections from World War II*, 132; and *Congressional Record* 88:1, 549.

17. Executive Order 8757, in Roosevelt, *Public Papers, 1941*, 162–6.

18. Ibid., 264–7. This was the precursor of the Office of Strategic Services, eventually the CIA.

19. Winkler, *Politics of Propaganda*, 26.

20. Executive Order 8922, in Roosevelt, *Public Papers, 1941*, 425–9; and Kane, "O.F.F."

21. Executive Order 8985, in Roosevelt, *Public Papers, 1941*, 574–9.

22. *Congressional Record* 88:3, 3868.

23. Ibid. 88:1, 550.

24. Memo to Judge Rosenman from Bernard L. Gladieux, chief of BOB Defense Organization Section, March 24, 1942, "Information" file, Rosenman Papers.

25. Letter from M. S. Eisenhower to Assistant Director Donald Stone, Feb. 20, 1942, Box 82, RG 51.

26. Conference with the president, March 7, 1942, 4, Smith Papers.

27. Conference with the president, April 4, 1942, 5, Smith Papers.

28. Memo for the files, June 6, 1942, Smith Papers. Tydings chaired the Special Committee on Fiscal Affairs of the Government during the Seventy-seventh Congress, a different committee from Byrd's (that held a hearing on the Information Center). It, too, focused on cutting government spending.

29. Memo for the president from Harold D. Smith, March 7, 1942. Reprinted in Gosnell, *Framing of the OWI Executive Order*, 17.

30. Ambrose, and Immerman, *Milton S. Eisenhower*, chapter 5. Milton's older brother was Dwight, then a fast rising General who at that time was heading the Army's war planning office. Dwight, it will be recalled, had been a key author of the original IMP (chapter 4).

31. Eisenhower, *The President Is Calling*, 93.

32. OGR, *Report of Operations, 1941*, 6–7, 9, Box 898, RG 44.

33. Danton, "Public Library War Information Centers."

34. Box Pr62, RG 287.

35. This is the author's reconstruction based on available evidence. Eisenhower routinely destroyed his personal files (e-mail message to the author from Thomas W. Branigar, Archivist, Dwight D. Eisenhower Library and Museum, May 28, 2002, author's files).

36. Letter from Milton S. Eisenhower to Donald C. Stone, Feb. 20, 1942, Box 82, RG 51.

37. Memo from Kehrli to Gladieux regarding information survey, Jan. 20, 1942, Box 82, RG 51.

38. Intra-office memo from Grady Durham to Kehrli regarding progress report for week from Feb. 7 to Feb. 14, Feb. 16, 1942, Box 82, RG 51.

39. Letter from M. S. Eisenhower to Donald C. Stone, Feb. 20, 1942, Box 82, RG 51.

40. Eisenhower, *Summary of Conclusions Reached*, Box 82, RG 51.

41. Gosnell, *Framing of the OWI Executive Order*, 26.

42. Letter from M. S. Eisenhower to Donald C. Stone, Feb. 20, 1942, Box 82, RG 51. Later, Eisenhower was associate director of OWI (Eisenhower, *The President Is Calling*, chapters 6–7).

43. Gosnell, *Framing of the OWI Executive Order*.

44. Draft memo for the president, drafted by H[erman] K[ehrli], Feb. 24, 1942, Box 82, RG 51.

45. Letter from Oscar Cox, assistant solicitor general, to Bernard Gladieux, chief, Defense Organization section, and four enclosures, March 7, 1942, "Information" File, Rosenman Papers.

46. Rosenman, *Working with Roosevelt*, 277; and Roosevelt, *Public Papers, 1942*, 278–81.

47. Draft of March 7, letter from Oscar Cox, assistant solicitor general, to Bernard Gladieux, chief, Defense Organization section, and four enclosures, March 7, 1942; draft of March 14, memo to Judge Rosenman from Bernard L. Gladieux, chief of BOB Defense Organization section, March 14, 1942, and March 24 briefing of Rosenman, Memo to Judge Rosenman from Bernard L. Gladieux, chief of BOB Defense Organization section, March 24, 1942, 3, "Information" File, Rosenman Papers; Conference with the president, April 4, 1942, Smith Papers; and conference at the White House, April 10, 1942, Smith Papers.

48. Fleming, *New Dealers' War*, chapter 6.

49. Catton, *War Lords of Washington*, 180.

50. Records of the White House Stenographer's Diary, *FDR: Day by Day: The Pare Lorentz Chronology*, Roosevelt Presidential Library.

51. Letter to the state directors and their staffs from Mellett, July 11, 1942, Box 889A, RG 44.

52. Memo for the president from BOB Director Harold Smith, April 27, 1942, OF 788.

53. Conference with the president, May 1, 1942, 2–3, Smith Papers.

54. Letter from Attorney General Francis Biddle to Smith, May 11, 1942, 1, Box 82, RG 51.

55. "Office of War Information, June 7, 1942," BOB summary for the files, 5, Box 82, RG 51.

56. Memo for the president from Harold Smith, June 1, 1942, Box 82, RG 44.

57. Roosevelt, *Public Papers, 1942*, 274–8; and "President Forms Top News Agency," *New York Times*, June 14, 1942, 1, 31.

58. House, Conference Committee, *Appropriation for the Executive Office and Sundry Independent Bureaus*, H. Rep. 2259.

59. 56 Stat. 394.

60. Intra-office memo from Herman Kehrli to Bernard Gladieux, May 13, 1942, Box 82, RG 51.

61. "Office of War Information, June 7, 1942," BOB summary for the files, 5, Box 82, RG 51.

62. Memo from Herman Kehrli to Bernard L. Gladieux, BOB, June 9, 1942, Box 82, RG 51.

63. Roosevelt, *Complete Presidential Press Conferences*, Vol. 19, Items 394–5.

64. Letter from Mellett to Lewis S. Hershey, July 1, 1942, Box 890, RG 44. Italics added.

65. Memo to all state directors from Philip C. Hamblet, July 1, 1942, Box 890, RG 44.

66. Confidential memo from Phillip Hamblet, July 7, 1942, Box 996, RG 44.

67. Mackay, *Domestic Operations of the OWI*, Ph.D. dissertation, 67–70.

68. Gosnell, *Office of Government Reports*, 36. Microfilm reproduction, Woodbridge, CT: Research Publications, 1976.

69. Mackay, *Domestic Operations of the OWI*, Ph.D. dissertation, 67.

70. House Appropriations Committee, *National War Agencies Appropriation Bill for 1944*, 917; and memo to George Barnes from McGee, Subject: Mellett statistics, Nov. 14, 1942, Mellett Papers.

71. Roosevelt, *Complete Presidential Press Conferences*, Vol. 19, Item 198.

72. Ibid., item 395.

73. Weinberg, *Wartime Propaganda in Democracy*, Ph.D. dissertation, 313.

74. Winkler, *Politics of Propaganda*, 36.

75. Koppes and Black, "Blacks, Loyalty, and Motion-Picture Propaganda," 384, footnote 3.

76. Winkler, *Politics of Propaganda*, 66.

Chapter 10: Truman's Office of Government Reports, 1946–48

1. Memo for the president, Aug. 18, 1945 and conference with the president, Aug. 18, 1945, Smith Papers.

2. Cover note to Judge Rosenman, Aug. 20, 1945, Smith Papers.

3. Memo on demobilization of emergency agencies, BOB, Aug. 17, 1945, 5, Smith Papers.

4. Executive order 9608, promulgated in *Federal Register*, 10:173 (Sept. 1, 1945) 1.

5. Truman, *Public Papers, 1945*, 253.

6. *U.S. Government Manual*, 1945, second ed., 88.

7. House Appropriations Committee, *Independent Offices Appropriations Bill for 1947: Hearings*, 48.

8. Sander, *Staff for the President*, 52.

9. "Estimates for [FY]1947," 2, BOB, Box 150, PSF-Truman.

10. "Conversation with Mrs. Berenguer re OWI Transfer," Robert C. Sampson, BOB Personnel Officer, Aug. 31, 1945, Box 1873, RG 44.

11. *U.S. Government Manual*, 1945, second ed., iii. After 1967, the building was called the Old Executive Office Building. It was renamed the Eisenhower Executive Office Building in 1999.

12. *Budget of the U.S., 1948*, 76–7.

13. *Congressional Record* 92:1, 353–4; and House Appropriations Committee, *Independent Offices Appropriations Bill for 1947: Hearings*, 21.

14. Boxes 1021–29, RG 44.

15. *Congressional Record* 92:1, 353; House Appropriations Committee, *Independent Offices Appropriations Bill for 1947: Hearings*, 22; and memo to the director from F. J. Lawton, BOB administrative assistant, regarding Government Information Service, Dec. 4, 1946, Box 1873, RG 44.

16. "Government Information Service, Activities of Press Intelligence Division, Report for Month of Dec., 1945," Box 1006, RG 44.

17. "Estimates for 1947," BOB, Box 150, PSF-Truman.

18. House Appropriations Committee, *Independent Offices Appropriations Bill for 1947: Hearings*, 21–2.

19. Conference with the president, Nov. 28, 1945, Smith Papers.

20. *Budget of the U.S., 1948*, 39, 50–1.

21. House Appropriations Committee, *Independent Offices Appropriations Bill for 1947: Hearings*, 48.

22. Ibid., 47–50.

23. House Appropriations Committee, *Independent Offices Appropriations Bill, 1947*, H. Rep. 1484, 3.

24. *Congressional Record* 92:1, 353.

25. Box 22, RG 233.

26. *Congressional Record* 92:1, 355.

27. This is the normal scenario that would have been expected to happen—but didn't—when the House was considering the the fiscal year 1943 Conference Committee Report for OGR. See chapter 9.

28. *Congressional Record* 92:1, 368–9.

29. Senate Appropriations Committee, *Independent Offices Appropriations Bill for 1947: Hearings*, 20–36.

30. Senate Appropriations Committee, *Independent Offices Appropriations Bill, 1947*, S. Rep. 926, 3.

31. House, Conference Committee, *Independent Offices Appropriations Bill, 1947*, H. Rep. 1794, 1, 4.

32. 60 Stat. 61.

33. Jackall and Hirota, *Image Makers*, 36–44.

34. Repplier, "Advertising Dons Long Pants."

35. House Appropriations Committee, *Third Deficiency Appropriation for 1946: Hearings*, 155.

36. Letter to James W. Young, Chairman, War Advertising Council from President Truman, Oct. 16, 1945, Box 322, RG 250.

37. Somers, *Presidential Agency*.

38. However, his office was in the East Wing, whereas the Oval Office and high-level presidential aides are in the West Wing. Now (2005), the East Wing is exclusively for the staff of the First Lady.

39. Byrnes had resigned from the Supreme Court when FDR named him to head OWMR. Byrnes, while still on the Court, had tried to mediate between FDR and Senator McKellar over the US Information Center. See chapter 8.

40. It had originally been established by executive order. OWMR's creation by executive order and then re-establishment by statute was the same process that OGR had undergone (chapter 5).

41. Calkin, *Preliminary Inventory of the Records of OWMR*, 31.

42. Dictated comments by Charles Jackson, Media Programming Division for talk to Advertising Council meeting in New York City, Nov. 28, 1945, Box 1, Jackson Papers.

43. "Media Programming Division: One Year, 1945—1946," Box 7, Jackson Papers.

44. "Steelman Speech Draft: 1 Nov. 1946," Box 1, Halverstadt Papers.

45. "Proposed Annual Budget for Media Programming Division" and "IV. Budget" in Media Programming Division Report, April 1946, Box 5, Jackson Papers.

46. House Appropriations Committee, *Third Deficiency Appropriation for 1946: Hearings*, 159.

47. Conference program, Box 13, Jackson Papers.

48. Press Release, OWMR, Sept. 17, 1946, Box 323, RG 250.

49. Press Release, OWMR, Nov. 2, 1945, OF 73.

50. "Motion Picture Memo," April 26, 1946, 4, Box 1, Halverstadt Papers.

51. "Steelman Speech Draft: 1 Nov. 1946," 6, Box 1, Halverstadt Papers.

52. Memo to John Steelman from Anthony Hyde, Oct. 16, 1946, Box 1, Halverstadt Papers.

53. "Films in the Reconversion Program," n.d., OWMR, Box 1, Halverstadt Papers.

54. Memo for Steelman from Anthony Hyde, July 3, 1946, Box 1, Halverstadt Papers.

55. House Appropriations Committee, *Third Deficiency Appropriation for 1946: Hearings*, 159.

56. Letter to John Steelman, OWMR director from President Truman, July 8, 1946, OF 122-K.

57. Letter to President Truman from John Steelman, July 8, 1946, Box 666, OF 122-K.

58. Letter to Bernard Friend from Arch Mercey, Aug. 15, 1946, Box 7, Halverstadt Papers.

59. "Memo on Government Motion Picture Program: OWMR Participation," to Anthony Hyde from Arch Mercey and Dallas Halverstadt, Oct. 3, 1946, Box 1, Halverstadt Papers.

60. Letter to Major General Erskine from Arch Mercey, Dec. 3, 1946, Box 1, Halverstadt Papers.

61. Truman, *Memoirs*, 24–7.

62. Smith had resigned in mid-June. Webb headed NASA in the JFK and LBJ administrations.

63. Memo to the president from James E. Webb on Organization of the Executive Office of the President, Oct. 28, 1946, Box 150, PSF-Truman.

64. Somers, *Presidential Agency*, 100.

65. Donaldson, *Truman Defeats Dewey*, 13–6.

66. Letter to the Attorney General from BOB Director Webb, Dec. 6, 1946; and letter to the president from the attorney general, Dec. 7, 1946, Folder 1585, OF 1172.

67. Memo to Steelman from Hyde, Nov. 15, 1946, 1, Box 322, RG 250.

68. "Resolution of the Motion Picture Committee," Nov. 21, 1946, 1, Box 1, Halverstadt Papers.

69. Memo to Steelman from Anthony Hyde regarding permanent status of Media Programming Division, Nov. 15, 1946, 1, Box 322, RG 250.

70. Ibid.

71. Sander, *Staff for the President*, 52.

72. Senate Appropriations Committee, *Independent Offices Appropriations Bill for 1948: Hearings*, 180.

73. "Schedule A, Order with Respect to Certain Matters Under Executive Order No. 9809," BOB, Dec. 26, 1946, Box 1873, RG 44.

74. Letter to the attorney general from Director Webb, Dec. 6, 1946, Folder 1585, OF 1172.

75. Donaldson, *Truman Defeats Dewey*, 17–8, 146, 149.

76. Truman, *Memoirs*, 491–5.

77. Felix Belair, "War Agencies Put in Unit for Liquidation," *New York Times*, Dec. 13, 1946, 1.

78. At the press conference, Truman incorrectly referred to the Media Programming Division as the Advertising Division (Truman, *Public Papers*, 492). The executive order got the title right.

79. *Federal Register* 11:242 (Dec. 13, 1946): 14281.

80. Memo for Miss Katherine C. Blackburn from the president, Dec. 19, 1946, OF 1173.

81. "Order with Respect to Certain Matters Under Executive Order No. 9809," BOB, Dec. 26, 1946; and accounts and procedures letter No. 11221, Accounting and Bookkeeping Division, general accounting office, Jan. 21, 1947, Box 1873, RG 44.

82. Memo to Anthony Hyde from Dallas Halverstadt, Jan. 20, 1947, Box 1, Halverstadt Papers.

83. "1948 Budget for OGR," Box 1, Halverstadt Papers; *Budget of the U.S., 1948*, 41, 76–7.

84. Memo to all OGR employees from Katherine Blackburn, April 4, 1947, Box 1873, RG 44. The identical titles can lead to confusion. The 1945–6

GIS was part of BOB and consisted of all the pre-war OGR functions (press clipping, information-answering, *U.S. Government Manual*) while the 1946–7 GIS was only the information-answering component within the post-war OGR.

85. House Appropriations Committee, *Independent Offices Appropriations Bill for 1948: Hearings*, Part 1, 182.

86. Ibid., 183.

87. Congressional, Joint Committee on Reduction, *Reduction: Hearings*, Part 4, 1239.

88. Ibid., 1233.

89. Memo to the Staff from Anthony Hyde, Oct. 29, 1946, Box 5, Jackson Papers.

90. Letter to K. C. Blackburn from Arch A. Mercey, Jan. 10, 1947, Box 1, Halverstadt Papers.

91. Memo from Katherine C. Blackburn, Jan. 16, 1947, Box 1873, RG 44.

92. Letter to the president from James W. Young, Chairman, Advertising Council, Dec. 17, 1946, Box 1586, OF 1173A.

93. Letter to Special Committee members from Mercey, Dec. 13, 1946, Box 1, Halverstadt Papers.

94. Letter to Blackburn from S. H. Fabian, Interim Chair, Motion Picture Industry Coordinating Committee, March 6, 1947, OF 73.

95. House Appropriations Committee, *Independent Offices Appropriations Bill for 1948: Hearings*, Part 1, 184.

96. Ibid., 185.

97. Ibid.; and boxes 1005 and 1007, RG 44.

98. Box 1023, RG 44; and OF 1173.

99. House Appropriations Committee, *Independent Offices Appropriations Bill for 1948: Hearings*, Part 1, 185–6.

100. *1947 Annual Report, Advertising Liaison, OGR*, Folder (1947), OF 196.

101. *1947 Annual Report, Motion Picture Liaison, OGR*, Box 1586, OF 1173.

102. "Insert for Miss Blackburn's Speech," 2–3, Box 1, Halverstadt Papers.

103. *Budget of the U.S., 1948*, 41.

104. "Report from Washington," *Tide: The Newsmagazine of Advertising, Marketing, and Public Relations* 21:14 (April 4, 1947): 73–4; and "Government Film Program to End," *Motion Picture Herald* 166:6 (Feb. 8, 1947): 32. For the GOP's critical view of agency public relations, see House Committee on Expenditures in the Executive Departments, *Final Report of the Subcommittee on Publicity and Propaganda*, H. Rep. 2474.

105. Memo to Dr. Steelman from James O. Cole, March 27, 1947, OF 1173.

106. Memo—confidential—to Dr. Steelman from Hyde, Dec. 14, 1946, Box 322, RG 250.

107. House Appropriations Committee, *Independent Offices Appropriations Bill for 1948: Hearings*, Part 1, 180–6.

108. Ibid., 186–209.

109. House Appropriations Committee, *Independent Offices Appropriations Bill, 1948*, H. Rep. 589, 35.

110. Letter to Congressman Carl Albert from Blackburn, June 18, 1947, Albert Papers.

111. Letter to Charles Jackson from T. E. Repplier, June 20, 1947, 2, Thomas Papers.

112. *Congressional Record* 93:6, 7175.

113. Ibid., 7181.

114. Letter to Elmer Thomas from T. S. Repplier, June 23, 1947, Thomas Papers.

115. Senate Appropriations Committee, *Independent Offices Appropriations Bill for 1948: Hearings*, 175.

116. Ibid., 178–9.

117. Ibid., 183.

118. Ibid., 181–97.

119. 61 Stat. 244.

120. Senate Appropriations Committee, *Independent Offices Appropriations Bill, 1948*, S. Rep. 475, 1.

121. Letter to Truman from Blackburn, July 18, 1947, underlining in original, Box 1586, OF 1173.

122. Letter to Blackburn from Matthew J. Connelly, July 19, 1947, Box 1586, OF 1173.

123. House, Conference Committee, *Independent Offices Appropriations Bill, 1948*, H. Rep. 1049, 5.

124. 61 Stat. 588.

125. Donaldson, *Truman Defeats Dewey*, Chapter 11.

126. Letter to Webb from Truman, Feb. 10, 1948, Box 1873, RG 44; and Sander, *Staff*, 52.

127. *Budget of the U.S., 1949*, 47.

128. Memo to S. T. Adams, assistant personnel officer, BOB from Blackburn, Box 1873, RG 44. As it turned out, Blackburn had cut OGR's budget slightly more than needed. When FY1948 ended, OGR had spent only $188,426 of the $230,000 appropriation (*Budget of the U.S., 1950*, 64). With the more than $40,000 unspent, she could have kept a few more staff on the payroll.

129. Neustadt became a special assistant to President Truman and then a professor. Those experiences contributed to his book *Presidential Power*. He had no particular recollection of this incident relating to OGR (handwritten note to the author, Sept. 10, 2002, author's files).

130. Memo to Dr. John R. Steelman from Malcolm Morrow, Aug. 19, 1947, Box 1586, OF 1173.

131. Letter to the president from Katherine C. Blackburn, July 25, 1947, Box 1586, OF 1173.

132. Letter to Blackburn from President Truman, Aug. 6, 1947, Box 1586, OF 1173.

133. "Head of Reports Agency Quits," *New York Herald Tribune*, Aug. 8, 1947, Archives of Media Industries.

134. Letter from Steelman to agency heads, Aug. 27, 1947, OF 1173; and Letter to Dr. John R. Steelman from T. S. Repplier, Aug. 5, 1947, OF 196.

135. Letter to John T. Gibson from John R. Steelman, Oct. 9, 1947, Box 1586, OF 1173.

136. Memo to Steelman from Dallas Halverstadt, Oct. 13, 1947, Box 1, Halverstadt Papers.

137. Letter to BOB Director Webb from President Truman, Feb. 10, 1948, Box 1873, RG 44.

138. In 1942, when OWI had absorbed OGR, it discontinued the *retention* of clippings. That collection is now (2005) in 791 boxes at the National Archives (Helton, *Preliminary Inventory of the Records of OGR*, 23–4; Helton, *Preliminary Inventory of the Records of OWI*, 50, 115).

139. House Appropriations Committee, *Independent Offices Appropriations Bill for 1949: Hearings*, 1173.

140. House Appropriations Committee, *Independent Offices Appropriations Bill, 1949*, H. Rep. 1288, 18–9.

141. Memo to Samuel T. Adams, BOB Personnel Officer, from C. William Taylor regarding termination notices for OGR employees, May 20, 1948 and office memo on delivery of OGR salary checks paid on July 2, 1948, Box 1873, RG 44.

142. Memo for Steelman from Jackson, Report of Activities, Aug. 24, 1948, OF 1173.

143. Letter to Lawrence Tipton from Halverstadt, June 8, 1948, Box 1, Halverstadt Papers.

144. E-mail from David J. Haight, archivist, Eisenhower Library, Aug. 29, 2002; phone call with Stephen Plotkin, Research Archivist, Kennedy Library, Oct. 8, 2002; and e-mail from Shannon Jarrett, archives specialist, Johnson Library, Oct. 11, 2002, author's files.

145. E-mail from William McNitt, archivist, Ford Library, June 2, 2003, author's files.

146. E-mail from Megann K. Strajcher, associate manager, Ad Council, Oct. 1, 2002, author's files.

147. House Appropriations Committee, *Independent Offices Appropriations Bill for 1950: Hearings*, Part 1, 276.

148. Memo to Samuel T. Adams, BOB personnel officer, from C. William Taylor regarding termination notices for OGR employees, May 20, 1948, Box 1873, RG 44; and *Budget of the U.S., 1949*, 105.

149. *Budget of the U.S., 1950*, 50.

150. House Appropriations Committee, *Independent Offices Appropriations Bill for 1950: Hearings*, Part 1, 275–6.

151. Senate Appropriations Committee, *Independent Offices Appropriations Bill, 1949*, S. Rep. 984, 3.

152. *Congressional Record* 94:2, 2829.

153. Ibid. 94:3, 4239.

154. House, Conference Committee, *Independent Offices Appropriations Bill, 1949*, H. Rep. 1695, 3.

155. Letter to President Truman from Harley Kilgore, Feb. 17, 1948, Box 1586, OF 1173.

156. Letter to Senator Kilgore from Truman, Feb. 19, 1948, BOB, Box 150, PSF-Truman.

157. Letter to Webb from George Straubinger, Senate Librarian, Jan. 22, 1948, U.S. Senate Library.

158. Letter to Jess Larson, Administrator, War Assets Administration from Leslie Riffle, executive director, Minority [Party] Policy Committee, U.S. Senate, Feb. 17, 1948, U.S. Senate Library.

159. Letter to Dr. Luther H. Evans, Librarian of Congress from Carl A. Loeffler, secretary of the Senate, May 21, 1948, U.S. Senate Library.

160. Crosby Noyes, "Miss Clara Edmunds Loses Fight to Save Information Library," *Washington Evening Star*, May 27, 1948, OF 569.

161. Library of Congress, *Report of the Exchange and Gift Division Processing Department for the Year Ending June 30, 1948*, typescript, 15, Manuscript Division, Library of Congress Archives.

162. Form letter to remaining OGR employees from S. T. Adams, BOB Budget Officer, May 31, 1948, Box 1873, RG 44.

163. *Budget of the U.S., 1951*, A36; and office memo on delivery of OGR salary checks paid on July 2, 1948, Box 1873, RG 44.

164. *Budget of the U.S., 1951*, A36.

165. Somers, *Presidential Agency*, 209n.

166. *Public Law* 89–554.

167. Rossiter, "The Constitutional Significance of the Executive Office of the President," 1209.

Chapter 11: Since Then, Till Now

1. Arnold, *Making the Managerial Presidency*, chapter 5; Ingraham, "Commissions, Cycles, and Change," 192–4; and Moe, *Hoover Commissions Revisited*.

2. Stanley and Sullivan, *Information Services in the Executive Branch of the Government*, 2, 8, 13–14. Sullivan was an unlikely source for these recommendations. He had previously authored two books that included criticisms of government public relations in general and OGR in particular (*Dead Hand of Bureaucracy*, chapter 14 and *Bureaucracy Runs Amuck*, chapter IV).

3. Later, Price was dean of Harvard's Kennedy School of Government and author of the influential book, *The Scientific Estate* (Cambridge, MA: Harvard University Press, 1965).

4. Commission on Organization of the Executive Branch, *Hoover Commission Report*, 505.

5. Memo for Hoover From Don K. Price, Oct. 1, 1948, "Subject: Report from Stanley and Sullivan on Information Services," 1, Information Services File, Rowe Papers.

6. Memo for Hoover, Sept. 30, 1948, "Subject: Field Coordination and Government Information," Field Coordination and Government Information Folder, Box 13, Hoover Commission series.

7. Ibid., 1.

8. Price, "Democratic Administration" (1946), 80, italics added. He repeated the observation 13 years later in "Democratic Administration" (1959), 73.

9. Hoover never responded to Price's memo. (E-mail from Brad Bauer, archivist, Hoover Presidential Library, May 30, 2002, author's files.)

10. "Outline for Discussion of Report on Info. Services," Information Services File, Rowe Papers.

11. Commission on Organization of the Executive Branch of the Government, *Hoover Commission Report*, 47.

12. Ibid., 26.

13. Hensel and Millett, "Recommendations for the Improvement of Departmental Management," 17.

14. Millett, "Departmental Management in Practice," 57.

15. Retrieved, May 27, 2004: http://www.gpoaccess.gov/gmanual/browse-gm-03.html.

16. Retrieved, May 27, 2004: http://www.adcouncil.org/campaigns.

17. Walcott and Hult, "White House Staff Size"; Kessel, "Structures of the Reagan White House" and "Structures of the Carter White House"; and Brown, "Party and Bureaucracy," 292–3.

18. Dizard, *Strategy of Truth*; "USIS: The Front Line" in Henderson, *U.S. Information Agency*, 129–62. In 1999, it was merged into the State Department and the USIS title was discontinued.

19. See Daniels, "Policy Termination" and "Policy and Organizational Termination"; and Kaufman, *Time, Chance, and Organizations*.

20. Gould, *Modern American Presidency*, 160.

21. Kumar, "Office of Communications"; and Maltese, *Spin Control*.

22. "President Expands Emergency Council," *New York Times*, Dec. 20, 1933, 4.

23. Krock, "Events Suggest Need of a Bureau of Explanation," *New York Times*, Feb. 20, 1934, 20.

24. Bonafede, "White House Report," 910.

25. Maltese, *Spin Control*.

26. Williams, " 'The President's' OGR," 561–2.

27. Bonafede, "Men Behind Nixon," 258.

28. Winfield, "The New Deal Publicity Operation."

29. Winfield, *FDR and the News Media*, 238.

30. Millett, *Government and Public Administration*, 280. This was written a decade after his work as a staff member of the Hoover Commission. See endnotes 13 and 14 of this chapter.

31. Patterson, *Congressional Conservatism and the New Deal*.

32. Lee, "When Congress Tried to Cut Pentagon Public Relations"; Murphy, *Forest Service Violations of Section 303 of 1998 Interior Department Appropriations Act*; Yarwood and Enis, "Problems in Regulating Federal Executive Branch Publicity" and "Advertising and Publicity Programs"; Fulbright, *Pentagon Propaganda Machine*; Pimlott, *Public Relations and American Democracy*, 69–95; and McCamy, *Government Publicity*, 5–10.

33. Dimock and Dimock, *Public Administration*, fourth edition, 593.

34. Feinberg, "Mr. Justice Brandeis and the Creation of the *Federal Register*"; and Weinberg, *Wartime Propaganda in Democracy*, Ph.D. dissertation, 126.

35. Schlesinger, *The Crisis of the Old Order*, 57. This author was unsuccessful at confirming the quote independently. In 2002, Schlesinger—understandably—was unable to identify the source of the quote (correspondence, June 21, 2002, author's files).

36. MacCann, *People's Films*, 108.

37. *Congressional Record* 87:3, 2560.

38. Weinberg, *Wartime Propaganda in Democracy*, Ph.D. dissertation, 280, italics added.

39. Gosnell, *Office of Government Reports*, 37.

40. MacCann, *People's Films*, 114–7.

41. Pimlott, *Public Relations and American Democracy*, 72.

42. White, *Introduction to the Study of Public Administration*, third ed., 228.

43. Redford, *Ideal and Practice in Public Administration*, 89.

44. Redford, *Democracy in the Administrative State*, 70–1.

45. Pfiffner, *Public Administration*, revised ed., 582, italics added.

46. House Committee on Public Buildings and Grounds, *To Prohibit: Hearings*, 7.

47. "Information Building Irks Congress," *The [Washington, DC] News*, March 10, 1942.

48. Mellett, "Government Propaganda," 312.

49. Simon, Smithburg and Thompson, *Public Administration*, 416.

50. Weiss, "Public Information," 246; and Gormley and Balla, *Bureaucracy and Democracy*, 19–21, 177–8.

51. Herring, "Official Publicity," 170 and *Public Administration and the Public Interest*, 367.

52. McCamy, *Government Publicity*, 24.

53. McCamy, "Public Relations in Public Administration," 319–20, italics added.

54. Wann, *President as Chief Administrator*, 54.

55. *Congressional Record* 84:7, 7340.

56. Ibid. 86:5, 5191.

57. Ibid. 88:1, 549.

58. Ibid. 92:1, 274.

59. Richard, "Public Relations Value of the Annual Report," 150.

60. Graham, "Trends in Teaching of Public Administration," 73.

61. Pfiffner and Presthus, *Public Administration*, third ed., 130–44.

62. Dimock, "Building Program Support," 39.

63. Rourke, *Bureaucracy, Politics, and Public Policy*, 50.

64. Weinberg, *Wartime Propaganda in Democracy*, Ph.D. dissertation, 124.

65. Lepawsky, *Administration* (1949), 563.

66. Lepawsky, *Administration* (1960 and 1965).

67. Millett, *Government and Public Administration*, 280.

68. Dimock and Dimock, *Public Administration*, third ed., 334–5.

69. Simon, *Technique of Municipal Administration*, third ed., 527.

70. Lepawsky, *Administration*, 549–54; White, *Introduction to the Study of Public Administration*, third ed., 231; Millett, *Management in the Public Service*, 141–4; Nimmo, *Newsgathering in Washington*, 22; and Christofferson, "Municipal Reports and Events."

71. Campbell, "San Diego's 1951 Annual Report."

72. Rosen, "Public Relations Activities and Means."

73. House Appropriations Committee, *Defense Department Appropriation for 1969: Hearings*, Part 4, 201.

74. House Appropriations Committee, *Department of Defense Appropriation Bill, 1971*, H. Rep. 91–1570, 47.

75. Gilbert, "Special Reports and Events," 166.

76. Lee, "Public Relations in Public Administration."

77. Shafritz, *International Encyclopedia of Public Policy and Administration*; and Rabin, *Encyclopedia of Public Administration and Public Policy*.

78. Heise, "Toward Closing the Confidence Gap," 209.

79. Garnett, "Epilog."

80. Schachter, *Reinventing Government or Reinventing Ourselves*, 85–8.

81. Behn, "What Right Do Public Managers Have to Lead?"

82. Government Finance Officers Association, "GFOA Awards for Recognition." Retrieved May 27, 2004: http://www.gfoa.org/services/awards.shtml.

83. Washington, *Consultation and Communications*, 35.

84. Édes, "The Role of Government Information Officers."

85. Lee, "Reporters and Bureaucrats," 458–9.

86. Lee, *E-Reporting*.

87. Caddy and Vergez, *Citizens as Partners*, 20.

88. Gramberger, *Citizens as Partners: OECD Handbook*.

Bibliography

Books and Articles

Ambrose, Stephen E., and Richard H. Immerman. *Milton S. Eisenhower: Educational Statesman*. Baltimore: Johns Hopkins University Press, 1983.

Arnold, Peri E. *Making the Managerial Presidency: Comprehensive Reorganization Planning, 1905–1996*, second ed. Lawrence: University Press of Kansas, 1998.

Aronson, Steven M. L. *Hype*. New York: Morrow, 1983.

Badger, Anthony J. *The New Deal: The Depression Years, 1933–40*. New York: Hill & Wang, 1989.

Barry, Amanda. *PR Power: Inside Secrets from the World of Spin*. London: Virgin Books, 2002.

Barry, John M. *Rising Tide: The Great Mississippi Flood of 1927 and How it Changed America*. New York: Simon & Schuster, 1997.

Behn, Robert D. "What Right Do Public Managers Have to Lead?" *Public Administration Review* 58 (1998): 209–24.

Bennett, Linda L. M., and Stephen Earl Bennett. *Living with Leviathan: Americans Coming to Terms with Big Government*. Lawrence: University Press of Kansas, 1990.

Beyle, Herman C. *Governmental Reporting in Chicago*. Chicago: University of Chicago Press, 1928.

Blum, Albert A. "Birth and Death of the M-Day Plan." In *American Civil-Military Decisions: A Book of Case Studies*, edited by Harold Stein, 63–94. University: University of Alabama Press for the Inter-University Case Program, 1963.

Bonafede, Dom. "Men Behind Nixon: Herbert G. Klein: Spokesman for the Administration." *National Journal* 1 (1969): 258–62.

———. "White House Report: Administration tries public relations to reestablish image and promote its efforts." *National Journal* 5 (1973): 908–12.

Boorstin, Daniel J. *The Image: A Guide to Pseudo-Events in America*. New York: Harper & Row, 1964.

Brown, Roger G. "Party and Bureaucracy: From Kennedy to Reagan." *Political Science Quarterly* 97 (1982): 279–94.

Brownlow, Louis. *A Passion for Anonymity: The Autobiography of Louis Brownlow, Second Half*. Chicago: University of Chicago Press, 1958.

Budget of the United States Government for the Fiscal Year Ending June 30, 19__. Washington, DC: Government Printing Office.

Burns, James MacGregor. *Roosevelt: The Lion and the Fox*. New York: Harcourt, Brace & World, 1956.

Caddy, Joanne, and Christian Vergez. *Citizens as Partners: Information, Consultation and Public Participation in Policy-Making*. Paris: Organisation for Economic Co-operation and Development, 2001.

Campbell, O. W. "San Diego's 1951 Annual Report." *Public Administration Review* 13 (1953): 30–2.

Caro, Robert A. *The Years of Lyndon Johnson: Master of the Senate*. New York: Alfred A. Knopf, 2002.

Carroll, Gordon. "Dr. Roosevelt's Propaganda Trust." *American Mercury* 42:165 (1937): 1–31.

Catton, (Charles) Bruce. *The War Lords of Washington*. New York: Harcourt, Brace, 1948.

Childs, Harwood L. "Public Information and Opinion." *American Political Science Review* 37 (1943): 56–68.

Christofferson, Robert M. "Municipal Reports and Events." Chapter 12 in *Municipal Public Relations*, edited by Desmond L. Anderson. Chicago: International City Managers' Association, 1966.

Clawson, Marion. *New Deal Planning: The National Resources Planning Board*. Baltimore: Johns Hopkins University Press, 1981.

Clinton, William J. *Public Papers of the Presidents of the United States, 1996 Volume, Book I*. Washington, DC: Government Printing Office, 1997.

Committee on Public Information, U. S. *The Creel Report: Complete Report of the Chairman of the Committee on Public Information*. New York: Da Capo Press, 1972 [1920].

Commission on Organization of the Executive Branch of the Government. *The Hoover Commission Report*. New York: McGraw-Hill, 1949.

Cooke, Morris L. *Our Cities Awake: Notes on Municipal Activities and Administration*. Garden City, NY: Doubleday, Page, 1919.

Cooper, Phillip J. *By Order of the President: The Use and Abuse of Executive Direct Action*. Lawrence: University Press of Kansas, 2002.

Creel, George. *How We Advertised America*. New York: Arno Press, 1972 [1920].

Cutlip, Scott M. *The Unseen Power: Public Relations, A History*. Hillsdale, NJ: Erlbaum, 1994.

———. *Public Relations History: From the 17th to the 20th Century: The Antecedents*. Hillsdale, NJ: Erlbaum, 1995.

Daniels, Mark R. *Creating Sustainable Community Programs: Examples of Collaborative Public Administration*. Westport, CT: Praeger, 2001.

———, ed. "Policy and Organizational Termination." *International Journal of Public Administration* 24 (2001): 247–339.

———. "Policy Termination." In *Encyclopedia of Public Administration and Public Policy*, edited by Jack Rabin, 943–6. New York: Marcel Dekker, 2003.

Danton, Emily Miller. "Public Library War Information Centers." *American Library Association Bulletin* 36 (1942): 500–7.

Davenport, Walter. "You Can't Say That!" *Collier's* 107:7 (1941): 19, 62–5.

Delorme, Denise E., and Fred Fedler. "Journalists' Hostility Toward Public Relations: An Historical Analysis." *Public Relations Review* 29 (2003): 99–124.

Dimock, Marshall E. "Building Program Support." In *Communication in Public Administration*, edited by Robert B. Highsaw and Don L. Bowen, 39–48. University: Bureau of Public Administration, University of Alabama, 1965.

Dimock, Marshall E., and Gladys O. Dimock. *Public Administration*, third ed. New York: Holt, Rinehart and Winston, 1964.

———. *Public Administration*, fourth ed. New York: Holt, Rinehart and Winston, 1969.

Dizard, Wilson P. *The Strategy of Truth: The Story of the U.S. Information Service*. Washington, DC: Public Affairs Press, 1961.

Donaldson, Gary A. *Truman Defeats Dewey*. Lexington: University Press of Kentucky, 1999.

Drury, Allen. *A Senate Journal, 1943–1945*. New York: Da Capo Press, 1972 [1963].

Édes, Bart W. "The Role of Government Information Officers." *Journal of Government Information* 23 (2000): 455–69.

Eisenhower, Milton S. *The President is Calling*. Garden City, NY: Doubleday, 1974.

Emmerich, Herbert. *Federal Organization and Administrative Management*. University: University of Alabama Press, 1971.

Ewen, Stuart. *PR! A Social History of Spin*. New York: Basic Books, 1996.

Federal Register. Washington, DC: National Archives, 1938–42.

Feinberg, Lotte E. "Mr. Justice Brandeis and the Creation of the *Federal Register*." *Public Administration Review* 61 (2001): 359–70.

Fenno, Richard F., Jr. *The Power of the Purse: Appropriations Politics in Congress.* Boston: Little, Brown, 1966.

Fesler, James W. "Executive Management and the Federal Field Service." In President's Committee on Administrative Management, *Report of the Committee with Studies of Administrative Management in the Federal Government*, 273–94. Washington, DC: Government Printing Office, 1937.

———. *Area and Administration*. University: University of Alabama Press, 1949.

———. "The Brownlow Committee Fifty Years Later." *Public Administration Review* 47 (1987): 291–6.

———, et al. *Industrial Mobilization for War: History of the War Production Board and Predecessor Agencies, 1940–1945. Volume I: Program and Administration*. Washington, DC: Government Printing Office, 1947.

Fleming, Thomas. *The New Dealers' War: Franklin D. Roosevelt and The War Within World War II*. New York: Basic Books, 2001.

Foner, Eric. *Reconstruction: America's Unfinished Revolution, 1863–1877*. New York: Harper & Row, 1988.

Fuhrman, Candice Jacobson. *Publicity Stunt! Great Staged Events that Made the News*. San Francisco: Chronicle Books, 1989.

Fulbright, J. William. *The Pentagon Propaganda Machine*. New York: Vintage, 1971.

Garnett, James L. "Administrative Communication: Domain, Threats, and Legitimacy." Chapter 1 in *Handbook of Administration Communication*, edited by James L. Garnett and Alexander Kouzmin. New York: Marcel Dekker, 1997.

———. "Epilog: Directions and Agendas for Administrative Communication." Chapter 33 in *Handbook of Administration Communication*, edited by James L. Garnett and Alexander Kouzmin. New York: Marcel Dekker, 1997.

Gilbert, William H. "Special Reports and Events." Chapter 10 in *Public Relations in Local Government*, edited by William H. Gilbert. Washington, DC: International City Management Association, 1975.

Glaser, Comstock [Kurt]. *Administrative Procedure: A Practical Handbook for the Administrative Analyst*. Washington, DC: American Council on Public Affairs, 1941.

Gormley, William T., Jr., and Steven J. Balla. *Bureaucracy and Democracy: Accountability and Performance*. Washington, DC: CQ Press, 2004.

Gould, Lewis L. *The Modern American Presidency*. Lawrence: University Press of Kansas, 2003.

Graham, George A. "Trends in Teaching of Public Administration." *Public Administration Review* 10 (1950): 69–77.

Gramberger, Marc R. *Citizens as Partners: OECD Handbook on Information, Consultation and Public Participation in Policy-Making*. Paris: Organisation for Economic Co-operation and Development, 2001.

Graves, W. Brooke. "Public Reporting in the American States." *Public Opinion Quarterly* 2 (1938): 211–28.

Gulick, Luther. *Administrative Reflections from World War II*. University: University of Alabama Press, 1948.

Hamblet, Philip C. "The Nerve Center for National Facts." *Future: The Magazine for Young Men* 4:11 (1942): 10–11, 21.

Harris, Joseph P. "The Emergency National Defense Organization." *Public Administration Review* 1 (1940): 1–24.

Heise, J. Arthur. "Toward Closing the Confidence Gap: An Alternative Approach to Communication Between Public and Government." *Public Administration Quarterly* 9 (1985): 196–217.

Henderson, John W. *The United States Information Agency*. New York: Frederick A. Praeger, 1969.

Hensel, H. Struve, and John D. Millett. "Recommendations for the Improvement of Departmental Management." Part One in *Departmental Management in Federal Administration: A Report with Recommendations*, edited by H. Struve Hensel and John D. Millett. Washington, DC: Government Printing Office, 1949.

Herring, E. Pendleton. "Official Publicity Under the New Deal." *The Annals of the American Academy of Political and Social Science* 179 (1935): 167–75.

———. *Public Administration and the Public Interest*. New York: Russell & Russell, 1967 [1936].

Hiebert, Ray Eldon. *Courtier to the Crowd: The Story of Ivy Lee and the Development of Public Relations*. Ames: Iowa State University Press, 1966.

High, Stanley. "You Can't Beat the Government." *Saturday Evening Post* 210:21 (1937): 5–7, 34–8.

Hobbs, Edward H. *Behind the President: A Study of Executive Office Agencies*. Washington, DC: Public Affairs Press, 1954.

Holland, Matthew F. *Eisenhower Between the Wars: The Making of a General and Statesman*. Westport, CT: Praeger, 2001.

Holt, Daniel D., ed. *Eisenhower: The Prewar Diaries and Selected Papers, 1905–1941*. Baltimore: Johns Hopkins University Press, 1998.

Horn, Stephen. *Unused Power: The Work of the Senate Committee on Appropriations*. Washington, DC: Brookings Institution, 1970.

Ickes, Harold L. *The Secret Diary of Harold L. Ickes: The Inside Struggle, 1936–1939*, vol. II. New York: Simon and Schuster, 1954.

Industrial Mobilization Plan, Revised 1936. Washington, DC: Government Printing Office, 1936.

Ingraham, Patricia W. "Commissions, Cycles, and Change: The Role of Blue-Ribbon Commissions in Executive Branch Change." Chapter 9 in *Agenda* for Excellence: Public Service in America*, edited by Patricia W. Ingraham and Donald F. Kettl. Chatham, NJ: Chatham House, 1992.

Jackall, Robert, and Janice M. Hirota. *Image Makers: Advertising, Public Relations, and the Ethos of Advocacy*. Chicago: University of Chicago Press, 2000.

Jordan, Philip D. "Teacher's Section: Keeping Up with the War News." *Mississippi Valley Historical Review* 29 (1942): 407–9.

Journal of the Executive Proceedings of the Senate of the United States of America. Volume 80. Washington, DC: Government Printing Office, 1939.

Kane, R. Keith. "The O.F.F." *Public Opinion Quarterly* 6 (1942): 204–20.

Kaufman, Herbert. *Time, Chance, and Organizations: Natural Selection in a Perilous Environment*, second ed. Chatham, NJ: Chatham House, 1991.

Kessel, John H. "The Structures of the Carter White House." *American Journal of Political Science* 27 (1983): 431–63.

———. "The Structures of the Reagan White House." *American Journal of Political Science* 28 (1984): 231–58.

Kilpatrick, Wylie. *Reporting Municipal Government*. New York: Municipal Administration Service, 1928.

King, Cheryl Simrell, and Camilla Stivers, eds. *Government Is Us: Public Administration in an Anti-Government Era*. Thousand Oaks, CA: Sage, 1998.

Kirst, Michael W. *Government without Passing Laws: Congress' Nonstatutory Techniques for Appropriations Control*. Chapel Hill: University of North Carolina Press, 1969.

Knepper, Cathy D. *Greenbelt, Maryland: A Living Legacy of the New Deal*. Baltimore: Johns Hopkins University Press, 2001.

Koistinen, Paul A. C. *Planning War, Pursuing Peace: The Political Economy of American Warfare, 1920–1939*. Lawrence: University Press of Kansas, 1998.

Koppes, Clayton R., and Gregory D. Black. "Blacks, Loyalty, and Motion-Picture Propaganda in World War II." *Journal of American History* 73 (1986): 383–406.

———. *Hollywood Goes to War: How Politics, Profits, and Propaganda Shaped World War II Movies*. New York: Free Press, 1987.

Kreidberg, Marvin A., and Merton G. Henry. *History of Military Mobilization in the United States Army 1775–1945*. Washington, DC: Department of the Army, 1955.

Krock, Arthur. "Press vs. Government—A Warning." *Public Opinion Quarterly* 1 (1937): 45–9.

Kumar, Martha Joynt. "The Office of Communications." *Presidential Studies Quarterly* 31 (2002): 609–34.

Kurtz, Howard. *Spin Cycle: Inside the Clinton Propaganda Machine*. New York: Free Press, 1998.

Larson, Cedric. "Publicity for National Defense: How It Works." *Journalism Quarterly* 18 (1941): 245–55.

———. "Official Information for America at War: The Graphic Materials and Current Channels on which Washington Depends for Progress." *Print: A Quarterly Journal of the Graphic Arts* 2:3–4 (October–December 1941): 66–86.

Lee, Mordecai. "Public Relations in Public Administration: A Disappearing Act in Public Administration Education." *Public Relations Review* 24 (1998): 509–20.

———. "Reporters and Bureaucrats: Public Relations Counter-Strategies by Public Administrators in an Era of Media Disinterest in Government." *Public Relations Review* 25 (1999): 451–63.

———. "Public Information in Government Organizations: A Review and Curriculum Outline of External Relations in Public Administration." *Public Administration and Management: An Interactive Journal* [*www.pamij.com*] 5 (2000): 183–214.

———. "When Congress Tried to Cut Pentagon Public Relations: A Lesson from History." *Public Relations Review* 26 (2000): 131–54.

———. "The Federal Public Relations Administration: History's Near Miss." *Public Relations Review* 28 (2002): 87–98.

———. "Intersectoral Differences in Public Affairs: The Duty of Public Reporting in Public Administration." *Journal of Public Affairs* 2:2 (2002): 33–43.

———. "Is There Anything New Under the Sun? Herbert Simon's Contributions in the 1930s to Performance Measurement and Public Reporting of Performance Results." *Public Voices* 6:2–3 (2003): 73–82.

———. "The First Federal Public Information Service, 1920–33: At the US Bureau of Efficiency!" *Public Relations Review* 29 (2003): 415–25.

———. "E-Reporting: Using Managing-for-Results Data to Strengthen Democratic Accountability." Chapter 4 in *Managing for Results 2005*, edited by John M. Kamensky and Al Morales. Lanham, MD: Rowman & Littlefield, 2004. Also available online as a monograph, accessed May 27, 2004: http://www.businessofgovernment.org/pdfs/Lee_Report.pdf.

Lepawsky, Albert. *Administration: The Art and Science of Organization and Management*. New York: Alfred A. Knopf, 1949.

———. New York: Alfred A. Knopf, 1960.

———. Calcutta, India: Oxford & Ibh, 1965.

Levine, Michael. *A Branded World: Adventures in Public Relations and the Creation of Superbrands*. Hoboken, NJ: J. Wiley, 2003.

Lindstrom, Matthew, and Martin A. Nie. "Public Participation and Agency Planning." *Public Manager* 29:1 (2000): 33–6

MacCann, Richard Dyer. *The People's Films: A Political History of U.S. Government Motion Pictures*. New York: Hastings House, 1973.

Macmahon, Arthur W. "The Future Organizational Pattern of the Executive Branch." *American Political Science Review* 38 (1944): 1179–91.

Mallinson, Bill. *Public Lies and Private Truths: An Anatomy of Public Relations.* London: Cassell, 1996.

Maltese, John Anthony. *Spin Control: The White House Office of Communications and the Management of Presidential News*, second ed. Chapel Hill: University of North Carolina Press, 1994.

Marchand, Roland. *Creating the Corporate Soul: The Rise of Public Relations and Corporate Imagery in American Big Business.* Berkeley: University of California Press, 1998.

McCamy, James L. *Government Publicity: Its Practice in Federal Administration.* Chicago: University of Chicago Press, 1939.

———. "Public Relations in Public Administration." In *Current Issues in Library Administration*, edited by Carleton B. Joeckel, 301–21. Chicago: University of Chicago Press, 1939.

McDonald, William F. *Federal Relief Administration and the Arts: The Origins and Administrative History of the Arts Projects of the Works Progress Administration.* Columbus: Ohio State University Press, 1969.

McKinzie, Richard D. *The New Deal for Artists.* Princeton, NJ: Princeton University Press, 1973.

McLuhan, Marshall. *Understanding Media: The Extensions of Man.* Cambridge, MA: MIT Press, 1994 [1964].

Mellett, Lowell. "Government Propaganda." *Atlantic Monthly* 168:3 (1941): 311–3.

———. "The Office of Government Reports." *Public Administration Review* 1 (1941): 126–31.

Message of the President of the United States Transmitting the Budget for the Service of the Fiscal Year Ending June 30, 1935. Washington, DC: Government Printing Office, 1934.

Millett, John D. "Departmental Management in Practice." Part Two in *Departmental Management in Federal Administration: A Report with Recommendations*, edited by H. Struve Hensel and John D. Millett. Washington, DC: Government Printing Office, 1949.

———. *Management in the Public Service: The Quest for Effective Performance.* New York: McGraw-Hill, 1954.

———. *Government and Public Administration: The Quest for Responsible Performance.* New York: McGraw-Hill, 1959.

Milner, Henry. *Civic Literacy: How Informed Citizens Make Democracy Work.* Hanover, NH: University Press of New England, 2002.

Mock, James R., and Cedric Larson. *Words That Won the War: The Story of The Committee on Public Information, 1917–1919.* New York: Russell & Russell, 1968 [1939].

Moe, Ronald C. *The Hoover Commissions Revisited*. Boulder, CO: Westview, 1982.

Moynihan, Donald P. "Normative and Instrumental Perspectives on Public Participation: Citizen Summits in Washington, D.C." *American Review of Public Administration* 33 (2003): 164–88.

Nimmo, Dan D. *Newsgathering in Washington: A Study in Political Communication*. New York: Atherton, 1964.

Nixon, Richard M. *Public Papers of the Presidents of the United States: Richard Nixon, 1970*. Washington, DC: Government Printing Office, 1971.

Patterson, James T. *Congressional Conservatism and the New Deal: The Growth of the Conservative Coalition in Congress, 1933–1939*. Westport, CT: Greenwood Press, 1981 [1967].

Penkower, Monty N. *The Federal Writers' Project: A Study in Government Patronage of the Arts*. Urbana: University of Illinois Press, 1997.

Pfiffner, John M. *Public Administration*. New York: Ronald, 1935.

———. *Public Administration*, revised ed. New York: Ronald, 1946.

Pfiffner, John M., and R. Vance Presthus. *Public Administration*, third ed. New York: Ronald, 1953.

Pierce, Robert N. *A Sacred Trust: Nelson Poynter and the St. Petersburg Times*. Gainesville: University Press of Florida, 1993.

Pimlott, J. A. R. *Public Relations and American Democracy*. Port Washington, NY: Kennikat, 1972 [1951].

Polenberg, Richard. *Reorganizing Roosevelt's Government: The Controversy Over Executive Reorganization, 1936–1939*. Cambridge, MA: Harvard University Press, 1966.

President's Committee on Administrative Management. *Report of the Committee with Studies of Administrative Management in the Federal Government*. Washington, DC: Government Printing Office, 1937.

Price, Don K. "Democratic Administration." Chapter 4 in *Elements of Public Administration*, edited by Fritz Morstein Marx. New York: Prentice-Hall, 1946.

———. "Democratic Administration." Chapter 4 in *Elements of Public Administration*, second ed., edited by Fritz Morstein Marx. Englewood Cliffs, NJ: Prentice-Hall, 1959.

Price, Vincent, Joseph N. Cappella and Lilach Nir. "Does Disagreement Contribute to More Deliberative Opinion?" *Political Communication* 19 (2002): 95–112.

Rabin, Jack, ed. *Encyclopedia of Public Administration and Public Policy*, 2 vols. New York: Marcel Dekker, 2003.

Redfield, Charles E. "The Theory of Communication: Its Application to Public Administration." In *Communication in Public Administration*, edited by Robert B. Highsaw and Don L. Bowen, 11–25. University: Bureau of Public Administration, University of Alabama, 1965.

Redford, Emmette S. *Ideal and Practice in Public Administration.* University: University of Alabama Press, 1958.

———. *Democracy in the Administrative State.* New York: Oxford University Press, 1969.

Relyea, Harold C., ed. *The Executive Office of the President: A Historical, Biographical, and Bibliographical Guide.* Westport, CT: Greenwood, 1997.

Repplier, Theodore S. "Advertising Dons Long Pants." *Public Opinion Quarterly* 9 (1945): 269–78.

Richard, Oscar. "The Public-Relations Value of the Annual Report." *Public Personnel Review* 8 (1947): 144–50.

Ridley, Clarence E. "Municipal Reports." *National Municipal Review* 16 (1927): 243–5.

———. "Appraising Municipal Reports." *National Municipal Review* 17 (1928): 150–3.

———. "Municipal Reporting Taken Seriously." *Public Opinion Quarterly* 1 (1937): 112–6.

Robertson, David. *Sly and Able: A Political Biography of James F. Byrnes.* New York: W. W. Norton, 1994.

Roosevelt, Elliot, ed. *F.D.R., His Personal Letters, 1928–1945*, vol. II. New York: Duell, Sloan and Pearce, 1950.

Roosevelt, Franklin D. *Complete Presidential Press Conferences of Franklin D. Roosevelt.* New York: Da Capo Press, 1972.

———. *The Public Papers and Addresses of Franklin D. Roosevelt, The Year of Crisis, 1933.* New York: Random House, 1938.

———. *The Advance of Recovery and Reform, 1934.* New York: Random House, 1938.

———. *The Court Disapproves, 1935.* New York: Random House, 1938.

———. *The Constitution Prevails, 1937.* London: Macmillan, 1941.

———. *The Continuing Struggle for Liberalism, 1938.* London: Macmillan, 1941.

———. *War—And Neutrality, 1939.* New York: Macmillan, 1941.

———. *War—And Aid to Democracies, 1940.* New York: Macmillan, 1941.

———. *The Call to Battle Stations, 1941.* New York: Harper & Brothers, 1950.

———. *Humanity on the Defensive, 1942.* New York: Harper & Brothers, 1950.

Root, Harriet M. "The United States Information Center." *American Library Association Bulletin* 36 (1942): 517–9.

Rosen, Abe S. "Public Relations Activities and Means." In *The Public Relations of Local Governments—Papers presented at the World Conference of Local Governments, Washington, DC, June 15–20, 1961*, 34–7. The Hague, Netherlands: Martinus Nijhoff for the International Union of Local Authorities, 1962.

Rosen, Bernard. *Holding Government Bureaucracies Accountable*, third ed. Westport, CT: Praeger, 1998.

Rosenman, Samuel I. *Working with Roosevelt*. New York: Harper & Brothers, 1952.

Rossiter, Clinton L. "The Constitutional Significance of the Executive Office of the President." *American Political Science Review* 43 (1949): 1206–17.

Rourke, Francis E. *Bureaucracy, Politics, and Public Policy*, third ed. Boston: Little, Brown, 1984.

Sander, Alfred Dick. *A Staff for the President: The Executive Office, 1921–1952*. New York: Greenwood, 1989.

Schachter, Hindy Lauer. *Reinventing Government or Reinventing Ourselves: The Role of Citizen Owners in Making a Better Government*. Albany: State University of New York Press, 1997.

Schlesinger, Arthur M. *The Age of Roosevelt: The Crisis of the Old Order, 1919–1933*. Boston: Houghton Mifflin, 2003 [1957].

Seligman, Lester G. "Introduction." In *New Deal Mosaic: Roosevelt Confers with His National Emergency Council, 1933–1936*, edited by Lester G. Seligman and Elmer E. Cornwell Jr., xiii–xxix. Eugene: University of Oregon Books, 1965.

Seligman, Lester G., and Elmer E. Cornwell Jr., eds. *New Deal Mosaic: Roosevelt Confers with His National Emergency Council, 1933–1936*. Eugene: University of Oregon Books, 1965.

Shafritz, Jay M., ed. *International Encyclopedia of Public Policy and Administration*, 4 vols. Boulder, CO: Westview, 1998.

Shils, Edward A. "A Note on Governmental Research on Attitudes and Morale." *American Journal of Sociology* 47 (1941): 472–80.

Short, K. R. M. "Washington's Information Manual for the Motion Picture Industry, 1942." *Historical Journal of Film, Radio and Television* 3 (1983): 171–80.

Shull, Steven A., and Thomas C. Shaw. *Explaining Congressional-Presidential Relations: A Multiple Perspectives Approach*. Albany: State University of New York Press, 1999.

Siebert, Fredrick S. "Federal Information Agencies—An Outline." *Journalism Quarterly* 19 (1942): 28–33.

Simon, Herbert A. "Inter-City Contests." In *Municipal Year Book: 1937*, edited by Clarence E. Ridley and Orin F. Nolting, 137–44. Chicago: International City Manager's Association, 1937.

———. "Municipal Reporting." In *Municipal Year Book: 1938*, edited by Clarence E. Ridley and Orin F. Nolting, 47–51. Chicago: International City Manager's Association, 1938.

———. "Municipal Reporting." In *Municipal Year Book: 1939*, edited by Clarence E. Ridley and Orin F. Nolting, 38–42. Chicago: International City Manager's Association, 1939.

——— (reviser). *The Technique of Municipal Administration*, third ed. Chicago: International City Managers' Association, 1947.

Simon, Herbert A., and Clarence E. Ridley. "Trends in Municipal Reporting." *Public Opinion Quarterly* 2 (1938): 465–8.

Simon, Herbert A., Donald W. Smithburg and Victor A. Thompson. *Public Administration*. New Brunswick, NJ: Transaction, 1991 [1958].

Simonsen, William, and Mark D. Robbins. *Citizen Participation in Resource Allocation*. Boulder, CO: Westview, 2000.

Sinclair, Barbara. "Hostile Partners: The President, Congress, and Lawmaking in the Partisan 1990s." Chapter 7 in *Polarized Politics: Congress and the President in a Partisan Era*, edited by Jon R. Bond and Richard Fleisher. Washington, DC: CQ Press, 2000.

Snyder, Robert L. *Pare Lorentz and the Documentary Film*. Norman: University of Oklahoma Press, 1968.

Somers, Herman Miles. *Presidential Agency: The Office of War Mobilization and Reconversion*. New York: Greenwood Press, 1969 [1950].

Stauber, John C., and Sheldon Rampton. *Toxic Sludge is Good for You: Lies, Damn Lies, and the Public Relations Industry*. Monroe, ME: Common Courage Press, 1995.

Steele, Richard W. "Preparing the Public for War: Efforts to Establish a National Propaganda Agency, 1940–41." *American Historical Review* 75 (1970): 1640–53.

———. "The Pulse of the People. Franklin D. Roosevelt and the Gauging of American Public Opinion." *Journal of Contemporary History* 9 (1974): 195–216.

———. *Propaganda in an Open Society: The Roosevelt Administration and the Media, 1933–1941*. Westport, CT: Greenwood, 1985.

Stoke, Harold W. "Executive Leadership and the Growth of Propaganda." *American Political Science Review* 35 (1941): 490–500.

Sullivan, Lawrence. *The Dead Hand of Bureaucracy*. Indianapolis, IN: Bobbs-Merrill, 1940.

———. *Bureaucracy Runs Amuck*. Indianapolis, IN: Bobbs-Merrill, 1944.

Talese, Gay. *The Kingdom and the Power*. New York: World Publishing Company, 1969.

Thatcher, Harold W. *Planning for Industrial Mobilization, 1920–1940*. Washington, DC: Historical Section, General Administrative Services Division, Office of the Quartermaster General, US Army, 1943.

Thomson, Oliver. *Easily Led: A History of Propaganda*. Thrupp, Stroud, Gloucestershire, UK: Sutton, 1999.

Tobin, Harold J., and Percy W. Bidwell. *Mobilizing Civilian America*. New York: Council on Foreign Relations, 1940.

Truman, Harry S. *Memoirs: Years of Trial and Hope*, volume 2. Garden City, NY: Doubleday, 1956.

Truman, Harry S. *Public Papers of the Presidents of the United States: Harry S Truman, 1945*. Washington, DC: Government Printing Office, 1961.

Tye, Larry. *The Father of Spin: Edward L. Bernays & the Birth of Public Relations*. New York: Crown, 1998.

The United States at War: Development and Administration of the War Program by the Federal Government. Washington, DC: War Records Section of the Bureau of the Budget, 1947.

"United States Information Center." *American Foreign Service Journal* 20:1 (1943): 18–9, 41.

Vaughn, Stephen. *Holding Fast the Inner Lines: Democracy, Nationalism, and the Committee on Public Information*. Chapel Hill: University of North Carolina Press, 1980.

Venn, Fiona. *The New Deal*. Edinburgh, UK: Edinburgh University Press, 1998.

Walcott, Charles E., and Karen M. Hult. "White House Staff Size: Explanations and Implications." *Presidential Studies Quarterly* 29 (1999): 638–56.

Walton, Douglas. "What is Propaganda, and What Exactly is Wrong with it?" *Public Affairs Quarterly* 11 (1997): 383–413.

Wann, A. J. *The President as Chief Administrator: A Study of Franklin D. Roosevelt*. Washington, DC: Public Affairs Press, 1968.

Warken, Philip W. *A History of the National Resources Planning Board, 1933–1943*. New York: Garland, 1979.

Washington, Sally. *Consultation and Communications: Integrating Multiple Interests into Policy, Managing Media Relations—Public Management Occasional Papers No. 17*. Paris: Organisation for Economic Co-operation and Development, 1997.

Webb, Robert N. "U.S. Information Please." *Rockefeller Center Magazine* (March 1941): 12–3.

Weiss, Janet A. "Public Information." Chapter 7 in *The Tools of Government: A Guide to the New Governance*, edited by Lester M. Salamon. New York: Oxford University Press, 2002.

White, Leonard D. *The City Manager*. Chicago: University of Chicago Press, 1927.

———. *Trends in Public Administration*. New York: McGraw-Hill, 1933.

———. *Introduction to the Study of Public Administration*, third ed. New York: Macmillan, 1949.

Wiener, Norbert. *The Human Use of Human Beings: Cybernetics and Society*. New York: Avon, 1967.

Williams, Daniel W. "Measuring Government in the Early Twentieth Century." *Public Administration Review* 63 (2003): 643–59.

Williams, Margaret H. " 'The President's' Office of Government Reports." *Public Opinion Quarterly* 5 (1941): 548–62.

Wills, Garry. *A Necessary Evil: A History of American Distrust of Government.* New York: Simon & Schuster, 1999.

Wilson, Woodrow. "The Study of Administration." *Political Science Quarterly* 2 (1887): 197–222.

———. *Congressional Government: A Study in American Politics.* Boston: Houghton Mifflin, 1994 [1885].

Winfield, Betty Houchin. "The New Deal Publicity Operation: Foundation for the Modern Presidency." *Journalism Quarterly* 61 (1984): 40–8, 218.

———. *FDR and the News Media.* Urbana: University of Illinois Press, 1990.

Winkler, Allan M. *The Politics of Propaganda: The Office of War Information, 1942–1945.* New Haven, CT: Yale University Press, 1978.

Yarwood, Dean L., and Ben J. Enis. "Advertising and Publicity Programs in the Executive Branch of the National Government: Hustling or Helping the People?" *Public Administration Review* 42 (1982): 37–46.

———. "Problems in Regulating Federal Executive Branch Publicity and Advertising Programs." *American Review of Public Administration* 18 (1988): 29–45.

Unpublished Dissertations

Kiely, Edward S. "The Evolution of Federal Field Coordinating Agencies, 1921–1982." Ph.D. dissertation, University of Pittsburgh, 1982.

Mackay, LaMar Seal. "Domestic Operations of the Office of War Information in World War II." Ph.D. dissertation, University of Wisconsin-Madison, 1966.

Pope, Robert Dean. "Senatorial Baron: The Long Political Career of Kenneth D. McKellar." Ph.D. dissertation, Yale University, 1976.

Weinberg, Sydney S. "Wartime Propaganda in Democracy: America's Twentieth-Century Information Agencies." Ph.D. dissertation, Columbia University, 1969.

Congressional Publications

House. *Amendment to Estimates of Appropriations for the Office of Government Reports, 1942, Communication from the President.* 77th Congress, first session, 1941. H. Doc. 247.

———. *Documents by War Policies Commission.* 72nd Congress, first session, 1932. H. Doc. 271.

———. *Message from the President on Federal Government's Handling of Work-Relief Projects.* 76th Congress, first session, 1939. H. Doc. 270.

———. *Proposed Provision on Existing Appropriation, Office of Government Reports, 1942, Communication from the President.* 77th Congress, first session, 1941. H. Doc. 467.

———. *War Policies Commission.* 72nd Congress, first session, 1931. H. Doc. 163.

———. Committee of Conference. *Appropriations for the Executive Office and Sundry Independent Executive Bureaus, Boards, Commissions, and Offices.* 77th Congress, second session, 1942. H. Rep. 2259.

———. *Authorizing Expenditures for the Office of Government Reports in the Executive Office of the President.* 77th Congress, first session, 1941. H. Rep. 644.

———. *Independent Offices Appropriation Bill, 1943.* 77th Congress, second session, 1942. H. Rep. 2207.

———. *1947.* 79th Congress, second session, 1946. H. Rep. 1794.

———. *1948.* 80th Congress, first session, 1947. H. Rep. 1049.

———. *1949.* 80th Congress, second session, 1948. H. Rep. 1695.

———. *Second Deficiency Appropriation Bill, 1941.* 77th Congress, first session, 1941. H. Rep. 894.

———. Committee on Appropriations. *Additional Appropriations Incident to the National Defense, Fiscal Years 1942 and 1943.* 77th Congress, first session, 1941. H. Rep. 1549.

———. *Hearings.* 77th Congress, second session, 1941.

———. *Appropriations for Work Relief and Relief, Fiscal Year 1941.* 76th Congress, third session, 1940. H. Rep. 2186.

———. *Appropriations for Work Relief, Relief, and for Loans and Grants for Public Works Projects Fiscal Year 1940.* 76th Congress, first session, 1939. H. Rep. 833.

———. *Defense Department Appropriations for 1969: Hearings.* 90th Congress, second session, 1968.

———. *Department of Defense Appropriation Bill, 1971.* 91st Congress, second session, 1970. H. Rep. 91–1570.

———. *Emergency Relief Appropriation Act of 1938 and Public Works Administration Appropriation Act of 1938: Hearings.* 75th Congress, third session, 1938.

———. *Independent Offices Appropriation Bill, 1941.* 76th Congress, third session, 1940. H. Rep. 1515.

———. *Hearings.* 76th Congress, third session, 1940.

———. *Independent Offices Appropriation Bill, 1943.* 77th Congress, second session, 1942. H. Rep. 1643.

———. *Hearings.* 77th Congress, second session, 1941.

———. *Independent Offices Appropriation Bill, 1947.* 79th Congress, second session, 1946. H. Rep. 1484.

———. *Hearings.* 79th Congress, second session, 1946.

———. *Independent Offices Appropriation Bill, 1948.* 80th Congress, first session, 1947. H. Rep. 589.

———. *Hearings.* 80th Congress, first session, 1947.

———. *Independent Offices Appropriation Bill, 1949.* 80th Congress, second session, 1948. H. Rep. 1288.

———. *Hearings.* 80th Congress, second session, 1948.

———. *Independent Offices Appropriation Bill for 1950: Hearings.* 81st Congress, first session, 1949.

———. *Second Deficiency Appropriation Bill, 1941: Hearings.* 77th Congress, first session, 1941.

———. *Third Deficiency Appropriation for 1946: Hearings.* 79th Congress, second session, 1946.

———. *Work Relief and Relief Appropriation, 1941.* 76th Congress, third session, 1940. H. Rep. 2681.

———. *Work Relief and Relief for Fiscal Year 1940: Hearings.* 76th Congress, first session, 1939.

———. *Work Relief and Relief for Fiscal Year 1941: Hearings.* 76th Congress, third session, 1940.

———. Committee on Expenditures in the Executive Departments. *Authorizing Expenditures for the Office of Government Reports in the Executive Office of the President.* 77th Congress, first session, 1941. H. Rep. 177.

———. *Final Report of the Subcommittee on Publicity and Propaganda.* 80th Congress, second session, 1948. H. Rep. 2474.

———. *To Authorize Expenditures for Office of Government Reports: Hearings.* 77th Congress, first session, 1941.

———. Committee on Public Buildings and Grounds. *Prohibit Use of Money for Acquisition, Construction, and Equipment of any Building for Office of Government Reports: Hearings.* 77th Congress, second session, 1942.

Joint Committee on Reduction of Nonessential Federal Expenditures. *Reduction of Nonessential Federal Expenditures: Hearings.* 77th Congress, second session, 1942, Part 4.

Senate. *Communication from the President: Obligations by the Office of Government Reports.* 77th Congress, second session, 1942. S. Doc. 179.

———. *Industrial Mobilization Plan Revision of 1939*. 76th Congress, second session, 1939. S. Doc. 134.

———. Committee on Appropriations. *Additional Appropriations Incident to the National Defense, Fiscal Years 1942 and 1943*. 77th Congress, first session, 1941. S. Rep. 919.

———. *Emergency Relief Appropriation Act, Fiscal Year 1941*. 76th Congress, third session, 1940. S. Rep. 1754.

———. *Hearings*. 76th Congress, third session, 1940.

———. *First Deficiency Appropriation Bill, 1942*. 77th Congress, second session, 1942. S. Rep. 1086.

———. *Hearings*. 77th Congress, second session, 1942.

———. *Independent Offices Appropriation Bill, 1941*. 76th Congress, third session, 1940. S. Rep. 1177.

———. *Hearings*. 76th Congress, third session, 1940.

———. *Independent Offices Appropriation Bill, 1943*. 77th Congress, second session, 1942. S. Rep. 1266.

———. *Hearings*. 77th Congress, second session, 1942.

———. *Independent Offices Appropriation Bill, 1947*. 79th Congress, second session, 1946. S. Rep. 926.

———. *Hearings*. 79th Congress, second session, 1946.

———. *Independent Offices Appropriation Bill, 1948*. 80th Congress, first session, 1947. S. Rep. 475.

———. *Hearings*. 80th Congress, first session, 1947.

———. *Independent Offices Appropriation Bill, 1949*. 80th Congress, second session, 1948. S. Rep. 984.

———. *Second Deficiency Appropriation Bill for 1941: Hearings*. 77th Congress, first session, 1941.

———. *Work Relief and Public Works Appropriation Act of 1938: Hearings*. 75th Congress, third session, 1938.

———. *Work Relief and Public Works Appropriation Act of 1939*. 76th Congress, first session, 1939. S. Rep. 668.

———. *Hearings*. 76th Congress, first session, 1939.

———. Committee on Expenditures in the Executive Departments. *Authorizing Expenditures for the Office of Government Reports in the Executive Office of the President*. 77th Congress, first session, 1941. S. Rep. 264.

———. *To Authorize Expenditures for Office of Government Reports: Hearings*. 77th Congress, first session, 1941.

———. Special Committee Investigating the Munitions Industry. *Industrial Mobilization Plan: Revised—1933*. 74th Congress, first session, 1935. S. Comm. Print No. 2.

———. *Munitions Industry*. 74th Congress, second session, 1936. S. Rep. 944, Part 4.

Major Federal Documents

Calkin, Homer L., compiler. *Preliminary Inventory of the Records of the Office of War Mobilization and Reconversion*. Washington, DC: National Archives, 1951.

Eisenhower, Milton S. *Study of War Information Work: Supporting Data*. Washington, DC: Bureau of the Budget, February 20, 1942.

———. *Summary of Conclusions Reached in the Study of War Information Work*. Washington, DC: Bureau of the Budget, February 20, 1942.

General Accounting Office. "Chronology of GAO's Efforts to Obtain NEPDG Documents from the Office of the Vice President, April 19, 2001 to August 25, 2003." Accessed May 27, 2004: http://www.gao.gov/.

Gosnell, Harold F. *The Framing of the Office of War Information Executive Order*. Prepared for the Committee on Records of War Information, December 29, 1944.

———. *Office of Government Reports*. Washington, DC: Committee on War Records Section, Bureau of the Budget, December 31, 1943.

Helton, H. Stephen, compiler. *Preliminary Inventory of the Records of the Office of Government Reports (Record Group 44)*. Washington, DC: National Archives, 1951.

———. *Preliminary Inventory of the Records of the Office of War Information (Record Group 208)*. Washington, DC: National Archives, 1953.

Murphy, Robert P. *Forest Service Violations of Section 303 of 1998 Interior Department Appropriations Act—US General Accounting Office Legal Opinion B-281637*. Washington, DC: General Accounting Office, May 14, 1999.

National Emergency Council. *Report of Operations of the National Emergency Council: Calendar Year 1938*. Washington, DC: National Emergency Council, 1939.

Office of Government Reports. *Report of Operations of the Office of Government Reports: Calendar Year 1940*. Washington, DC: Office of Government Reports, January 1941.

———. *1941*. Washington, DC: Office of Government Reports, January 1942.

Stanley, Edward and Lawrence Sullivan. *Information Services in the Executive Branch of the Government*. Report to the Commission on Organization of the Executive Branch of the Government (Hoover Commission I), September 28, 1948.

War Films. Washington, DC: Office of the Coordinator of Government Films, April 14, 1942.

War Resources Board. *Report of the War Resources Board*. Washington, DC: 1940.

Archival Sources

(*Note:* To reduce repetition of identical information, here are the locations of the three main archival collections cited: the Roosevelt Presidential Library is in Hyde Park, NY; the Truman Library is in Independence, MO; and the National Archives II site is in College Park, MD.)

Albert, Carl, Papers of. Carl Albert Center, University of Oklahoma, Norman, OK.

Archives of Media Industries. Center for American History, University of Texas-Austin, Austin, TX.

Blackburn, Katherine C., Papers of. Roosevelt Library.

Cartwright, Wilburn, Papers of. Carl Albert Center, University of Oklahoma, Norman, OK.

FDR Memorial Foundation, Papers of. Roosevelt Library.

Halverstadt, Dallas C., Papers of. Truman Library.

Hoover Commission, First, series. Hoover Presidential Library, West Branch, IA.

Jackson, Charles W., Papers of. Truman Library.

Library of Congress Archives. US Congress, Washington, DC.

Mellett, Lowell, Papers of. Roosevelt Library.

Official Files (OF) 25, War Department. Roosevelt Library.

Official Files (OF) 73, Motion Pictures. Truman Library.

Official Files (OF) 79, Authorization, Treasury Department., Numbered Letters. Roosevelt Library.

Official Files (OF) 122, Mobilization and Reconversion, Office of War. Truman Library.

Official Files (OF) 196, Advertising. Truman Library.

Official Files (OF) 569, Libraries. Truman Library.

Official Files (OF) 788, National Emergency Council. Roosevelt Library.

Official Files (OF) 1172, Temporary Controls, Office of. Truman Library.

Official Files (OF) 1173, Government Reports, Office of. Truman Library.

Official Files (OF) 1275, Division of Press Intelligence. Roosevelt Library.

Official Files (OF) 4850, US Information Center. Roosevelt Library.

President's Committee on Administrative Management (PCAM), Papers of. Roosevelt Library.

President's Personal File (PPF). Roosevelt Library.

President's Secretary's Files (PSF-Roosevelt). Roosevelt Library.

President's Secretary's File (PSF-Truman). Truman Library.

Record Group (RG) 44, Office of Government Reports. National Archives II.

Record Group (RG) 51, Office of Management and Budget. National Archives II.

Record Group (RG) 233, U.S. House of Representatives, 1789-1989. Center for Legislative Archives, National Archives, Washington, DC.

Record Group (RG) 250, Office of War Mobilization and Reconversion. National Archives II.

Record Group (RG) 287, Publications of the US Government. National Archives II.

Rosenman, Samuel, Papers of. Roosevelt Library.

Rowe, James H., Jr., Papers of. Roosevelt Library.

Smith, Harold, Papers of. Roosevelt Library.

Thomas, Elmer, Papers of. Carl Albert Center, University of Oklahoma, Norman, OK.

US Senate Library, historical files of. Secretary of the Senate, US Senate, Washington DC.

Index